The Family Secret

Life Journeys of Giuseppe Giancola (1882 to 1959)

and Cleonice Mastrantuoni (1884 to 1964)

The Family Secret

Life Journeys of Giuseppe Giancola (1882 to 1959)

and Cleonice Mastrantuoni (1884 to 1964)

Clenise A. Stonitsch White

WHITE KNIGHT PRESS
HENRICO, VIRGINIA

Published by
White Knight Press
9704 Old Club Trace
Henrico, Virginia 23238
www.whiteknightpress.com
contact@whiteknightpress.com

ISBN: 978-1-937986-92-6 (hardback)
ISBN: 978-1-937986-93-3 (PDF file)

To: The Past, Present, and Future Generations

Contents

INTRODUCTION

Research for this book began around 1991 with trips to the National Archives in Washington, D. C. late at night after our small children were in bed for the night. Doctors at the National Institutes of Health in Bethesda, Maryland had asked a question for which I had no answer: Where were your grandparents from? My first response was that I would check with my mom. I called her (where she lived in Florida), and she became very quiet and hung up on me. We were very close and talked most days, and this seemed strange to me that she wouldn't talk to me—for almost a month! I tried calling my aunts and got similar responses with no new knowledge of our ancestors' origins. I was aware of more than a few genetic issues in the families of some of my cousins and that of one of my mom's brothers, who died at the age of two months. My husband and I were determined to see if we could help answer the doctors' questions and help with the scientific research involved. When I had the opportunity, I made trips for several years to the National Archives in Washington, D.C. searching for ship arrival and census records, and I would visit the Annandale, Virginia Mormon Family History Center requesting microfiche from the Utah Mormon Genealogical Center, searching the nondigitized Italian records, which were next to impossible to read. The machines to read the microfiche on were big and clunky. Eventually, my mom gave me a few hints that led to discoveries through more and more research off and on over these past 33 years.

I purchased books on genealogical research, wrote letters to historical societies and libraries, contacted various organizations in Chicago Heights, Illinois and Pennsylvania, purchased books about Italian families and the Italian language, read newspaper articles about various historical events in Pennsylvania and Chicago Heights, researched the families of names that I often heard from the "olden days." I read books about ships that provided passage from Europe to America in the late 1800's and early 1900's. I watched documentaries and read journal articles on the discrimination against Italians.

During the Covid-19 pandemic in 2020 - 2022 I signed up to reserve one of the limited number of computers at the local Richmond Mormon Family History Center to continue my study of the Italian records which I had begun in Annandale, VA. (Of course, I wore my mask.) With the records digitized, the task was made a bit less difficult. My headgear magnifiers have been my trusty friends all these years.

I want to thank Randy Yanikoski (Chuck and Linda's son) for the tremendously helpful listing that he compiled of names and birthdates of the Smith siblings (all of whom are deceased) and both their deceased and living family members. Also thank you to the cousins and family members who provided stories, emails, comments, photos, support, and collaboration, and to Rita Lepinskie who sent me selected documents, photos, negatives, and other items (from Uncle Smitty, Aunt Lucy, and Aunt Mandy's collections) on her visits to be with brother Joseph (Jay) Stonitsch in Orlando.

Without the journal entries and many conversations with my mom Josephine Stonitsch, I don't think I would have made as much progress as I was able to. Although she would not discuss the "family secret" with any of my siblings or cousins, she progressively, over time, seemed to really enjoy telling me her stories. (My mom lived with my husband Alex and me in Richmond, Virginia the last twelve years of her life of 106 years, 2 ½ months.) Giving me the few hints that helped me move forward with the research, she felt relieved knowing she was helping me, and she seemed relieved that she no longer felt totally constrained by the promise. The promise had its purpose way back then of keeping the family sheltered from the discrimination of the times, but it seemed to deprive each of the siblings of a sense of freedom, making them feel that they had to be guarded in their relationships all the time. My mom was at peace with her revelation, and I let her know that I would be sure no other generation would have that burden of secrecy.

Giuseppe Giancola in Castelpetroso, Isernia, Italy: from 1882 – 1897

Giuseppe Antonio Giancola was born at 5:00 a.m. 19 May 1882 to parents **Diamante Giancola** and Concetta **Illuminata Giancola di Genesio** in the house located in the hamlet of **Indiprete, Castelpetroso, Isernia, Italy**. Giuseppe was presented to the Administration of the Municipality of Castelpetroso by Donata Forte, a 70-year-old farmer who was a resident of this municipality, three hours after his birth. Giuseppe's father Diamante, a farmer also, was not present for the birth nor the civil registration of his son because of the necessity for him to go out of the area for personal business. See below: Figure 1: Birth Register <u>Atti Di Nascita 1882</u> cover; Figure 2: Page one of Register; Figure 3: Birth Certificate in Italian; and Figure 4: Birth Certificate translated to English by the author's former Northern Virginia neighbor's Italian Florida friends.

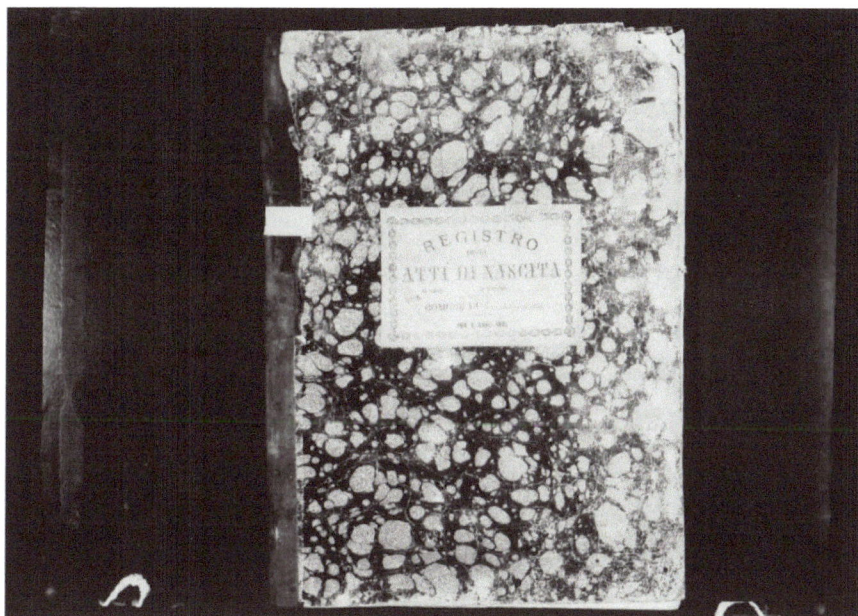

Figure 1. **Registro Atti Di Nascita 1882 cover**

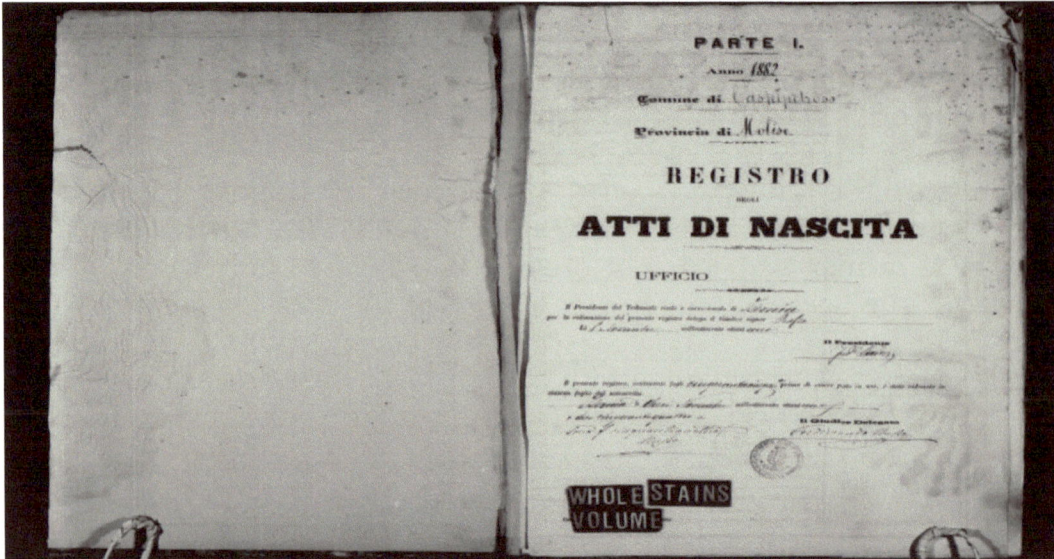

Figure 2. Page 1 of Castelpetroso 1882 Registro Atti Di Nascita

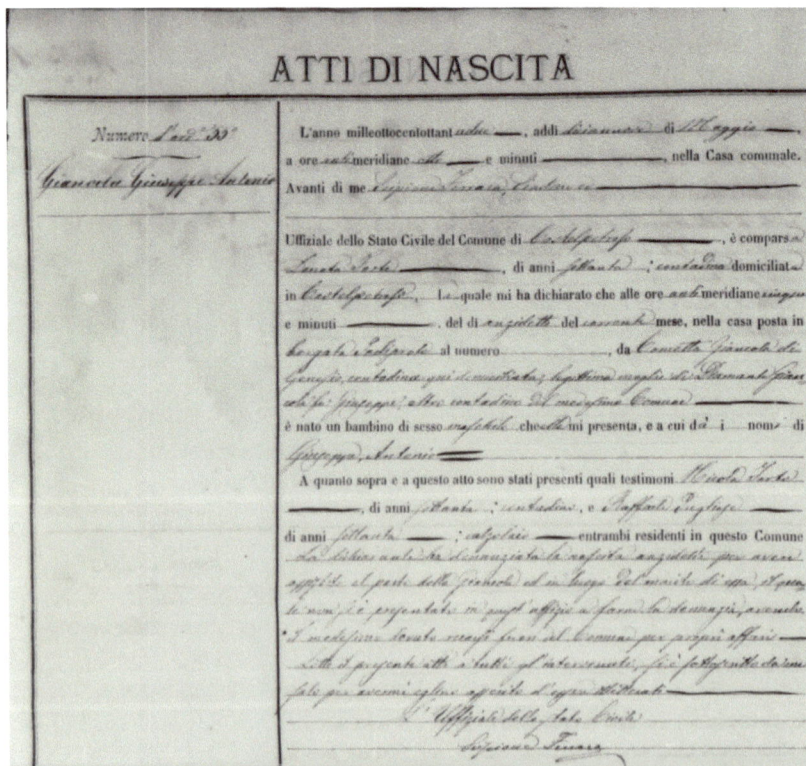

Figure 3. Birth Certificate of Giuseppe Antonio Giancola in Italian

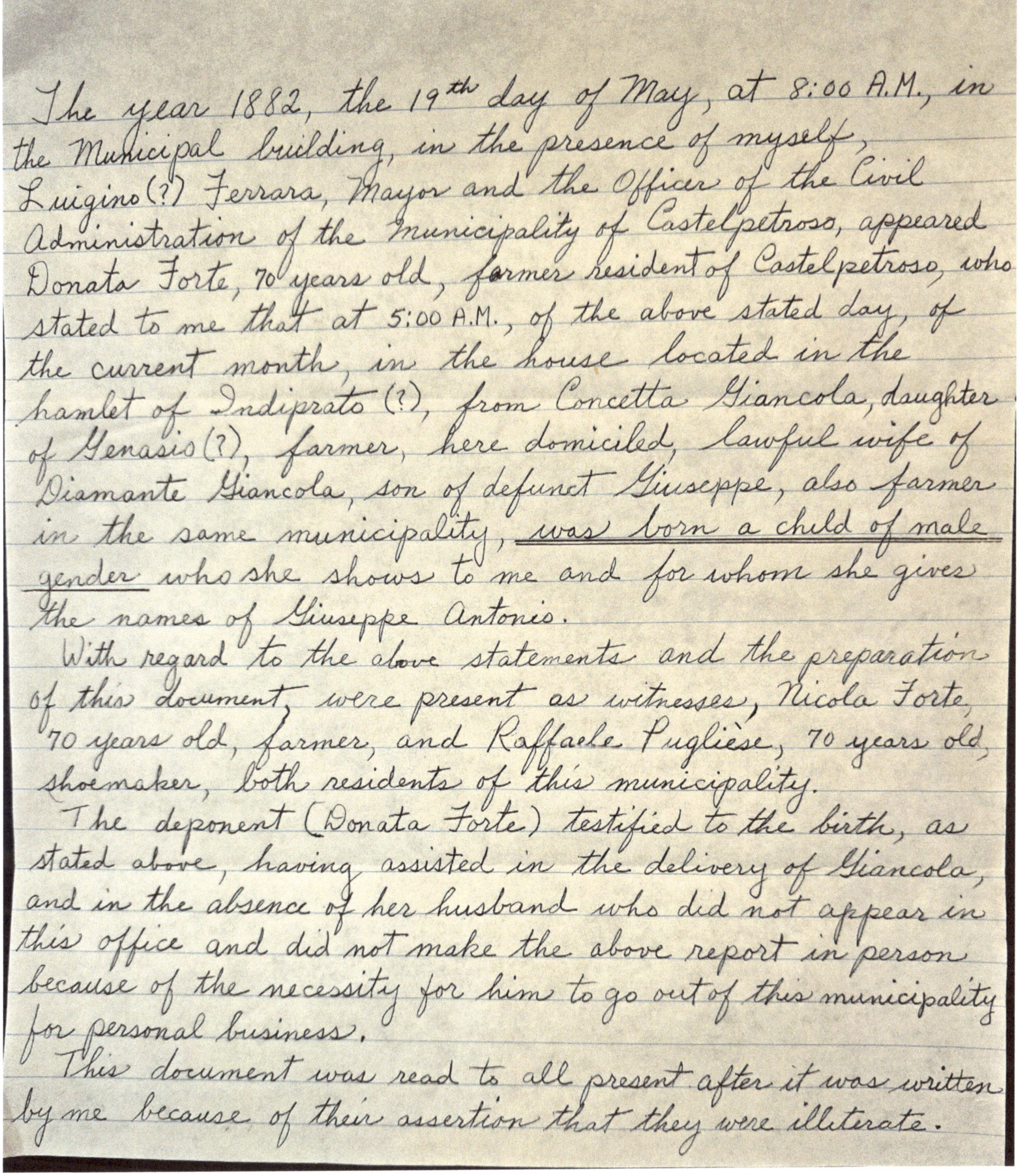

The year 1882, the 19th day of May, at 8:00 A.M., in the Municipal building, in the presence of myself, Luigino (?) Ferrara, Mayor and the Officer of the Civil Administration of the Municipality of Castelpetroso, appeared Donata Forte, 70 years old, farmer resident of Castelpetroso, who stated to me that at 5:00 A.M., of the above stated day, of the current month, in the house located in the hamlet of Indiprato (?), from Concetta Giancola, daughter of Genasio (?), farmer, here domiciled, lawful wife of Diamante Giancola, son of defunct Giuseppe, also farmer in the same municipality, <u>was born a child of male gender</u> who she shows to me and for whom she gives the names of Giuseppe Antonio.

With regard to the above statements and the preparation of this document, were present as witnesses, Nicola Forte, 70 years old, farmer, and Raffaele Pugliese, 70 years old, shoemaker, both residents of this municipality.

The deponent (Donata Forte) testified to the birth, as stated above, having assisted in the delivery of Giancola, and in the absence of her husband who did not appear in this office and did not make the above report in person because of the necessity for him to go out of this municipality for personal business.

This document was read to all present after it was written by me because of their assertion that they were illiterate.

Figure 4. Birth Certificate of Giuseppe Antonio Giancola translated to English by Angelo and Gloria Pardi

Although Giuseppe claimed various other locations as his birthplace during his lifetime (such as Argentina; Wilmerding, PA; and South America), Castelpetroso, Italy was his actual birthplace. Documents show different names at different points of his life including the following: Joe Giancola, Joseph Smith, Joseph A. Smith, Joseph Alfonso Smith, Gppe. Antonio Giancola, Giuseppe Gioncola, and Giuseppe Giansola. The name that came to be used most often was Joseph Anthony Smith. Indeed, he wanted to be looked upon as an American and not as an Italian. He had left that life behind. (More on this later.)

Castelpetroso is a community in the Province of Isernia in the Italian region of Molise, somewhat west of Campobasso and southeast of Isernia. The area was inhabited well before the conquest of the Lombards, which was in the latter part of the 6th century. See the Google Map below for the location of Castelpetroso in Italy.

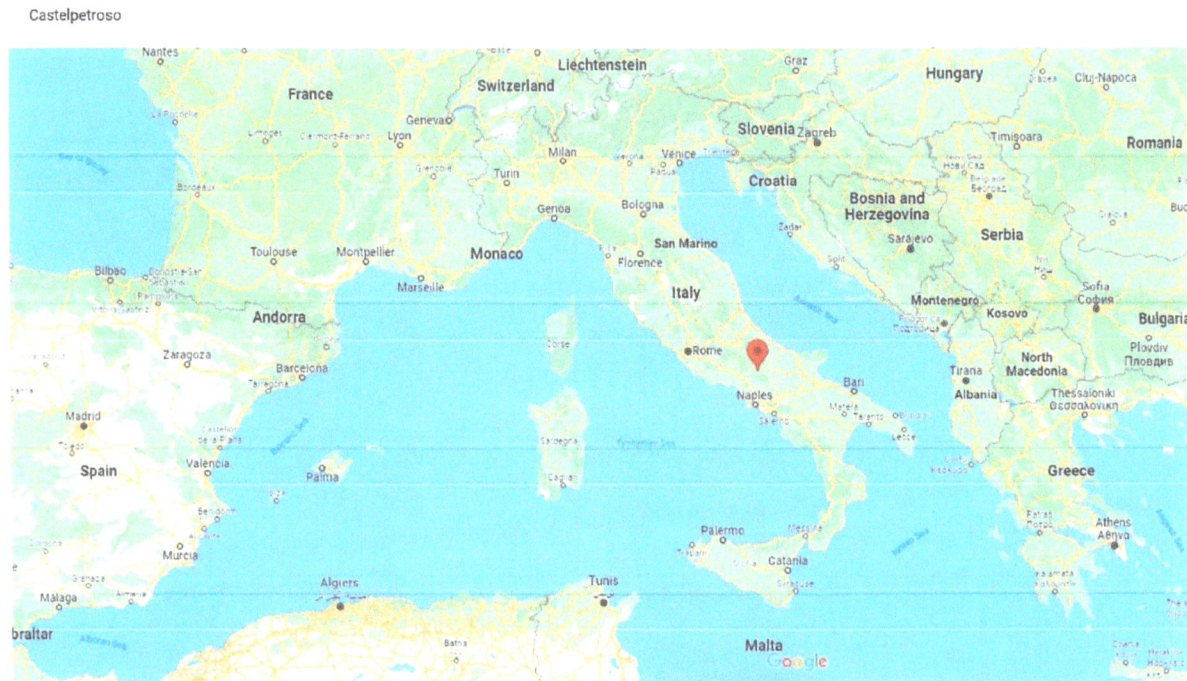

Figure 5. **Castelpetroso, Italy from Google Maps**

As stated above in the birth record, **Indiprete** (meaning "inside the rocks" in Italian) is the hamlet where Giuseppe's mother Concetta gave birth. It is one of the small hamlets in the hills of Molise that surround the medieval village of **Castelpetroso**. Many of the old buildings made of stone are still in existence, and the village of Castelpetroso is well known throughout the world for its famous Sanctuary of Our Lady of Sorrows, the construction of which began in 1890 and was completed around 1975. One document of a now deceased Forte relative (Nick Forte in Newport, Ohio) written on 10 August 1993 recalled that his mother's father Michele Arcangelo Giancola (1853-1940) worked on the construction of the sanctuary near the turn of the nineteenth century. (More details about the Forte family later.)

See below for Figure 6: Google Map of location of Indiprete in Italy; Figure 7: a Google Map photo of typical homes on Via Magnolia in Indiprete; Figure 8: map showing relative locations of Sanctuario di Maria Santissima Addolorata, Indiprete, and Castelpetroso; Figure 9: photo of Sanctuario.

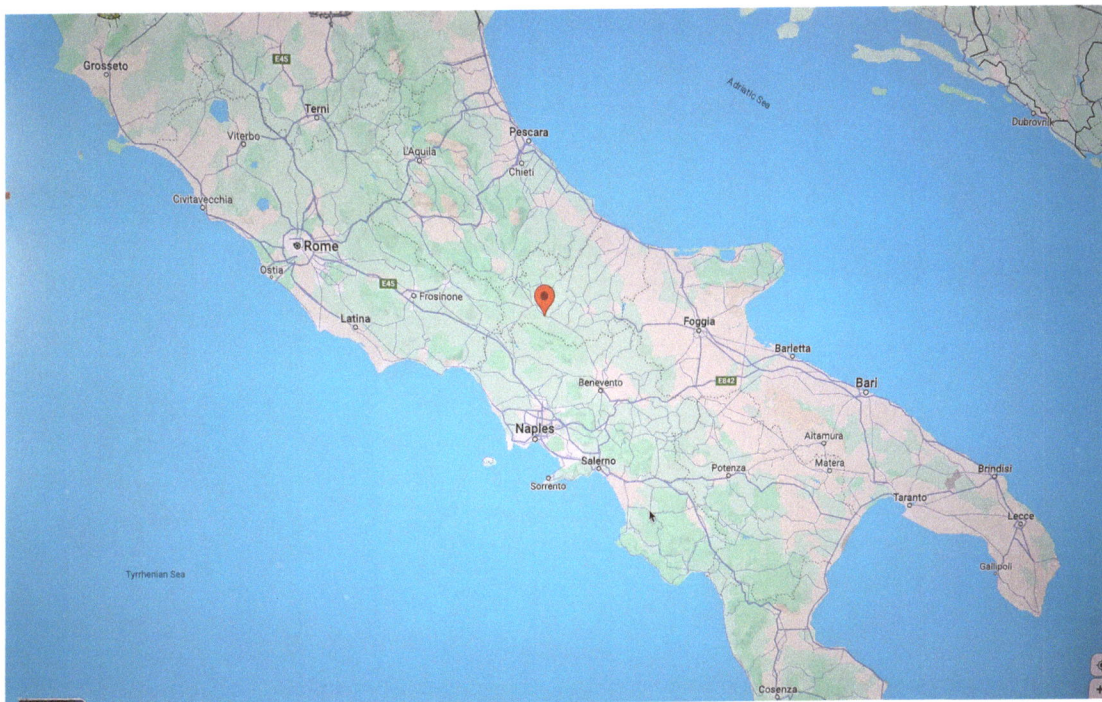

Figure 6. Google Map of Location of Indiprete in Italy

Figure 7. Photo of typical homes on Via Magnolia in Indiprete

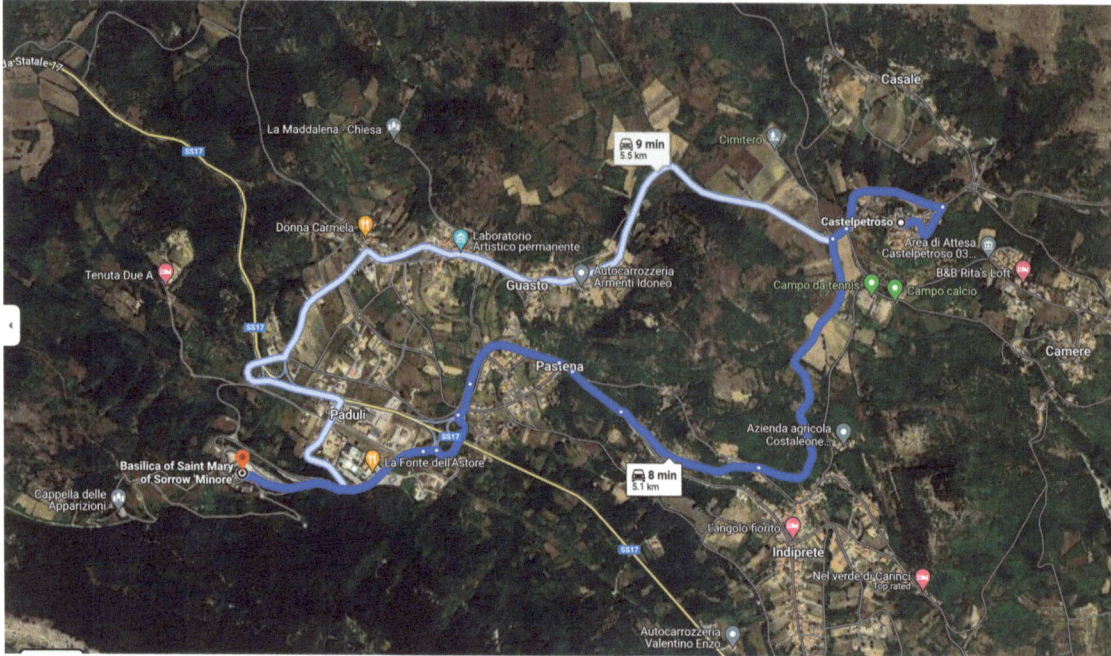

Figure 8. **Map showing relative locations of Sanctuario de Maria Santissima Addolorata, Indiprete, and Castelpetroso**

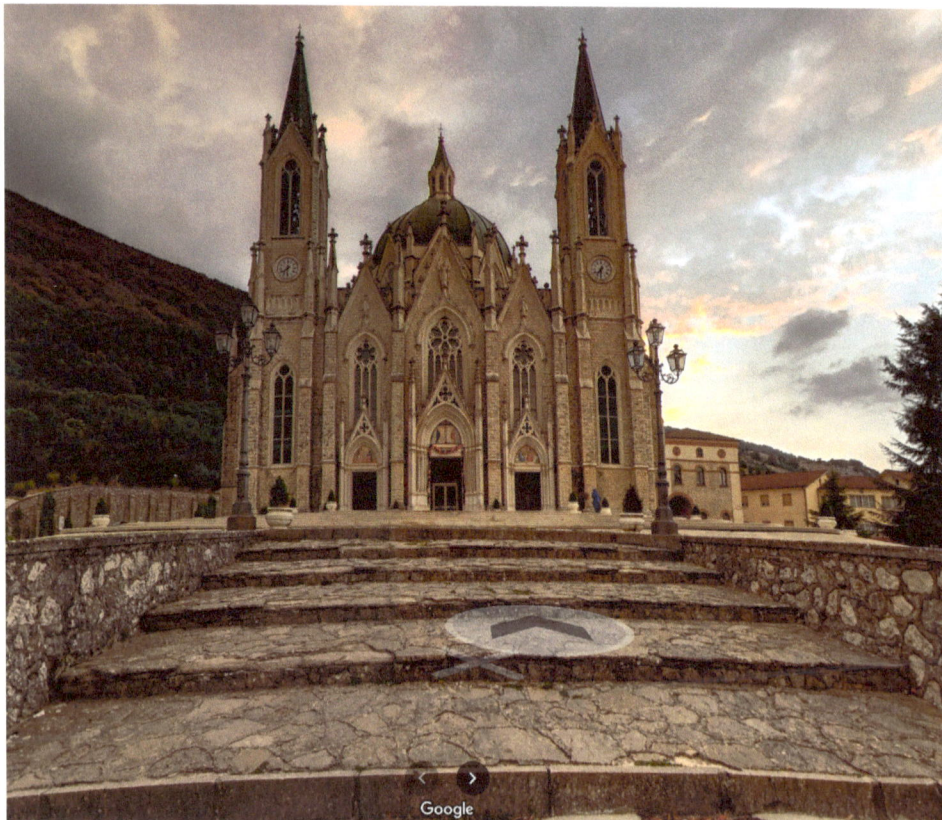

Figure 9. **Google photo of Basilica Minore dell'Addolorata di Castelpetroso**

Following is an article about the Sanctuary of Our Lady of Sorrows (Addolorata) describing the circumstances around the construction of this church. The beginning of the construction of the Basilica would have coincided with Giuseppe's life as a young boy (age 6 – 14) living in Castelpetroso. It is noteworthy that many Italians included Addolorata/o as part of their newborn's name at this time.

On this day: Apparition at Castelpetroso

Mar 22, 2011

by [Gerelyn Hollingsworth](#)

On this day in 1888, "two countrywomen belonging to Pastine, a hamlet in the diocese of Bojano, in Southern Italy, were sent to look for some sheep that had strayed on a neighboring hill, to which Castelpetroso is the nearest village. One was named Famiana Cecchino, and the other Serafina Giovanna Valentino; the former being a spinster aged thirty-five, and the latter a married woman a little younger. Before long they returned home, crying, sobbing, trembling, and terrified.

"People naturally inquired into the cause of their emotion, and heard from these women that they had seen a light issuing from some fissures in the rocks; and when they approached nearer the spot they saw distinctly the image of the Addolorata--a lady, young, very beautiful, pale, with disheveled hair, and bleeding from the wounds received from seven swords."

The Apparitions and Shrines of Heaven's Bright Queen: In Legend, Poetry and History: From the Earliest Ages to the Present Time, Volume Four, compiled by William J. Walsh, T. J. Carey Company, New York, 1904, page 173.

As the weeks went by, more and more people saw "the Blessed Virgin under the form known as Our Lady of Mount Carmel; others saw her as Our Lady of Grace, others as Our Lady of the Most Holy Rosary; but for the most part she appeared as Our Lady of Dolors. Generally, too, she was alone, but sometimes she was accompanied by St. Michael, sometimes by St. Anthony, sometimes by St. Sebastian, and sometimes by troops of angels. Among those who testified to these Apparitions was a well-known scoffer, who received the grace of seeing Our Lady four times in half-an-hour." Others favored with visions of the Lady were the archpriests of Castelpetroso and Bojano, the bishop of Bojano, his "Vicar-General, and many other ecclesiastics".

A spring appeared, and there was a miraculous cure. In 1890, the cornerstone for the Santuario dell'Addolorata was laid. In March 1995, Pope John Paul II visited the shrine. (End of Article)

Brothers and Sisters of Giuseppe Giancola (Giuseppe born 19 May 1882)

The brothers and sisters of Giuseppe included Antonio Nicole (born 23 June 1864 and died at age 1 on 23 November 1865); Anna Addolorata (born 26 July 1866 and died on 4 October 1866); Libera Addolorato (born 9 October 1868 and death certificate not found); Antonia Filomena (born 10 July 1871 and died at age 1 on 2 Nov 1872; boy Nicola (born 25 December 1873 and death certificate not found); boy Michele (born 26 June 1877 and died at age 2 on 13 March 1879); Maria Immacolata (born 16 Dec 1880 and died 22 Dec 1880); Vincenzo Addolorato (born 14 May 1885 and died at age 2 on 19 Sept 1886). No other births occurred from 1886 through 1895 for the couple Diamante and Concetta. Records show they had a total of 9 children from 1864 to 1885, at least six of whom died in infancy, and at least three had Addolorata/o in their names. The online records for Castelpetroso cover the years around 1800 to 1899. At least five of the children were deceased before Giuseppe was born, and Vincenzo Addolorato died when Giuseppe was four years old.

Cleonice Mastrantuoni in Roccamandolfi, Isernia, Italy: from 1884 – 1907

Figure 10. **Postcard from Roccamandolfi, Italy**

Roccamandolfi, the birthplace of Cleonice, is about 9 miles south of Castelpetroso, where Giuseppe was born. See map showing relative locations of the two towns below.

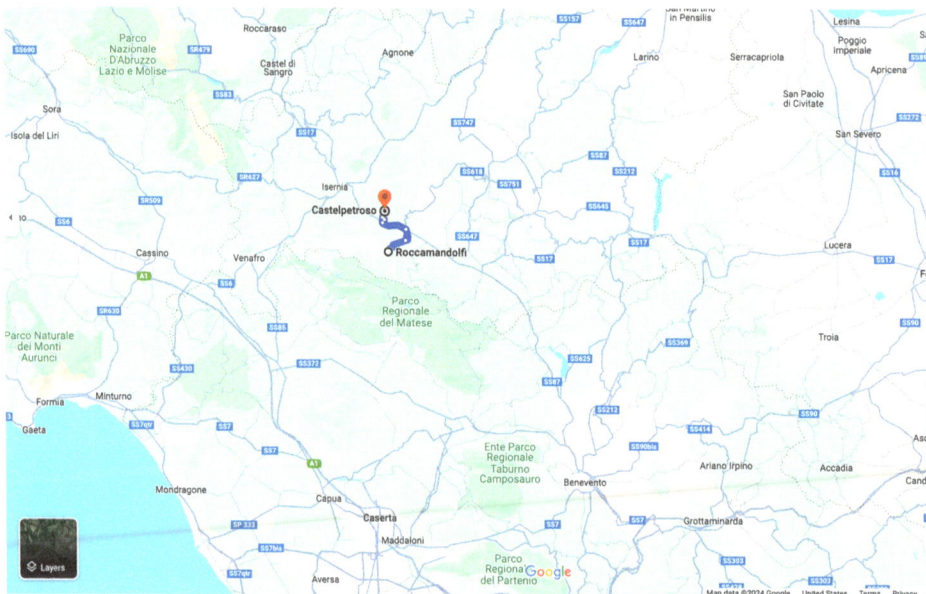

Figure 11. **About 9 miles distance between Castelpetroso and Roccamandolfi**

Roccamandolfi is in the center of Molise and has steep rock walls and green valleys surrounding it. It is said to have been founded in the early years of the 12th century, when a family named Mandolfus emigrated from Germany and built a fortress whose ruins are still there. It is called "Rocca Maginulfo." The Lombards ruled the area and then were conquered by the Normans. Various feudal lords ruled the area for centuries until feudalism was abolished around the 19th century. Here's a picture of Roccamandolfi with the mountains and valleys visible.

Figure 12. **Roccamandolfi, Italy**

Cleonice Mastrantuoni was born 11 November 1884 at 3:20 p.m. in Roccamandolfi, Isernia to parents Pasquale Mastrantuoni who was a bricklayer and was 31 at the time, and Elisabetta Martelli, a seamstress, who was 29. Their home was on Via Fontana. Cleonice's father presented her to the Administration of the Community of Roccamandolfi the next morning at 9:15. Roccamandolfi was a mountainous area. See Figure 13: Antenati Registry: 1884; Figure 14: Registry listing of Cleonice Mastrantuoni; Figure 15: Birth Certificate No. 86 of Cleonice Mastrantuoni. Note that at the end of the birth certificate, Pasquale's signature is Mastrantuoni, not Mastantuoni. The Registry and birth certificate misspelled the name.

Figure 13. **Antenati 1884 Registry**

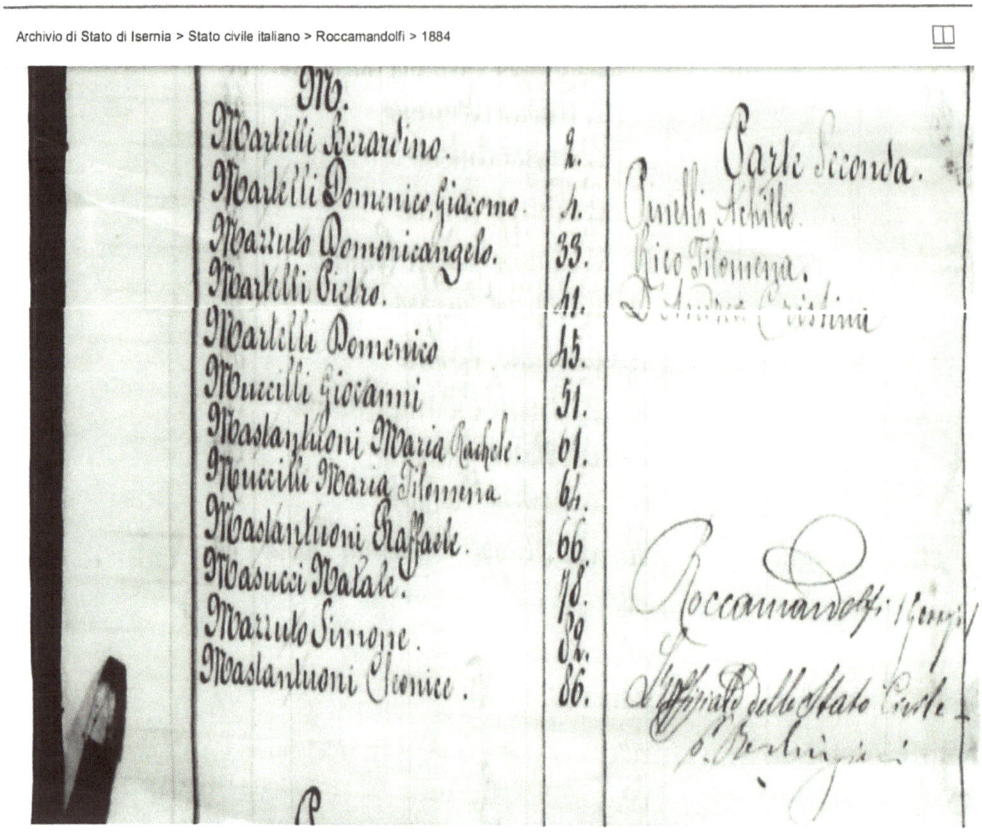
Archivio di Stato di Isernia > Stato civile italiano > Roccamandolfi > 1884

M.
Martelli Berardino. 2.
Martelli Domenico Giacomo. 4.
Marzullo Domenicangelo. 33.
Martelli Pietro. 41.
Martelli Domenico 45.
Mucilli Giovanni 51.
Mastantuoni Maria Rachele. 61.
Mucilli Maria Filomena 64.
Mastantuoni Raffaele. 66.
Masucci Natale. 78.
Marzullo Simone. 82.
Mastantuoni Cleonice. 86.

Parte Seconda.
Iannelli Achille.
Rico Filomena.
D'Andrea Cristina

Roccamandolfi
L'Uffiziale dello Stato Civile

Figure 14. **Registry Listing of Cleonice Mastrantuoni (with name misspelled)**

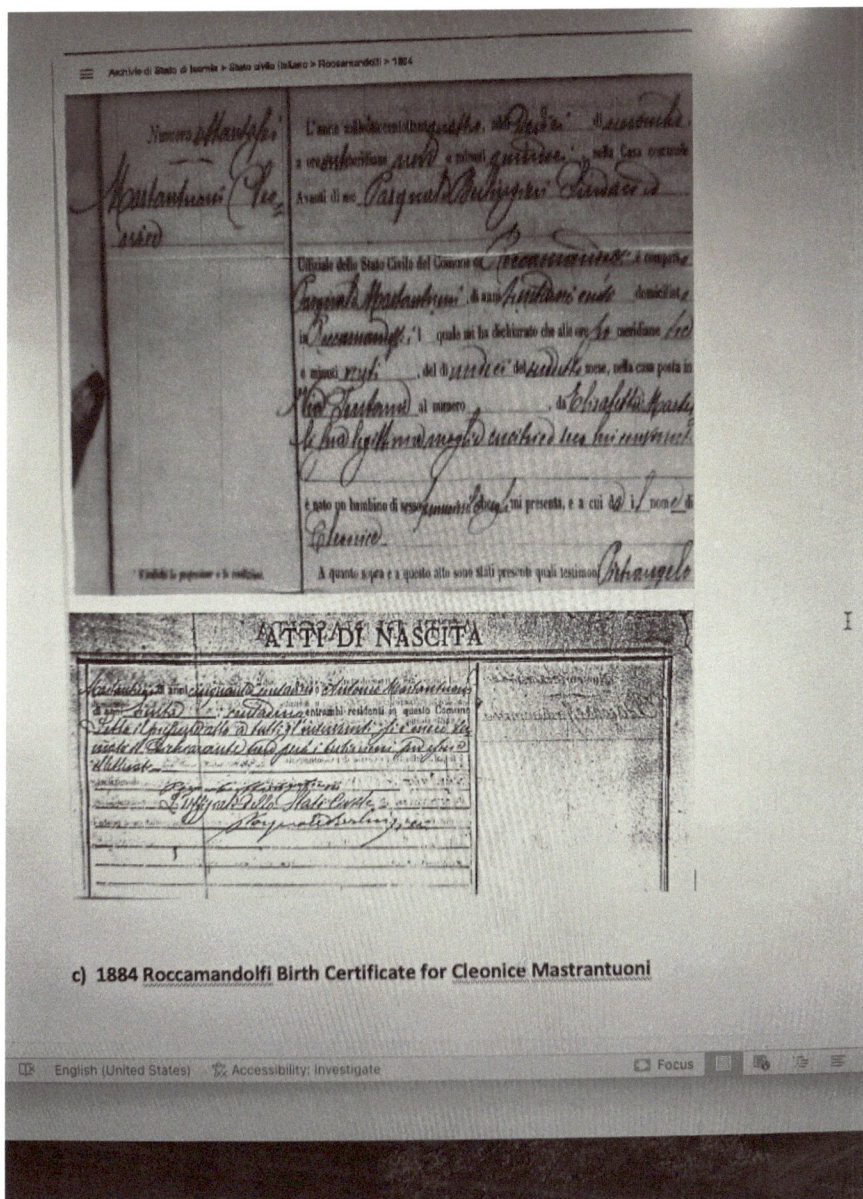

c) 1884 Roccamandolfi Birth Certificate for Cleonice Mastrantuoni

Figure 15. **1884 Roccamandolfi Birth Certificate for Cleonice Mastrantuoni**

It is reasonable to believe that Cleonice continued to live on Via Fontana with her parents until 1907. No travel records were found for Cleonice until 1907.

Documents show Cleonice Mastrantuoni's various names used during her lifetime included Cleonice Mastantuoni, Cleonice Giancola, Cleonice Giansola, Alice Smith, Clara A. Smith, Clara Smith, Alice De Maso, Clara Senas, Clara Alice Smith, and Clara Masters.

The following series of pictures will give a good idea of what it would have been like for Cleonice to stroll down her street in Roccamandolfi (minus the satellite dishes and the cars!) The road was quite narrow, and the buildings looked to be about what would be expected. The mountains can be seen in the background. At the end of the street, there was a square where the people used to meet. (One of my early memories is of the time I was sitting on our gray sofa in Orlando, Florida with Grandma, and she told me about the ladies in her little town all dressing in black and gathering in the square to meet after a death. She spoke to me in English, and it was very hard to understand her, I remember. She used to stay at our house on Manor Drive during the days when Aunt Lucy was working. I wasn't in school yet, so I spent a lot of time playing Bunco with her even though I had no idea how high I was supposed to count to win. She simply loved the game! More stories when I get to the days when she lived in Orlando, and our Stonitsch family saw her often.)

The Catholic Church in Roccamandolfi was in walking distance of the house where Cleonice's family lived, and it was at the end of the square with a set of steps leading to it. It was dedicated to San Giacomo Maggiore. "The church was built in Baroque style and hinges on a single nave inside, in which the relics of San Liberato are venerated. The body of the saint was obtained in 1780 by the Duchess Anna Pignatelli who had expressly requested the body of a saint from Pope Pius VI to be placed, inside a specific chapel, in the church of San Giacomo Maggiore. The church also houses an eighteenth-century altar inside, as well as a wooden sculpture by the sculptor Di Zinno and finally an original font dating back to the Renaissance period with a snake coiled on the bottom symbolizing sin. Not far from the church it is possible to admire the four ancient units of measurement used for grains, made of smooth stone and corresponding to the "tomolo" to the "Mezzetto" to the "quarter" and to the "measure.""

The last two of the series of pictures show the Chiesa di San Giacomo Maggiore where undoubtedly Cleonice, her parents, and relatives walked to for the various Catholic celebrations.

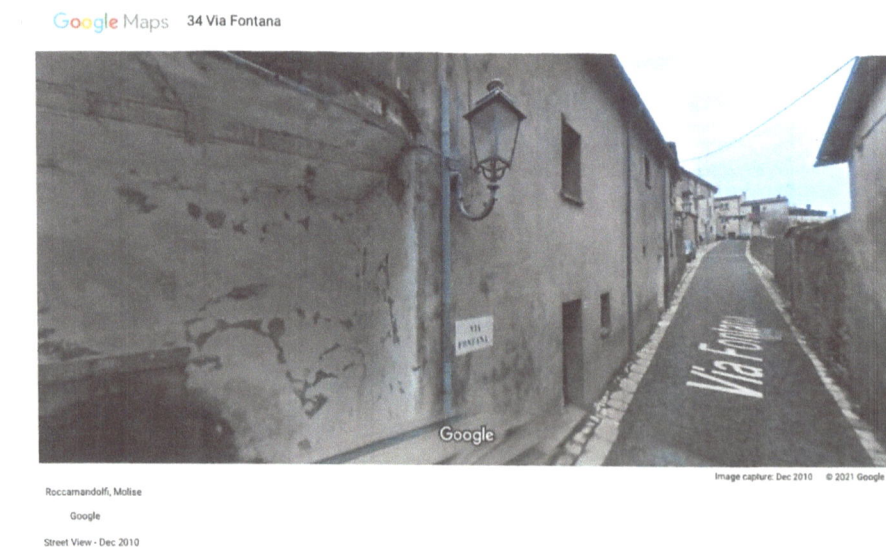

Figure 16. **34 Via Fontana**

Figure 17. **30 Via Fontana**

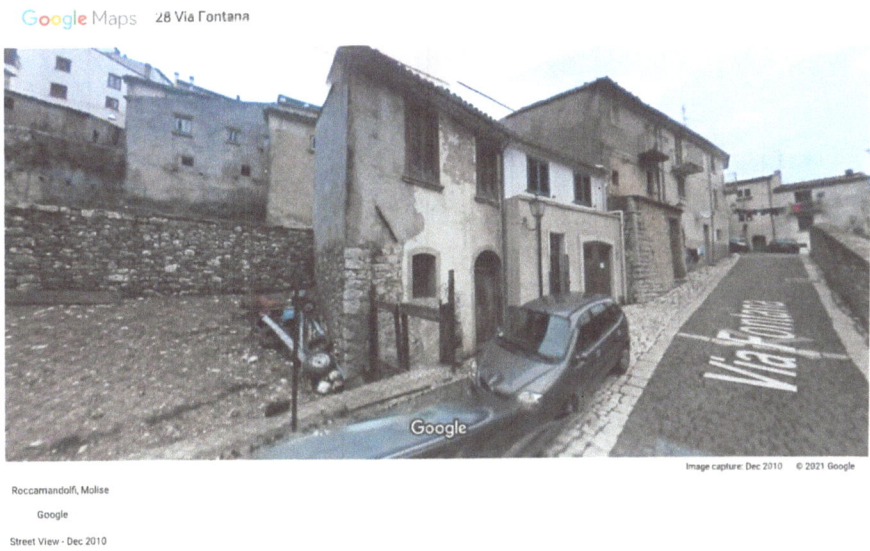

Figure 18. **28 Via Fontana (Looking up the street)**

Figure 19. **28 Via Fontana (looking down the street)**

Figure 20. **Roccamandolfi, Molise**

Figure 21. **Chiesa di San Giacomo Maggiore in Roccamandolfi, Italy**

Figure 22. **Closer View of Chiesa di San Giacomo Maggiore**

This may have been the Church where Cleonice and Giuseppe were married on 18 April of 1907. (The marriage records that are available online do not cover the years of the twentieth century. The search will continue for this certificate.) The bride's home Church was the usual place of marriage for couples in those days.

Brothers and Sisters of Cleonice Mastrantuoni (Cleonice born 11 Nov 1884)

The brothers and sisters of Cleonice included the following: Maria (born 1876 and died 1890 at age 14); Gaetano (born 1877 and died 1879 at age 2); Giuseppa (born 1878 and died in 1878 at 20 days old); Gaetano (born 1881 and died 1882 at 1 year old); Raffaele (born 1883 and died 1884 at 3 months old); Giovanna Gaetana (born and died in 1889 at 5 days old); Mario (born 29 March 1891); Maria (born 25 Aug 1893); Giovanina (born 1894). No records were found from 1895 to 1899 for any other children born to Pasquale and Elisabetta. (Most of the birth certificates have the correct spelling for the last name Mastrantuoni.) The children were all born at their home on Via Fontana. Most of the children died in infancy or childhood, but Cleonice's brother Mario lived to be an adult and was said to have moved to America, possibly to the New Jersey area. This has not been confirmed through research yet, but only through word-of-mouth. It was said that Mario had married and at some point, was divorced. This was something the family was not proud of and didn't discuss.

Giuseppe Giancola in Braddock, Pennsylvania: from 1897 – 1911

Giuseppe Giancola's first voyage from his home in Italy to the United States was in the year 1897 when he was 14 years old. He travelled from his home in Castelpetroso to Naples, Italy in late March/early April of 1897 and then sailed on a steamship called the Chateau Yquem to **Ellis Island, New York, New York,** arriving on April 26, 1897.

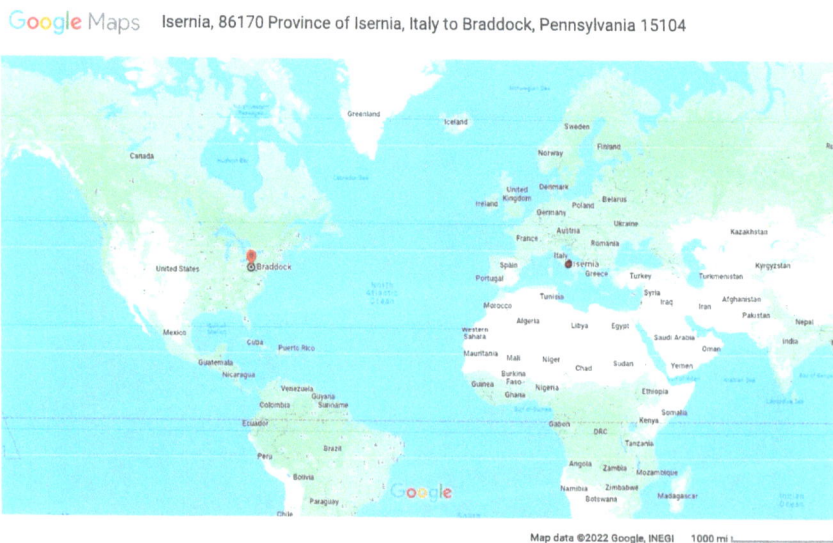

Figure 23. **Map Showing Voyage from Isernia, Italy, to Braddock, Pennsylvania**

Although various records claim that Giuseppe immigrated in an earlier year, such as 1893 or 1894, there is no evidence to support this. In fact, the website musee-aquitaine-bordeaux.fr/en/article/steam-packet-chateau-yquem shows the first Fabre Line trip of this vessel left Marseilles, Genoa, Leghorn 29 March 1897 and then from Naples, sailed on 16 April 1897 arriving in New York on 26 April 1897. Giuseppe was on this first voyage. Giuseppe could not have taken an earlier trip to America on this vessel. See the following history of the ship's voyages.

CHATEAU YQUEM (renamed GALLIA) ?

Builder: Chantiers & Ateliers de la Gironde, Bordeaux (engines by Schneider & Cie, Creuzot) in 1883
Launched: Launched on 17/11/1883 as the "Chateau Yquem" for the French owned Bordeaux Line
Description: 4,035 gross ship
length 386.5ft x beam 41ft, one funnel, three masts, iron construction, single screw and a speed of 12 knots.
Passenger accommodation for 50-1st and 1,200-3rd class.
Maiden Voyage: sailed from Bordeaux to New York on 30/6/1884.
Other Voyages: On 27/2/1886 she started a single Palermo - Naples - Valencia - New York round voyage
On 10/5/1887 started a single round voyage from Bordeaux to Naples and New York.
Her last Bordeaux - New York sailing started on 6/9/1887 and her last Naples - New York on 21/4/1888.
In the Autumn of 1888 she was chartered to Compagnie Generale Transatlantique (French Line) and sailed between Bordeaux, Havana
and Vera Cruz. Damaged in collision with the SPatersonish ship "Cristobal Colon" at Havana on 28/1/1889
on 3/11/1891 was offered for sale at Bordeaux but found no buyer.
Chartered to the French government in April 1895 and used as a transport for the Madagascar Expedition
9/10/1896 sailed from Havre to New York
Sold to the Fabre Line in 1896, she commenced her first Marseilles - Genoa - Leghorn - Naples - New York voyage on 29/3/1897
On 31/12/1897 she stranded at La Seyne, was refloated and had an extensive refit.
She resumed Marseilles - New York sailings on 21/1/1899 and started her last Marseilles -Naples - New York voyage on 3/6/1900.
Last Voyage: Marseilles -New York voyage in December 1909 (arr. NY 15/1/1910).
Sold/Scrapped: Sold and scrapped December 1910 in Italy.
Source: North Atlantic Seaway by N.R.P. Bonsor, vol.3, p.1064

Figure 24. History of Chateau Yquem

In addition to the above records, searches were made at Ellis Island by a researcher back in 1993 who also coordinated with the National Archives to assist in the search for a Giuseppe Giancola/Giansola on any earlier voyages on other ships. None were found. See letter below from Fort Monmouth, NJ.

```
                                        P O BOX 234
                                        FORT MONMOUTH, NJ 07703

                                        MARCH 15, 1993

        A. WHITE
        9931 S. PARK CI.
        FAIRFAX STATION, VA 22039

        DEAR MR. WHITE:

        REGARDING YOUR REQUEST FOR RESEARCH ASSISTANCE IN
        THE PASSENGER LISTS.

        NAME: GIUSEPPE GIANSOLA
        ARRIVED APRIL 1894
        FROM: ITALY
        TO: NY

        WE SEARCHED, ALL SHIPS FROM ITALY, FOR THE TIME FRAME
        APRIL 1894, BUT DID NOT FIND ANY PERSON NAMED GIUSEPPE
        GIANSOLA LISTED AS A PASSENGER.

        WE WILL BE AT ELLIS ISLAND THE END OF MARCH.  WHILE THERE
        WILL SEARCH THEIR RECORDS, AS WELL, FOR MENTION OF GIUSEPPE
        GIANSOLA.  IF ANYTHING IS LISTED HERE WILL SEND INFO POST
        HASTE.
        WE HAVE ALSO REQUESTED NATIONAL ARCHIVES TO ASSIST IN THE
        SEARCH.
        IF THEY COME UP WITH ANY ANSWERS WILL SEND INFO TO YOU.

        WHAT IS THE SOURCE FOR THE INFO THAT YOU SENT ON HIS
        ARRIVAL?

        ARE YOU 100% CERTAIN THAT IT IS CORRECT?

        SINCERELY YOURS,

        L. Pompfrell
```

Figure 25. Letter from Fort Monmouth, N.J., re Passenger Lists

The Statue of Liberty/Ellis Island records also provide information about passengers and ships that sailed from Naples, Italy to New York, New York during this time. Some pictures from the Statue of Liberty—Ellis Island Foundation website show the following: Giuseppe's information, a picture of the ship, the number of passengers, and information about the ship including its history. See below for that information.

10/27/2020   The Statue of Liberty & Ellis Island

8 1/2 x 11$29.00

If applicable please use promo code at checkout

[ADD TO CART >] [SAVE TO MY PROFILE]

- First Name : Gppi. Antonio
- Last Name : Giancola
- Nationality : Italy, Italian
- Date of Arrival : April 26th, 1897
- Age at Arrival : 14y
- Gender : Male
- Ship of Travel : Chateau Yquem
- Port of Departure : Naples
- Manifest Line Number : 0160

Annotations

Currently the Record has 0 Annotations.

This is a list of annotations for the passenger, created by visitors to the site. Annotations supplement information in the record, telling more about the passenger's background and life in the United States. Click a name to view an annotation.

[Request a TEXT correction]

The Statue of Liberty - Ellis Island Foundation

VISIT
- Statue of Liberty
- Ellis Island
- Statue of Liberty Museum
- National Immigration Museum

SUPPORT
- Donate
- Wall of Honor

DISCOVER
- Passenger · Ship search
- Stories · Oral Histories
- Famous Passengers
- Genealogy Primer
- Flag of Faces

THE FOUNDATION
- Mission

https://heritage.statueofliberty.org/passenger-details/czoxMjolMTAyODk5MDUwMzQ3ljs=/czo5OiJwYXNzZW5nZXIiOw==   2/3

Figure 26. Information from Ellis Island Foundation Website

○ 5 X 7 $10.00
○ 9 X 12 $12.50

[ADD TO CART >] [Save To My Profile]

Traveled
Not available

Number of Passengers
1,250

* **Please** note that ship images are smaller than the acid-free archival paper they are printed on. The ship image on 11" X 17" paper measures approximately 9" X 12". The ship image on 8 1/2" X 11" paper measures approximately 5" X 7". Measurements are approximate only. Our customized frames are guaranteed to fit every document.

About the Ship

Built by Chantiers et Ateliers de la Gironde, Bordeaux, France, 1883. 4,211 gross tons; 386 (bp) feet long; 41 feet wide. Compound engines, single screw. Service speed 13 knots. 1,250 passengers (50 first class, 1200 third class). One funnel, three masts, iron construction.

Ship History

Built for Compagnie Bordelaise de Navigation, French flag, in 1883 and named **Chateau Yquem**. Mediterranean-New York service.

Sold to Fabre Line, French flag, in 1900 and renamed **Gallia**.

Scrapped in 1910.

Dedicated to the Restoration and Preservation of the Statue of Liberty and Ellis Island.

-
-
-
-
-

Figure 27. **Information About the Chateau Yquem**

Chateau Yquem / Gallia

Ship Information

Built by Chantiers et Ateliers de la Gironde, Bordeaux, France, 1883. 4,211 gross tons; 386 (bp) feet long; 41 feet wide. Compound engine, single screw. Service speed 13 knots. 1,250 passengers (50 first class, 1,200 third class).One funnel, three masts, iron construction.

Ship History

Built for Compagnie Bordelaise de Navigation, French flag, in 1883 and named Chateau Yquem. Mediterranean-New York service.

Sold to Fabre Line, French flag, in 1900 and renamed Gallia.

Scrapped in 1910.

The Gallia/ Chateau Yquem

Figure 28. Information From Ellis Island Foundation Website

The New York Times newspaper also covers the arrival and departure of ships from the port of New York. A search of the Chateau Yquem was made for The New York Times and The Boston Globe newspapers for the mid- to late- 1890's. One in The Boston Globe dated 27 March 1896 mentions that, of the 1,203 Italians on the ship for that voyage in 1896 (which included only about 30 women), 400 Italians were detained, having no railway tickets west of Philadelphia which probably indicated that they had no intention of becoming citizens, according to the article. A man named de Luca of Naples chartered the ship from Funch, Edye & Co., and Commissioner Senner held the latter responsible for not having a contract with de Luca, and so the company had to pay for the expenses of the detained immigrants. The Chateau Yquem was not considered a reputable steamship and was "practically a tramp steamship." See The Boston Globe article below dated 27 March 1896.

The Boston Globe (Boston, Massachusetts) · 27 Mar 1898, Fri · Page 5

Printed on Jan 10, 2022

ITALIANS DETAINED.

A Hundred of Them Came on the Hindustan.

More Came on the Chateau Yquem and 400 Are Kept.

Commissioner Senner Will Hold Steamship Agents Responsible.

NEW YORK, March 26—Of 500 Italians who arrived on Sunday from Naples on the steamship Hindustan, 100 have been detained at Ellis Island, because they have no money and no definite idea of what they are going to do in America.

The 500 had an average of only $7 each, and many were without baggage. On the Chateau Yquem, which arrived on Tuesday, there were 1203 Italians, including only 30 women, only four of whom had railroad tickets west of Philadelphia.

They were a part of the multitude that hibernates in Italy and, when warm weather comes here, sets sail for New York. Most of them have no intention of becoming citizens.

Commissioner Senner has detained 400 of the Chateau Yquem's immigrants. The ship was chartered by a man named de Lucca of Naples from Punch, Edye & Co, her agents, and as Commissioner Senner does not know anything about de Lucca the expense of the detentions will fall on Punch, Edye & Co, who neglected to make a contract with de Lucca, providing that he should assume the responsibility for detained and deported immigrants.

Dr Senner says the Chateau Yquem and the Hindustan are practically tramp steamships and that he will not release the detained immigrants unless they produce bonds before the time set for their deportation.

In the case of reputable steamship lines, he says, bonds for detained immigrants would not be no necessary.

Figure 29. **The Boston Globe** Article Mentioning Chateau Yquem

Several articles in the April 1897 edition of <u>The New York Times</u> posted news about the progress of the Chateau Yquem steamship that Giuseppe was on in 1897, mentioning that it had passed various locations on its way to New York.

<u>The New York Times</u> dated 17 May 1899 has an article about a virulent case of scarlet fever on the Chateau Yquem which had just arrived in New York from Mediterranean ports. The three-year-old child was not diagnosed until after leaving the ship, and he and his family had mingled with the other passengers on the steamship during the voyage, exposing many to the dangers of scarlet fever.

SCARLET FEVER ON A SHIP.

Over Eight Hundred Immigrants Exposed to the Disease on the Chateau Yquem.

Dr. Williams of the medical staff at the Barge Office, yesterday afternoon discovered a well-developed case of scarlet fever among the steerage passengers of the steamship Chateau Yquem, which arrived here yesterday from Mediterranean ports. The case was not reported from Quarantine, and it was not until the 858 immigrants were landed at the Barge Office and were passing through the doctor's inspection that it was detected. Vito Di Stasio, three years old, was found to have the disease in a virulent form. The child was brought here in company with his father, mother, and his eight-months-old sister. The family was isolated from the other immigrants.

Up to the time of the discovery of the fever by the doctor, the family mingled with the other immigrants on the steamer and at the Barge Office. No attempt could be made to separate any who were exposed, save the family, as they passed before the register clerks and landed. Out of the 858 who arrived on the steamer, more than 700 had left the Barge Office before the case was discovered, and are now scattered throughout the city and country.

Health Officer Doty, when seen, said that the discovery of the case was a surprise to him, as the surgeon of the Chateau Yquem had not reported any sickness at Quarantine. Furthermore, there was no sickness discovered by the Quarantine doctors, and not a single child appeared with rash. "Scarlet fever is not legally a quarantinable disease at any rate," said Dr. Doty, "and had we found a case we would have simply reported it to the Board of Health and passed the steamer."

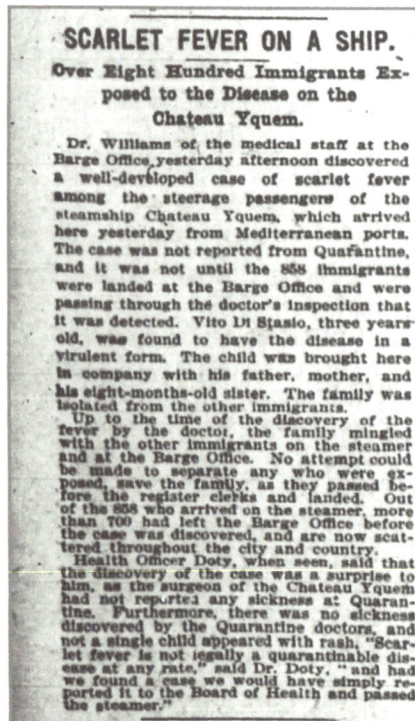

Figure 30. The New York Times 17 May 1899 Mentioning the Chateau Yquem

The risk of contracting diseases on the voyages was high. Fortunately, Giuseppe was only on the April 1897 Chateau Yquem voyage, which did not report a massive detention of Italian passengers nor any cases of scarlet fever.

This first steamship, the **Chateau Yquem**, that Giuseppe took to America left the port of Naples, Italy on 16 April 1897 and arrived in New York on 26 April 1897, shortly before Giuseppe's 15th birthday. His father would have been 58 years old (if he were indeed alive at this time), and his mother would have been 56. (Death certificates have not been located yet for either Diamante or Concetta.) The ship manifesto shows that neither of his parents accompanied Giuseppe on his journey to New York.

The following is a copy of the National Archives Microfilm Publications sheet which shows the vessel named Chateau Yquem, with the port of embarkation Naples, the date of arrival in New York as April 26, 1897. This is the ship that Giuseppe Giancola took to America.

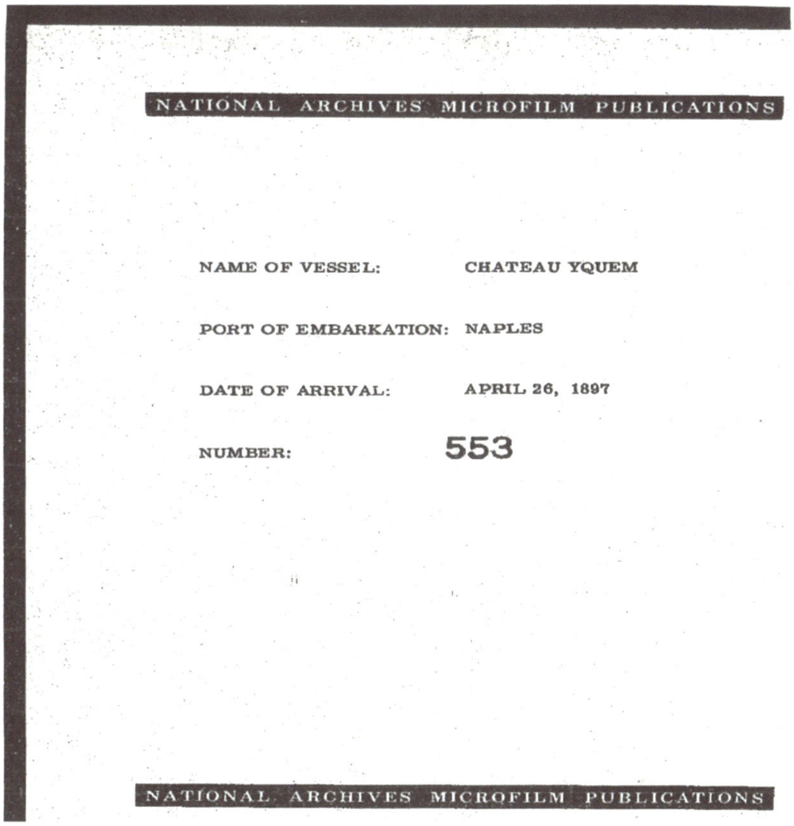

NATIONAL ARCHIVES MICROFILM PUBLICATIONS

NAME OF VESSEL: CHATEAU YQUEM

PORT OF EMBARKATION: NAPLES

DATE OF ARRIVAL: APRIL 26, 1897

NUMBER: **553**

NATIONAL ARCHIVES MICROFILM PUBLICATIONS

Figure 31. **National Archives Microfilm Record re Chateau Yquem**

The Ship Manifest shows the name Gppe. Antonio Giancola as passenger #160 out of 1,522. His ID number was 102899050347. His destination is listed as New York. Below is a page of the 1897 New York, U.S., Arriving Passenger and Crew Lists from Ancestry. com showing this initial trip of Giuseppe.

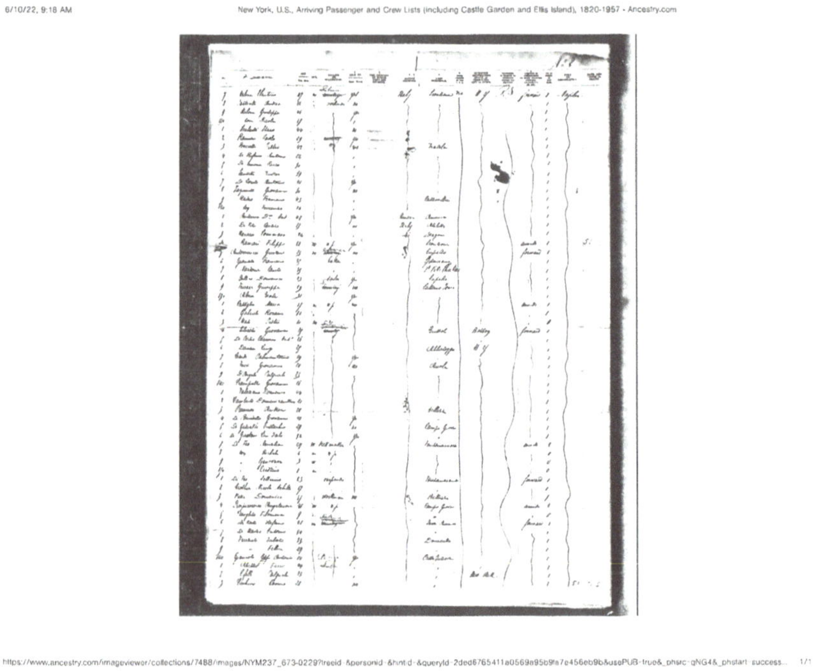

Figure 32. **Arrival Passenger List of Gppe. Antonio Giancola (Ancestry.com) to New York 26 April 1897**

He is listed as being 14 years old and able to read and write. It shows his last residence as being Castelpetroso. His name is located toward the bottom of this page. Three individuals from the same town of Castelpetroso that are listed below Giuseppe's name may have been relatives traveling to New York also: Cosmo Cicchino (age 21), Pasquale Cifelli (age 23), and Abessio Farro (age 44). All but Cosmo Cicchino were listed as being able to read and write. Each had one piece of baggage and occupied a forward position on the steamship Chateau Yquem. Here is an enlarged version of a portion of the bottom of the page.

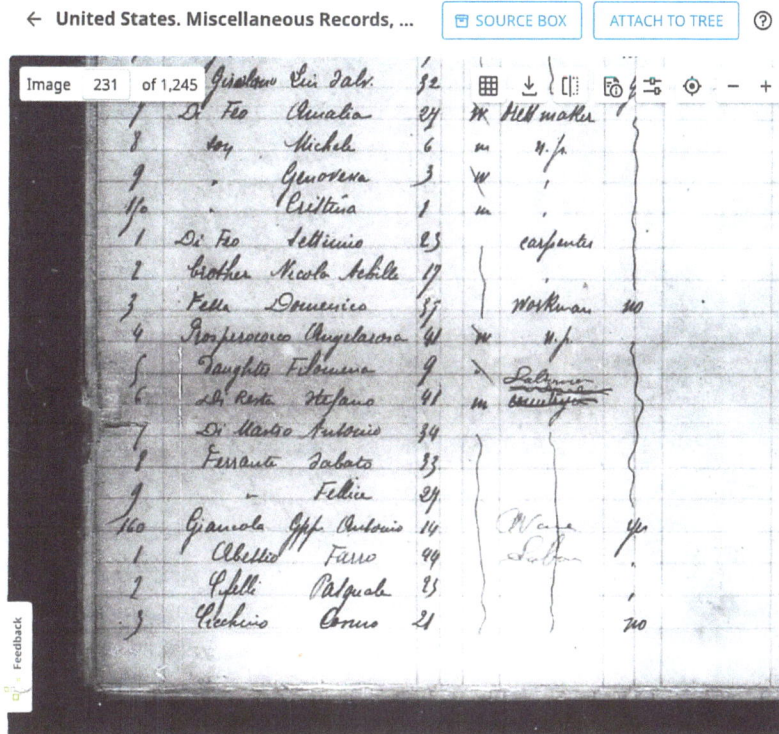

Figure 33. **Enlargement of bottom part of page of Arrival Passenger List from 26 April 1897**

The easily readable typed information from Ancestry.com shows the basic information from the list, and that is shown below.

Figure 34. **Ancestry.com Chateau Yquem Manifesto with Giuseppe's Information**

Here's the familysearch.org New York Passenger arrival List (Ellis Island) record:

Gppi. Antonio Giancola

Migration • New York Passenger Arrival Lists (Ellis Island), 1892-1924

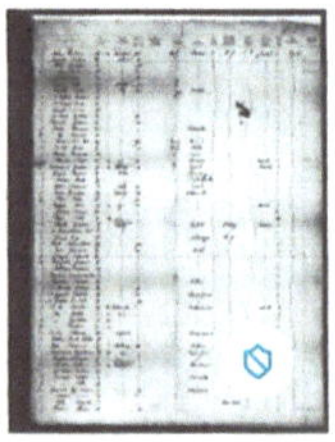

Document Information

Collection Information

[New York Passenger Arrival Lists (Ellis Island), 1892-1924]

Cite This Record

"New York Passenger Arrival Lists (Ellis Island), 1892-1924", , *FamilySearch* (https://www.familysearch.org/ark:/61903/1:1:JXWC-8P6 : Sat Mar 09 15:46:28 UTC 2024), Entry for Gppi. Antonio Giancola, 1897.

Name	**Gppi. Antonio Giancola**
Sex	**Male**
Age	**14 years**
Birth Date	**1883**
Nationality	**Italy, Italian**
Event Type	**Immigration**
Event Date	**1897**
Event Place	**Ellis Island, New York City, New York, United States**
Page Number	**553**
Series Number	**M237**
Affiliate Publication Title	**Passenger Lists of Vessels Arriving at New York, New York, 1820-1897**
Departure Port	**Naples**
Ship Name	**Chateau Yquem**

Family Tree

Similar Records

No similar records were found.

https://www.familysearch.org/ark:/61903/1:1:JXWC-8P6

https://www.familysearch.org/ark:/61903/1:1:JXWC-8P6

Figure 35. **Family Search New York Passenger Arrival List**

After landing at Ellis Island in 1897, it is most likely that, with help from relatives in New York, Giuseppe made his way to the Braddock area of western Pennsylvania to begin work there because the opportunities were abundant, and he would have heard about these work opportunities from the network of relatives and acquaintances who had already immigrated to the United States from Castelpetroso, where conditions were stagnant and oppressive. In any case, in the 1900 U.S. Federal Census for Pennsylvania, County of Allegheny, Township of Braddock, there is a listing for someone as a boarder at **307 Tenth Street** with the last name of Giancola and the first name that looks like it could have started out being Giu (seppe) and was overwritten by something that looks like Antonio. In transcriptions of that page of the census the name is written as Justonia. The age and birth year are overwritten also, but the birth month is listed as May. Joseph was 18 at the time of the 1900 census, but someone changed the date from 1882 to 1874 to coincide with an incorrect age of 26 years old. He is listed as being single and as a day laborer who had been employed for all the months (January through July) preceding the 21 July 1900 date of the enumeration. The head of the house was listed as Nicola D'Amore, and his wife was Dolorata, both of whom were of Italian descent. The remainder of the residents (which included Giancola) at that address were all listed as boarders, and all were Italian. Giancola's prior residence was Italy. He states that in 1900 he had been in the United States for two years and that his year of immigration was 1898 (but it was actually 1897). He held the status of being an alien in 1900, meaning that he was not yet naturalized. Giancola is on the seventh line of the page. The census also indicates that he is unable to read, write, or speak English yet.

United States Census, 1900 > United States Census, 1900 > Pennsylvania > Allegheny > ED 346 Braddock borough Ward 1

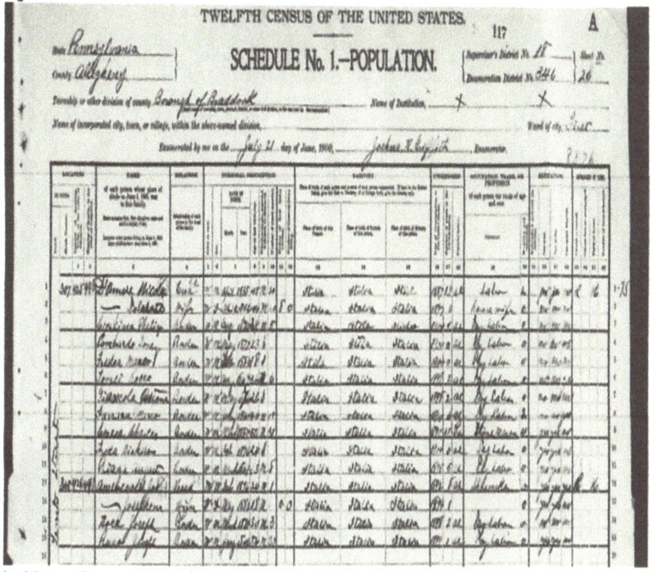
TWELFTH CENSUS OF THE UNITED STATES.

SCHEDULE No. 1.—POPULATION.

"United States Census, 1900," database with images, FamilySearch (https://familysearch.org/ark:/61903/3:1:S3HY-6P7C-DDS?cc=1325221&wc=9BW8-HZ4%3A1030550501%2C1030708501%2C1032716501 : 5 August 2014), Pennsylvania > Allegheny > ED 346 Braddock borough Ward 1 > image 51 of 51; citing NARA microfilm publication T623 (Washington, D.C.: National Archives and Records Administration, n.d.).

Figure 36. **United States Census, 1900: Pennsylvania, Allegheny, Braddock**

Next is a Google map showing where 307 Tenth Street is in Braddock, PA. Braddock is believed to be one of the first places that Giuseppe settled. It is a borough of Allegheny County in southwest PA, about eleven miles east of Pittsburgh. This is where Andrew Carnegie founded the Edgar Thomson Steel company in 1875. 307 Tenth Street is about .2 or .3 mile from the plant.

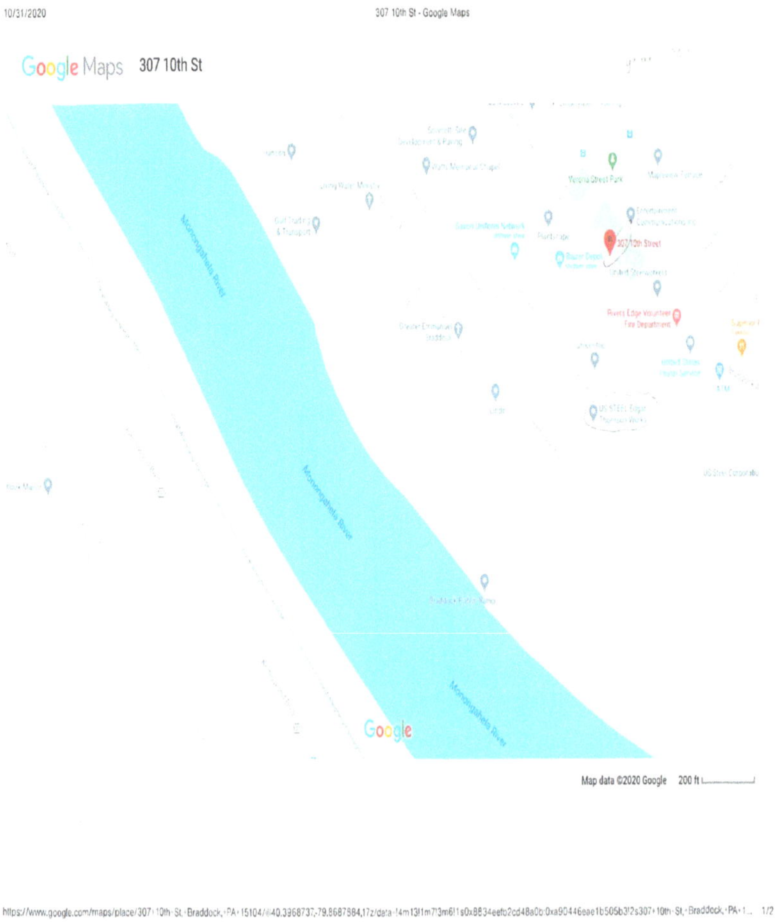

Figure 37. Google Maps showing 307 10ᵗʰ Street and US Steel Edgar Thompson Steel Company which was along the Monongahela River.

Here is a Welcome to Braddock sign from Google Maps with a picture of the U.S. Steel Edgar Thompson Works plant as it looked at that time.

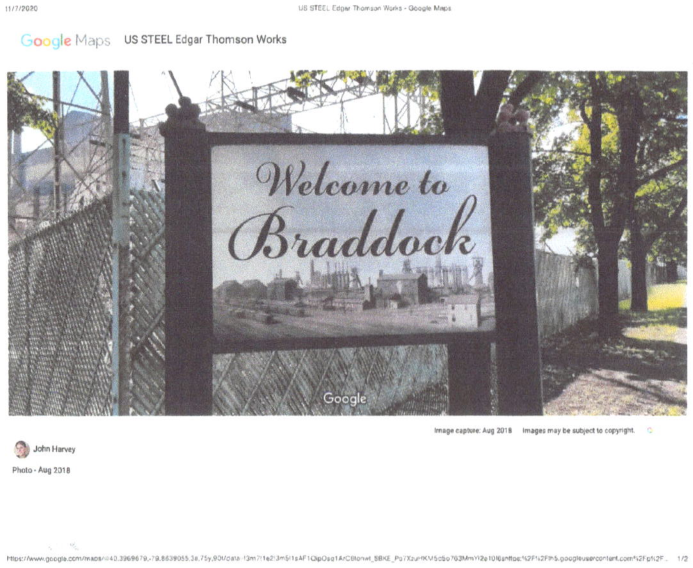

Figure 38. Google Maps Welcome to Braddock sign.

The following is a map showing the two-tenths of a mile walk from 307 Tenth Street to the steel plant.

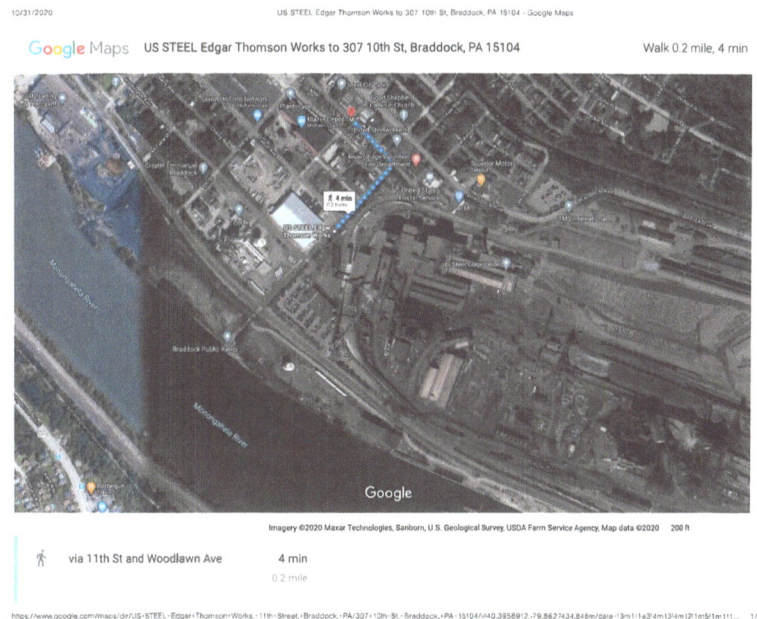

Figure 39. **Google Map Showing Distance Between 307 Tenth Street and the Steel Plant**

The Edgar Thomson Works plant was located on 152 11th St, Braddock, PA as shown on this Google.com/maps website. In 1883, Carnegie purchased the Homestead Steel Works plant which was the site of anti-union violence in 1892 when Carnegie threatened to substantially lower wages, increase working hours with no additional pay. This caused the union workers to go on strike along with nonunion workers who joined in. The steel company's management had hired the Pinkerton detective agents (similar to an army) whose job it was to settle labor disputes and strikes. When the agents confronted the employees, gun violence ensued, the plant was closed, and workers were fired. Meanwhile, Andrew Carnegie was vacationing in Scotland. This was all before Giuseppe arrived in the area which was about five years later around 1897. (It's no wonder there were plenty of job opportunities available with union workers and others being fired and wages being slashed! There were now lots of empty spaces to be filled.) The steel industry continued to grow, and by 1901 Carnegie sold his steel plants to J. P. Morgan. The plants were then called U. S. STEEL Edgar Thomson Works. (Later see postcard from 1924 with picture of Homestead Steel Works.)

Castelpetroso, Italy: 1903

Sometime before October 1903, Giuseppe travelled back to his hometown of Castelpetroso. This was not uncommon for Italian workers in America to return to their home country to visit with their relatives and share their newly earned wages. From 15 October 1903 to 31 October 1903 Giuseppe sailed back to the port of New York from Naples, Italy on the **Prinz Oscar** steamship. See picture of Prinz Oscar steamship below.

S.S. PRINZ OSKAR, 1902 Hamburg American Line
Courtesy The Peabody Museum of Salem

Figure 40. Prinz Oskar steamship for second known voyage of Giuseppe Giancola in 1903. Source: Ships of Our Ancestors by Michael J. Anuta

Next you will find a larger photo of the Prinz Oskar purchased from The Statue of Liberty-Ellis Island Foundation.

Figure 41. Photo of the Prinz Oskar Steamship Purchased from the Statue of Liberty-Ellis Island Foundation

The ship Prinz Oscar was described as "...a 6,026 gross ton ship, built in 1902 by Bremer Valkan, Vegesack for the Hamburg America Line of Hamburg. Her details were—length 403.4 ft x beam 49.2 ft, one funnel, two masts, twin screw and a speed of 13 knots. There was capacity for 60 1st and 1,200 3rd class passengers. Launched on 15 December 1902, she commenced her first Genoa – Naples – New York voyage and started her last voyage on this service on 29 June 1906."

Braddock, Pennsylvania: 1903

On the Ship Manifesto for that trip, Giuseppe's destination is listed as **Braddock, PA** to live with Peter Paul at **4 Tenth Street in Braddock, PA**. (See Ship Manifesto below.) Note that this location is on the same street as his thought-to-be previous address of 307 Tenth Street in Braddock, PA.

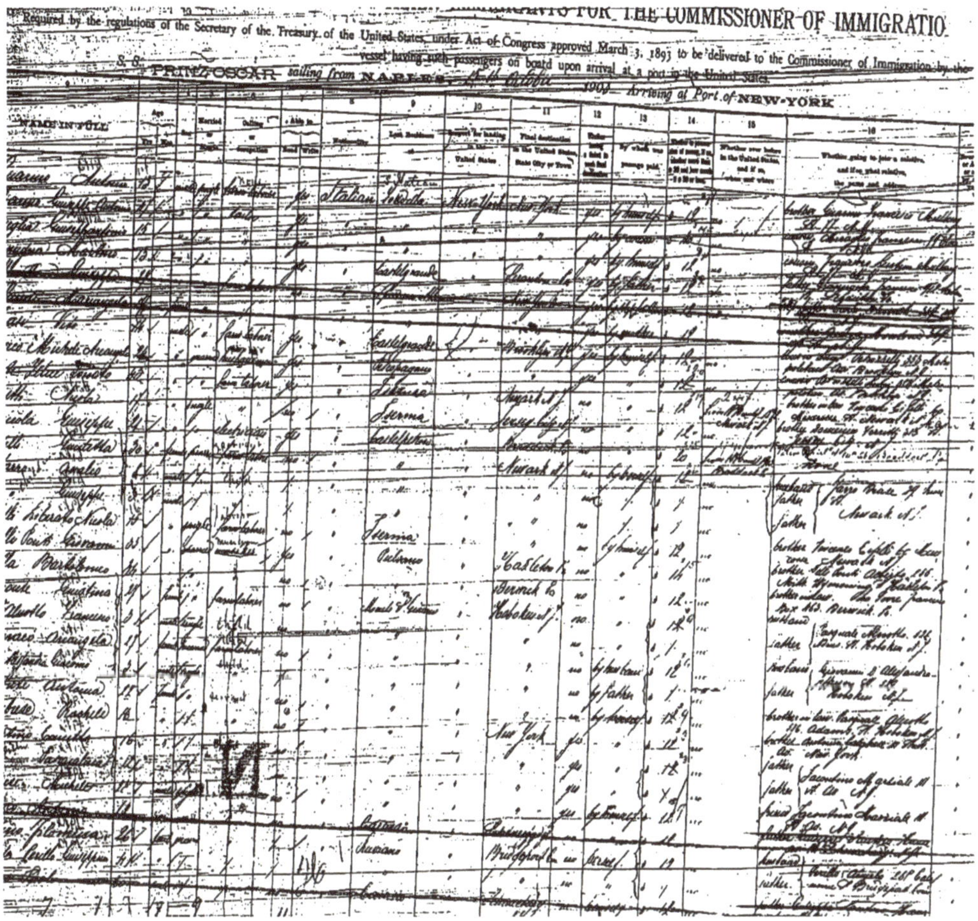
... FOR THE COMMISSIONER OF IMMIGRATIO...
Required by the regulations of the Secretary of the Treasury of the United States, under Act of Congress approved March 3, 1893 to be delivered to the Commissioner of Immigration by the ... vessel having such passengers on board upon arrival at a port in the United States.
PRINZ OSCAR sailing from NAPLES ... 1903 Arriving at Port of NEW YORK

Figure 42. **Prinz Oskar 1903 Ship Manifesto, Line 11—Giuseppe Giancola**

Peter Paul (the person that Giuseppe was planning to live with in Braddock) was not a relative of Giuseppe, but he was from Italy also, having been born in May 1866 as Pietro Paolo. Peter was 34 at the time of the 1900 Census, and had immigrated to the US in 1890, married, and had a large family. On the manifest it says that Giuseppe did not yet have a ticket to his final destination, but he did acknowledge that he was going to Braddock, PA to live with Peter Paul. It lists Giuseppe as 21, single, an electrician who could read and write, was born in Castelpetroso, paid for the passage by himself, had $20 with him, had spent 7 years in the U.S. from 1896 until 1903 (although we know that it was actually the year 1897 as previously discussed), that he was visiting Peter Paul at 4 Tenth Street in Braddock, PA. Giuseppe had not been in prison, nor in an almshouse, nor was supported by charity, nor was a polygamist. He was in good health and was neither deformed nor crippled.

Here is The Statue of Liberty-Ellis Island Foundation record for Giuseppe Giancola for this Prinz Oskar voyage.

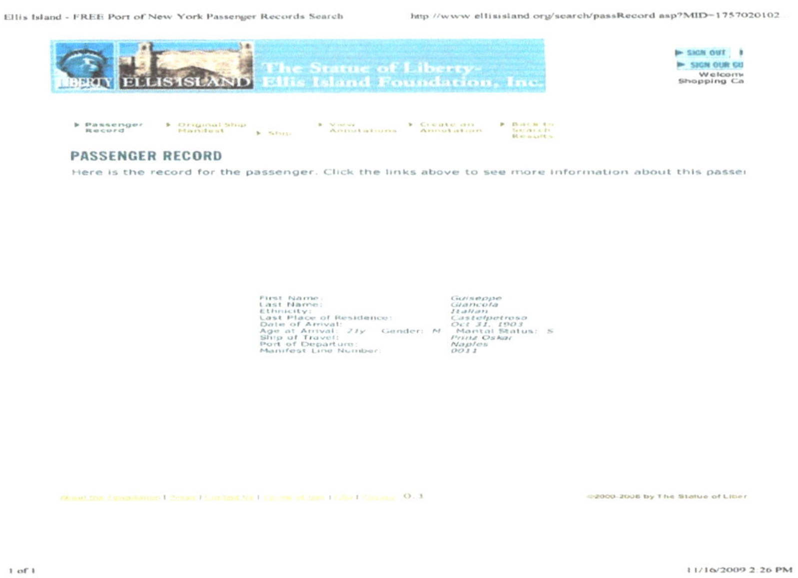

Ellis Island - FREE Port of New York Passenger Records Search http //www ellisisland.org/search/passRecord asp?MID=1757020102

The Statue of Liberty-Ellis Island Foundation, Inc.

▶ SIGN OUT
▶ SIGN OUR GU
Welcom
Shopping Ca

▶ Passenger Record ▶ Original Ship Manifest ▶ Ship ▶ View Annotations ▶ Create an Annotation ▶ Back to Search Results

PASSENGER RECORD

Here is the record for the passenger. Click the links above to see more information about this passe

First Name:	Guiseppe
Last Name:	Giancola
Ethnicity:	Italian
Last Place of Residence:	Castelpetroso
Date of Arrival:	Oct 31, 1903
Age at Arrival: 21y Gender: M	Marital Status: S
Ship of Travel:	Prinz Oskar
Port of Departure:	Naples
Manifest Line Number:	0011

©2000-2006 by The Statue of Liber

1 of 1 11/16/2009 2:26 PM

Figure 43. **Statue of Liberty-Ellis Island Foundation Record for Giuseppe Giancola for Prinz Oskar Voyage**

Braddock City directories and the 1900 and 1910 Censuses show Peter Paul living at 4 Tenth Street for the years 1900, 1902, 1903, and 1910. The 1920 Census shows Peter as an electrician living at 410 Talbot Ave about a half mile from his previous home.) It is unclear whether or how long Giuseppe lived with Peter Paul and his family at the 4 Tenth Street address, but it is reasonable that he could have moved there after boarding at 307 Tenth Street with D'Amore sometime between 1901-1903: the two addresses were only a distance of .2 miles apart. Both locations were close to the US STEEL Edgar Thomson Works, 152 11th St, Braddock, PA 15104. Giuseppe probably learned a lot to further his knowledge as an electrician both from his job and from Peter Paul with whom he lived as a boarder.

Clairton, PA: 1905

The Petition for Naturalization for Giuseppe Giancola in the Western District of Pennsylvania is dated 17 May 1905, and has his birthdate as 19 May 1882, with the place of landing as New York and his occupation as an electrician. It says that he is a native of Italy. His address in 1905 is listed as **#126 Clairton, PA**, and Adolorato Fato is his witness. Note that Giuseppe's last name is misspelled on the application as Gioncola. See the partial index to the names in the United States District Court Western District of Pennsylvania Petition for Naturalization (Figure 44, right hand side, line 7), and pages one and two for Giuseppe "Gioncola." Figures 45 and 46).

Film # 007790657

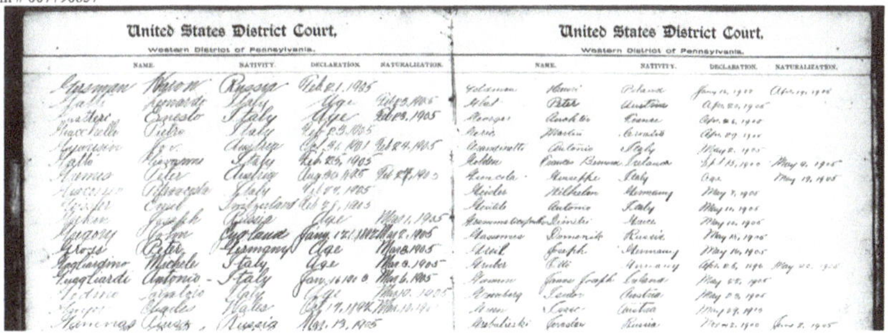

Figure 44. Partial Index to Names for Naturalization Petitions in Western District of Pennsylvania

The laws of naturalization changed over time. From 1855 until 1922, citizenship was automatically granted to the alien wife of U. S. citizens. (This was repealed in 1922.) Giuseppe would have been aware of this automatic granting of citizenship to a future spouse, and so made sure he satisfied the requirements for citizenship before he would be married. The Naturalization Act of 26 May 1824 allowed immigrants who had arrived in the United States before their 18th birthday (and Giuseppe arrived when he was 14) to, upon reaching their 21st birthday, petition for naturalization without prior declaration of intent. This was called "one paper naturalization." (See the website familysearch.org for more information about the naturalization process.) Giuseppe applied for his citizenship on May 17, 1905, two days short of his 21st birthday. This didn't seem to matter because the court allowed the process to go forward. And there is no declaration of intent in the records for Giuseppe. Under the column marked "declaration" is the word "Age" indicating that he qualified under the "one page naturalization" –almost! Five years of residency was required to petition for citizenship, and although his petition says that he arrived in 1894 (actually, it was 1897), he cleared the five-year mark (from 1897 to 1905). He was not required in 1905 to provide proof or a certificate of his arrival date of 26 April 1897. The law changed in 1906, and proof was required after this.

The Family Secret

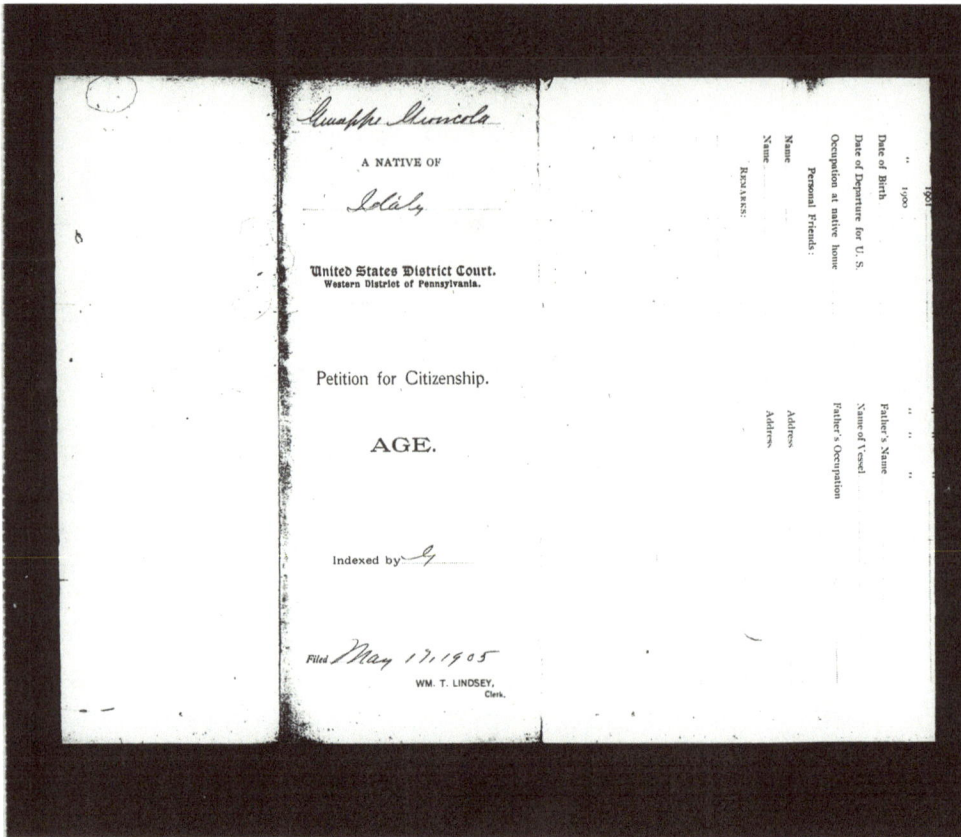

Figure 45. Giuseppe Giancola Petition for Naturalization Page 1

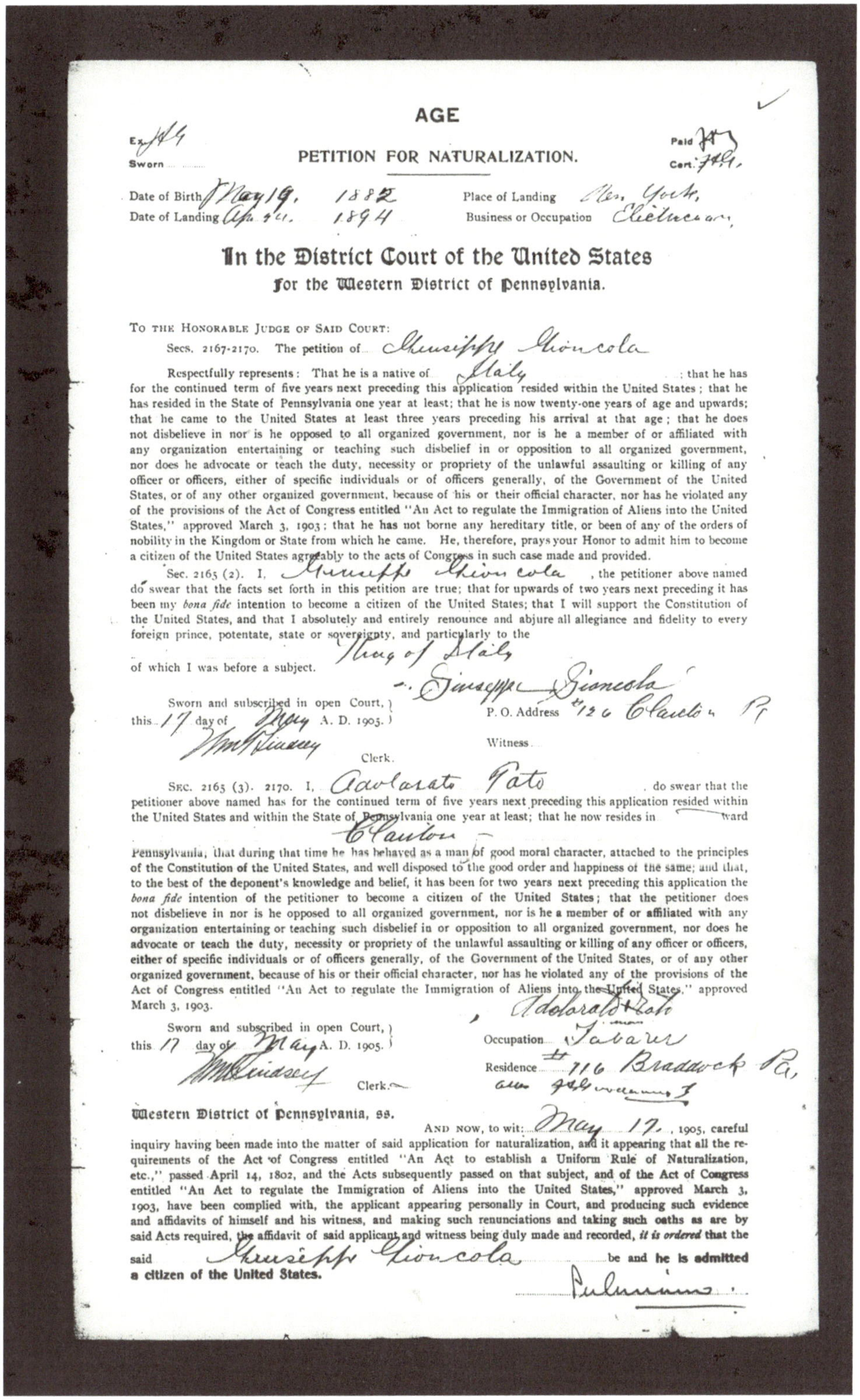

AGE

Ex. 44 PETITION FOR NATURALIZATION. Paid

Sworn Cert.

Date of Birth May 19, 1882 Place of Landing New York

Date of Landing Apr 20, 1894 Business or Occupation Electrician

In the District Court of the United States for the Western District of Pennsylvania.

To the Honorable Judge of Said Court:

Secs. 2167-2170. The petition of Giuseppe Giancola

Respectfully represents: That he is a native of Italy; that he has for the continued term of five years next preceding this application resided within the United States; that he has resided in the State of Pennsylvania one year at least; that he is now twenty-one years of age and upwards; that he came to the United States at least three years preceding his arrival at that age; that he does not disbelieve in nor is he opposed to all organized government, nor is he a member of or affiliated with any organization entertaining or teaching such disbelief in or opposition to all organized government, nor does he advocate or teach the duty, necessity or propriety of the unlawful assaulting or killing of any officer or officers, either of specific individuals or of officers generally, of the Government of the United States, or of any other organized government, because of his or their official character, nor has he violated any of the provisions of the Act of Congress entitled "An Act to regulate the Immigration of Aliens into the United States," approved March 3, 1903; that he has not borne any hereditary title, or been of any of the orders of nobility in the Kingdom or State from which he came. He, therefore, prays your Honor to admit him to become a citizen of the United States agreeably to the acts of Congress in such case made and provided.

Sec. 2165 (2). I, Giuseppe Giancola, the petitioner above named do swear that the facts set forth in this petition are true; that for upwards of two years next preceding it has been my *bona fide* intention to become a citizen of the United States; that I will support the Constitution of the United States, and that I absolutely and entirely renounce and abjure all allegiance and fidelity to every foreign prince, potentate, state or sovereignty, and particularly to the King of Italy of which I was before a subject.

Giuseppe Giancola

Sworn and subscribed in open Court, this 17 day of May A. D. 1905.

P. O. Address 126 Clairton Pa

Wm Lindsey Clerk.

Witness

Sec. 2165 (3). 2170. I, Adolarato Pato, do swear that the petitioner above named has for the continued term of five years next preceding this application resided within the United States and within the State of Pennsylvania one year at least; that he now resides in Clairton Ward Pennsylvania, that during that time he has behaved as a man of good moral character, attached to the principles of the Constitution of the United States, and well disposed to the good order and happiness of the same; and that, to the best of the deponent's knowledge and belief, it has been for two years next preceding this application the *bona fide* intention of the petitioner to become a citizen of the United States; that the petitioner does not disbelieve in nor is he opposed to all organized government, nor is he a member of or affiliated with any organization entertaining or teaching such disbelief in or opposition to all organized government, nor does he advocate or teach the duty, necessity or propriety of the unlawful assaulting or killing of any officer or officers, either of specific individuals or of officers generally, of the Government of the United States, or of any other organized government, because of his or their official character, nor has he violated any of the provisions of the Act of Congress entitled "An Act to regulate the Immigration of Aliens into the United States," approved March 3, 1903.

Adolarato Pato

Sworn and subscribed in open Court, this 17 day of May A. D. 1905.

Occupation Tabaier

Wm Lindsey Clerk.

Residence 716 Braddock Pa,

Western District of Pennsylvania, ss.

And now, to wit: May 17, 1905, careful inquiry having been made into the matter of said application for naturalization, and it appearing that all the requirements of the Act of Congress entitled "An Act to establish a Uniform Rule of Naturalization, etc.," passed April 14, 1802, and the Acts subsequently passed on that subject, and of the Act of Congress entitled "An Act to regulate the Immigration of Aliens into the United States," approved March 3, 1903, have been complied with, the applicant appearing personally in Court, and producing such evidence and affidavits of himself and his witness, and making such renunciations and taking such oaths as are by said Acts required, the affidavit of said applicant and witness being duly made and recorded, *it is ordered* that the said Giuseppe Giancola be and he is admitted a citizen of the United States.

Fulmimo

Figure 46. **Giuseppe Giancola Petition for Naturalization Page 2**

Clairton, PA is a city in Allegheny County, PA which is along the Monongahela River. The Carnegie Steel Company built a steel mill and coke production facility there around 1903. Below is a document from the Library of Congress showing the U.S. Steel Corp, Clairton Works which was west of the Monongahela River.

Figure 47. **Clairton Works, Clairton, PA (West of the Monongahela River) around the early 1900's**

Monongahela, Pennsylvania: 1907

Another document showing a place of residence for Giuseppe Giancola is his 4 March 1907 Application for Passport, in which it is stated that he is a naturalized and loyal citizen of the United States, was born at Castelpetroso, Italy on 19 May 1882, emigrated to the United States, sailing on board the French American line (the Chateau Yquem mentioned above) from Naples. He says that he lived uninterruptedly in the United States from 1894 to 1907. (This is incorrect. It should be 1897 instead of 1894.) He lived at **Braddock** and **Monongahela, Pennsylvania** during this time, and his permanent residence he states as **Monongahela City, PA**. His plan was to travel abroad (to Italy) and return to the United States by 1908 with his future wife Cleonice. He is described as 24 years old, 5 feet 6 ½ inches, with a regular mustache and a smooth square chin, a high forehead, blue eyes, a pointed, heavy nose, light, thin hair, a clear complexion, and a long, medium face. He lists his current address in 1907 as **301 Park Avenue, Monongahela City, PA.** See the Application for Passport below.

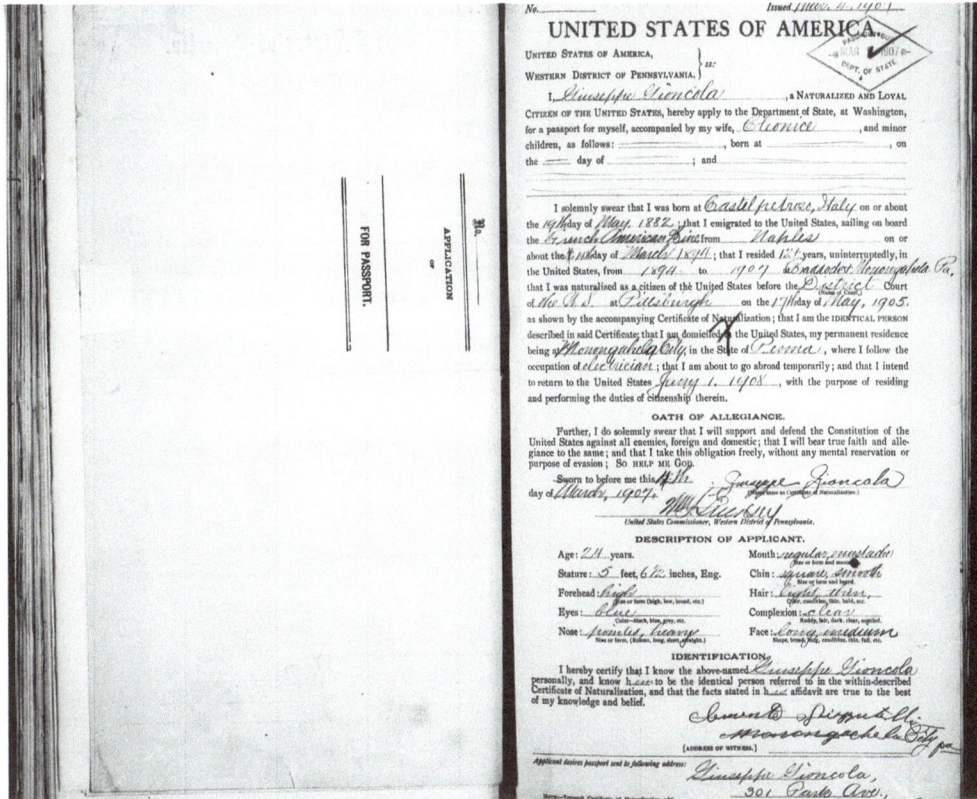

Figure 48. **Giuseppe Giancola Application for Passport in 1907**

The next five images show the enlarged version of the 1907 Application for Passport.

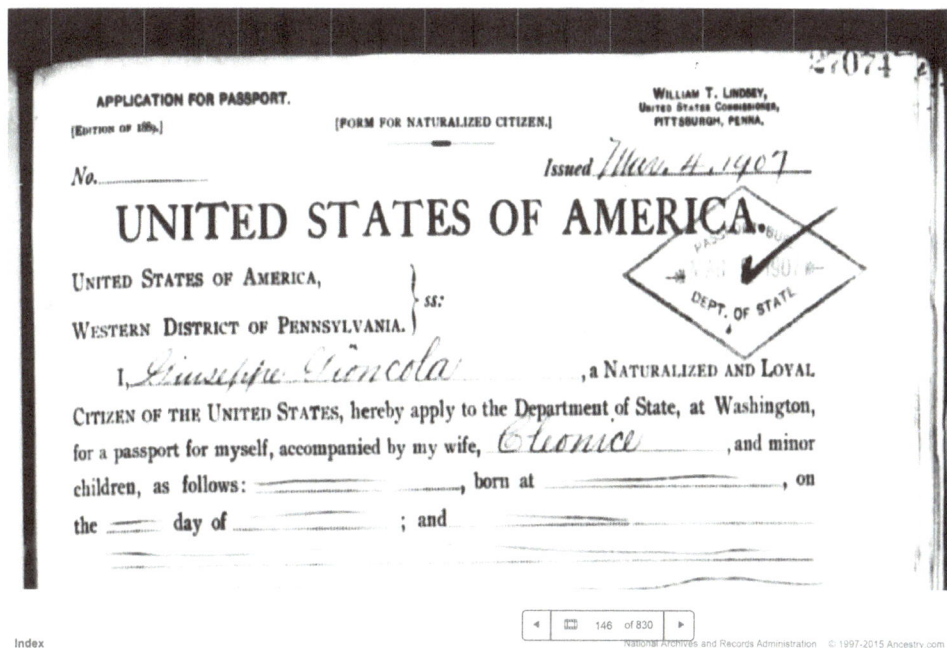

Figure 49. **Giuseppe Giancola Application for Passport, Enlarged Part 1**

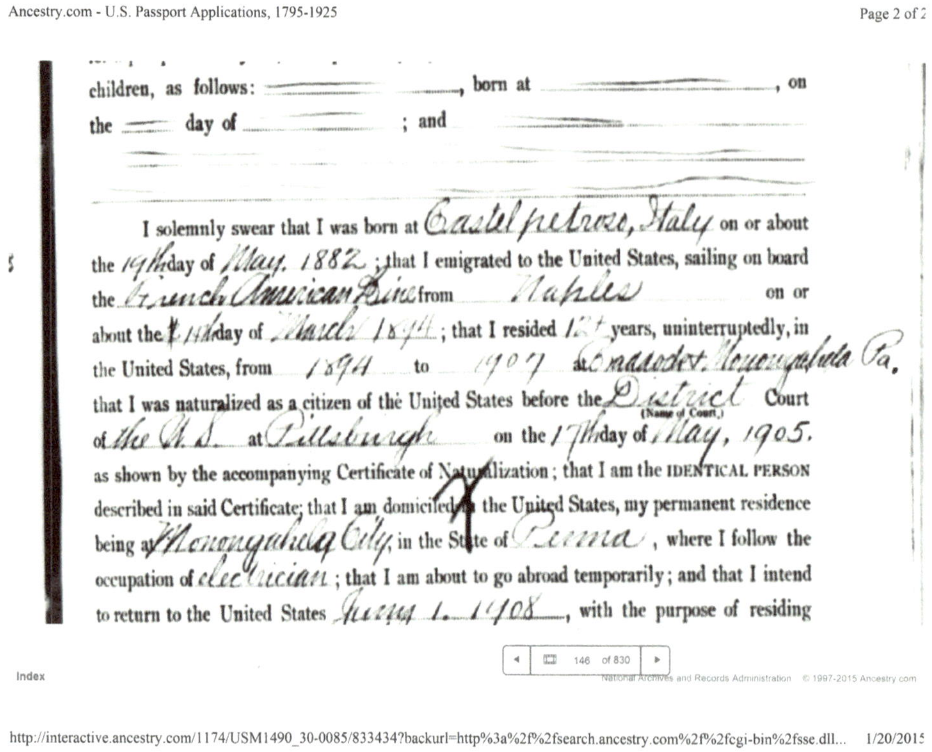

children, as follows: ———————, born at ———————, on
the ——— day of ———————; and ———————

I solemnly swear that I was born at *Castel petroso, Italy* on or about
the *19th* day of *May, 1882*; that I emigrated to the United States, sailing on board
the *French American Line* from *Naples* on or
about the *14th* day of *March 1894*; that I resided *12?* years, uninterruptedly, in
the United States, from *1894* to *1907* *at Monessen, Monongahela Pa.*
that I was naturalized as a citizen of the United States before the *District* Court
of *the U.S.* at *Pittsburgh* on the *17th* day of *May, 1905.*
as shown by the accompanying Certificate of Naturalization; that I am the IDENTICAL PERSON
described in said Certificate; that I am domiciled in the United States, my permanent residence
being at *Monongahela City*, in the State of *Penna*, where I follow the
occupation of *electrician*; that I am about to go abroad temporarily; and that I intend
to return to the United States *June 1. 1908*, with the purpose of residing

Figure 50. Giuseppe Giancola Application for Passport, Enlarged Part 2

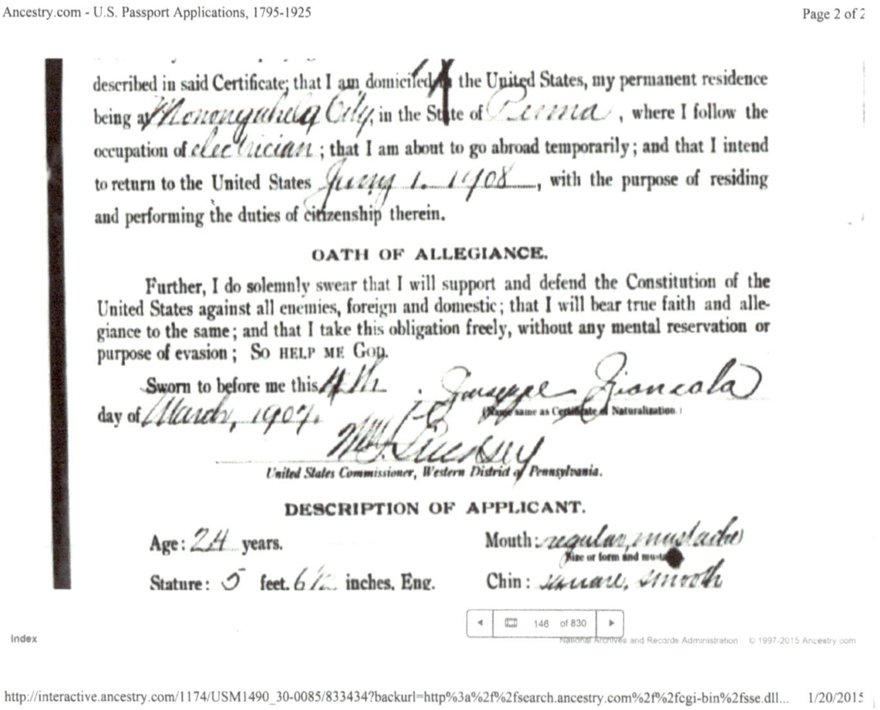

described in said Certificate; that I am domiciled in the United States, my permanent residence
being at *Monongahela City*, in the State of *Penna*, where I follow the
occupation of *electrician*; that I am about to go abroad temporarily; and that I intend
to return to the United States *June 1. 1908*, with the purpose of residing
and performing the duties of citizenship therein.

OATH OF ALLEGIANCE.

Further, I do solemnly swear that I will support and defend the Constitution of the
United States against all enemies, foreign and domestic; that I will bear true faith and allegiance to the same; and that I take this obligation freely, without any mental reservation or
purpose of evasion; So HELP ME GOD.

Sworn to before me this *4th*
day of *March, 1907.*

Giuseppe Giancola
(Same name as Certificate of Naturalization)

Wm Buckby
United States Commissioner, Western District of Pennsylvania.

DESCRIPTION OF APPLICANT.

Age: *24* years.

Mouth: *regular, mustache*
Size or form and mouth

Stature: *5* feet. *6½* inches, Eng.

Chin: *square, smooth*

Figure 51. Giuseppe Giancola Application for Passport, Enlarged Part 3

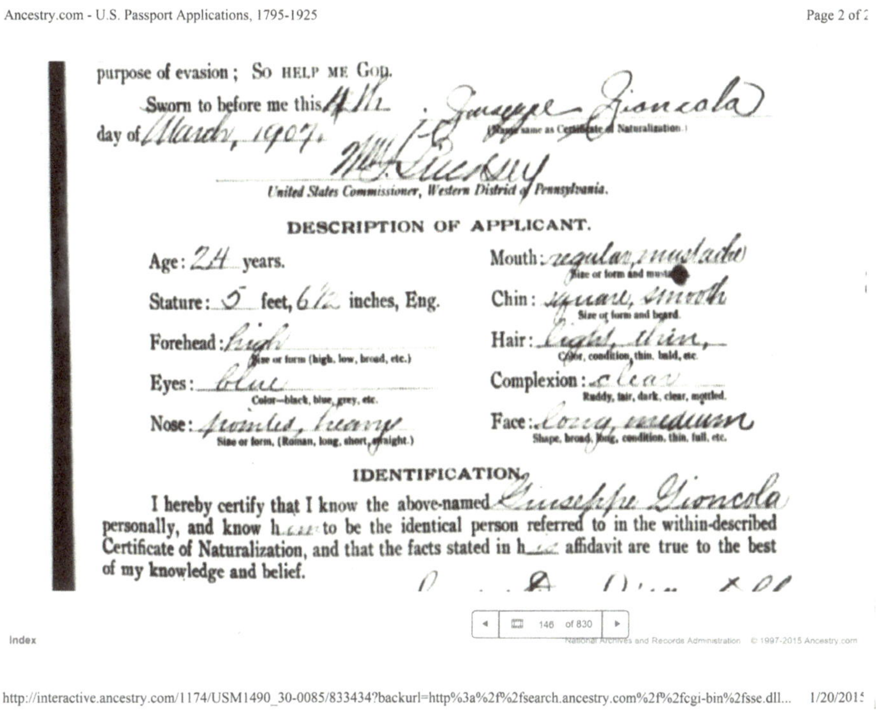

Figure 52. Giuseppe Giancola Application for Passport, Enlarged Part 4

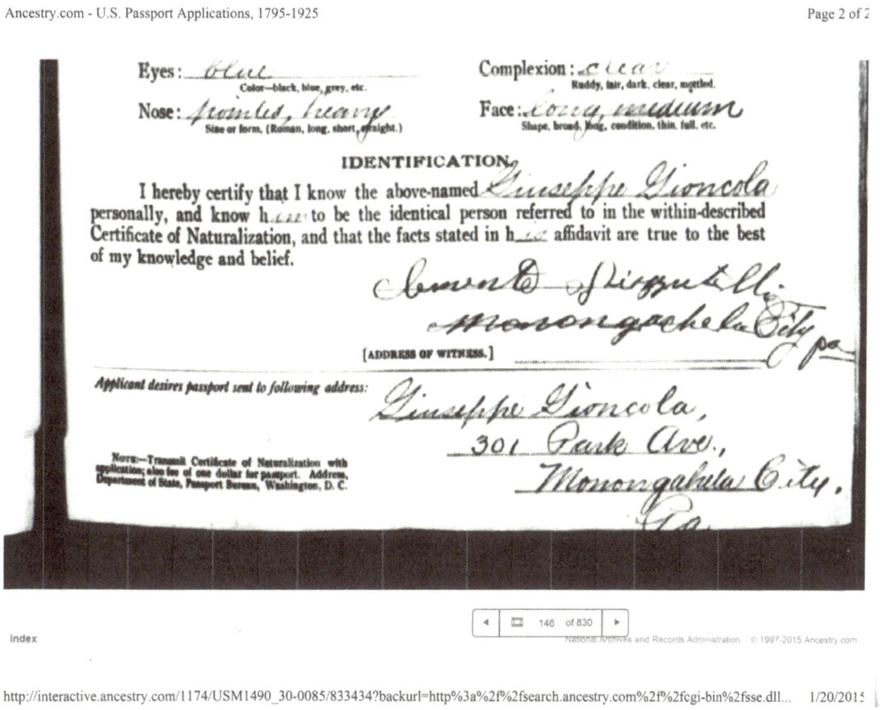

Figure 53. Giuseppe Giancola Application for Passport, Enlarged Part 5

The person who signed the application as a witness was named Clemente Pizzutelli of 431 Third Street, Monongahela City, PA. Clemente certified that he knew Giuseppe Giancola personally and could vouch for the facts that were provided on the application. Pizzutelli lived less than a half mile away from Giuseppe's 301 Park Avenue, Monongahela, PA address, and Clemente was 22 at the time that he acted as witness for Giuseppe. Clemente was born in Fosinone, Rome, IT, and had arrived in Monongahela when he was 16. The Daily Republic newspaper of Monongahela dated 27 Dec 1949 has Clemente's obituary which gives a short description of his life and that includes being a long-time merchant of a grocery store, being a member of the Italian Citizens of America, and being a member of the Sons of Italy. Clemente died at age 64. Monongahela was south of Clairton, the address that Giuseppe referred to in 1905 on his application for Naturalization. The cities were both on the Monongahela River with a railway system for easy transportation. Below is a 1902 Fowler and Moyer map of the City of Monongahela, PA. Both the Park Avenue and the Third Street addresses can be found in this drawing.

Monongahela City, Pennsylvania, 1902 Fowler and Moyer   ✕

Figure 54. **Map of City of Monongahela (above)**

From Naples, IT to PA: Giuseppe Giancola and Cleonice Giancola (26 May – 10 June 1907) As Husband and Wife

The most important voyage for Giuseppe was the one that he took to Italy in April of 1907 to marry Cleonice Mastrantuoni. He was 24, and she was 22. They were married on 18 April 1907, and they were in Naples on 26 May 1907 to travel to the New York port to start their life together as husband and wife in Allegheny County, Pennsylvania where he had been living for ten years. The journey across the ocean took fifteen days and Cleonice was very sick on board the ship **Nord America**. Giuseppe had the voyage and marriage all planned out: Having obtained his naturalization papers in 1905 in Pennsylvania and having obtained a passport for himself and his future wife, he had made things easy for Cleonice, so she did not have to apply for citizenship: it was automatic. She was an American citizen once she arrived with Giuseppe in the states. The Statue of Liberty – Ellis Island Foundation, Inc. passenger records for G. Antonio "Giansola" and Cleonice "Giansola" are shown below.

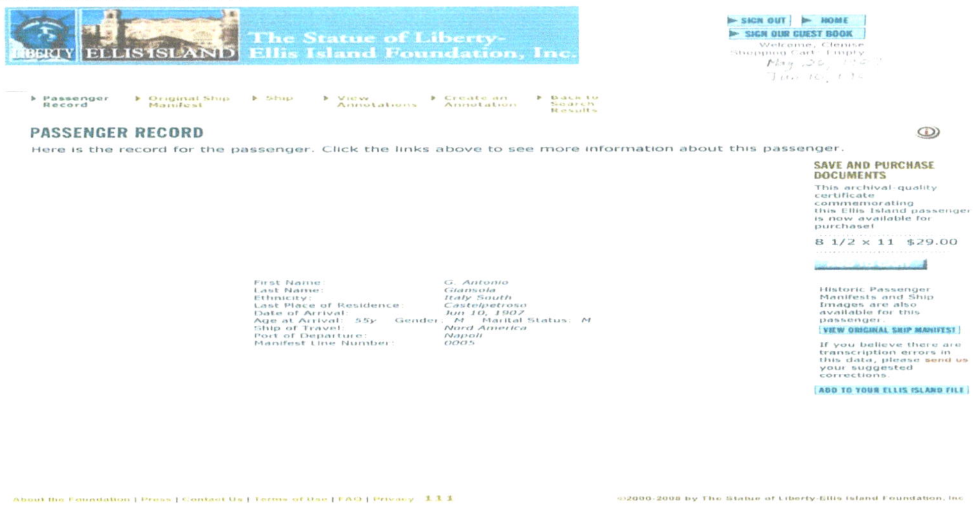
PASSENGER RECORD
Here is the record for the passenger. Click the links above to see more information about this passenger.

First Name: G. Antonio
Last Name: Giansola
Ethnicity: Italy South
Last Place of Residence: Castelpetroso
Date of Arrival: Jun 10, 1907
Age at Arrival: 55y Gender: M Marital Status: M
Ship of Travel: Nord America
Port of Departure: Napoli
Manifest Line Number: 0005

Figure 55. **Ship Arrival Record for Giuseppe Giancola on the Nord America 1907**

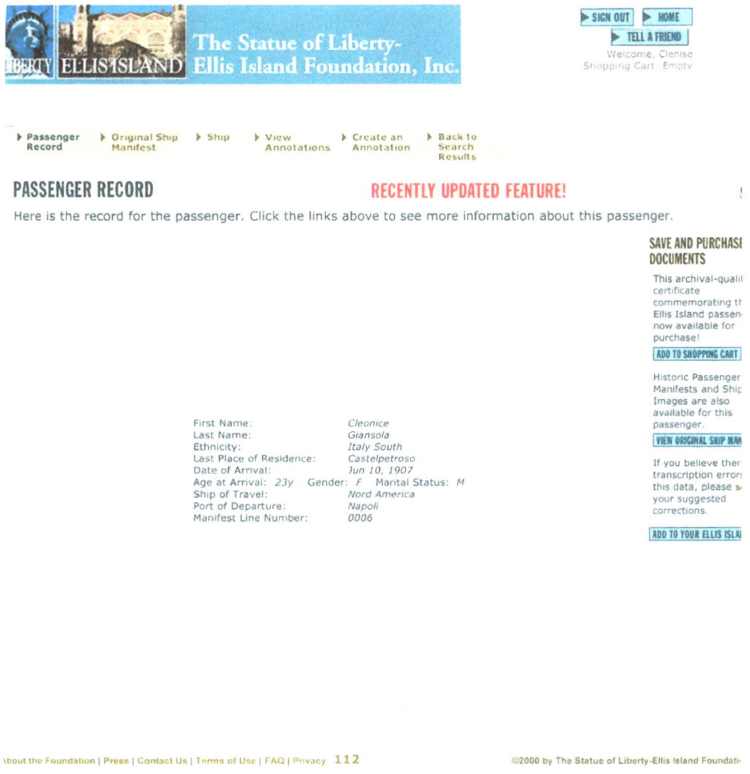
PASSENGER RECORD RECENTLY UPDATED FEATURE!
Here is the record for the passenger. Click the links above to see more information about this passenger.

First Name: Cleonice
Last Name: Giansola
Ethnicity: Italy South
Last Place of Residence: Castelpetroso
Date of Arrival: Jun 10, 1907
Age at Arrival: 23y Gender: F Marital Status: M
Ship of Travel: Nord America
Port of Departure: Napoli
Manifest Line Number: 0006

Figure 56. **Ship Arrival Record for Cleonice Giancola on the Nord America 1907**

The Manifest of Passengers for this May-June 1907 trip from the heritage.statueofliberty. org website is shown below with the relevant lines being lines 5 and 6.

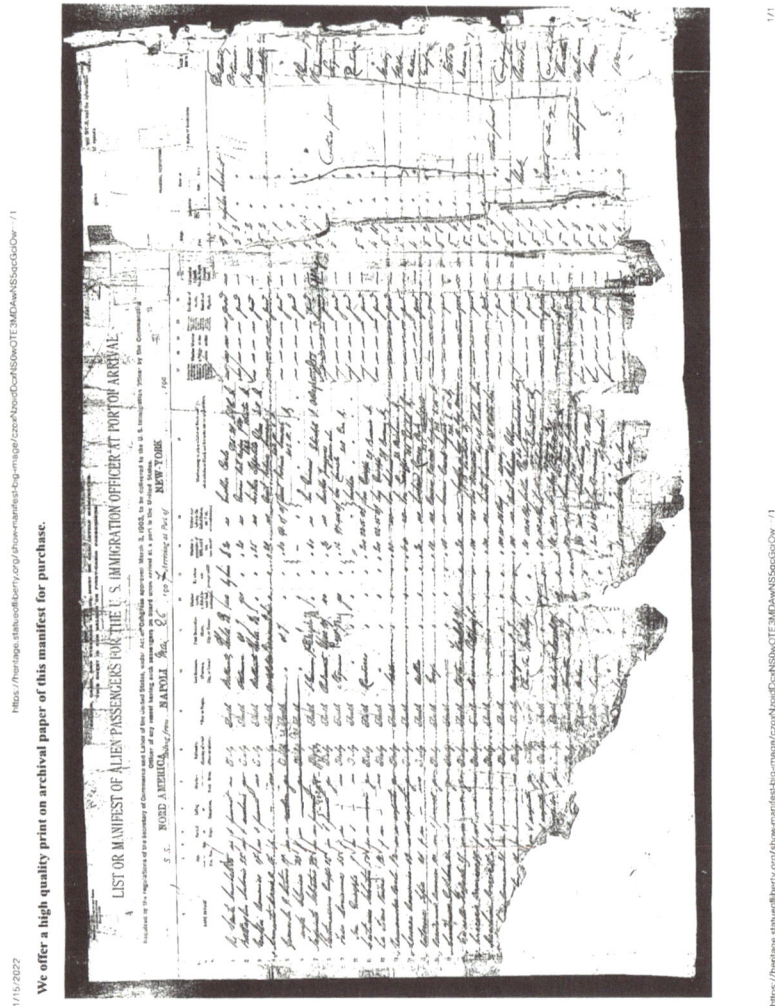

Figure 57. **Manifest of Passengers for May-June Ocean Voyage**

Note that on the Nord America passenger manifest, the age of Giuseppe is listed as 55 (probably due to the messy handwriting of the transcriber) instead of his proper age of 25. Cleonice's age is correct as 23. Their last name is recorded as Giansola, which makes it more difficult to find the record. This was probably not intentional: the writer did not take proper care in making the words and numbers legible in the manifest. The passenger manifest shows that Giuseppe had $40 in his possession on the voyage, that he and Cleonice were both in good mental and physical health, were on their way to be with Aunt Rosina Armenti (Nick Forte's grandmother who was married to Michele Archangelo Giancola) in New York at 602 W 6th Street, that they were both from Castelpetroso (although Cleonice was actually born in Roccamandolfi), and that Cleonice was 4 feet 9 inches and Giuseppe was 5 feet 5 inches.

Next is a picture of the Nord America ship.

S.S. NORD AMERICA, 1882 La Veloce Line
Courtesy Steamship Historical Society Collection, Univ. of Baltimore Library

Figure 58. **The S.S. Nord America, from <u>Ships of Our Ancestors</u>, by Anuta**

Allegheny County, PA

From their aunt's location in New York, Giuseppe and Cleonice made their way to Allegheny County, the Borough of East Pittsburgh, Ward 3. The birth certificate of their first child shows the date of birth as 22 March 1909 at 11:30 a. m., and their address as 216 Birch Street. This was filed on April 2, 1909, and it is hand-written.

The infant's name is recorded as Maria Smith with her parents' names being Joseph Smith and Alice Mastantuoni of 216 Birch Street, the Borough of E. Pittsburgh, ages 27 and 25, respectively, and the birthplace of both parents is Italy. The father's occupation is an electrician, and the mother's is a housewife. A physician attended the birth, and the registrar Hadfield signed the certificate on 2 April 1909. See Commonwealth of Pennsylvania Bureau of Vital Statistics Certificate of Birth below.

Figure 59. **Original Birth Certificate of Maria Smith 22 March 1909**

Here is a Google Map showing 1.4 miles from prior addresses of Joseph Smith on Tenth Street, near the US STEEL Edgar Thomson Works, and Birch Road. Recall that 307 Tenth Street was the likely address for Joseph in 1900 when he lived as a boarder in the house of D'Amore, and 4 Tenth Street when he lived with the Peter Paul family around 1903. The Braddock area around Birch Road would have been quite familiar to Joseph. By the time of the birth of his first daughter in 1909, he would have been well established in Braddock. He was determined to succeed in his new country and provide for his wife and daughter. As you may notice, this is the first time that we have seen Giuseppe Giancola changing his name to Joseph Smith on the legal birth certificate of Maria. It is believed that he was trying to make sure that his family would have a chance to assimilate into America without having to take on the discrimination that befell Italians during those early years of the twentieth century. (More on this later.)

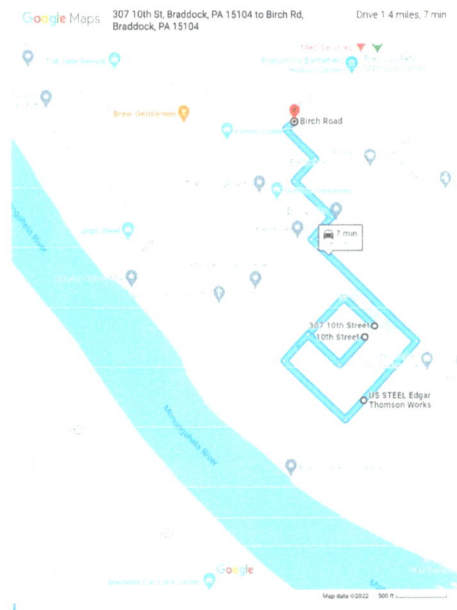

Figure 60. **Google Map Showing 307 10th St., Braddock, PA to Birch Rd, Braddock, PA**

There is another version of the birth certificate that is listed as a "Delayed Birth Certificate" that was certified on 18 March 1960, signed, and sworn to by Marie Dolores Smith whose residence was 2612 Jackson Avenue, South Chicago Heights, Ill. The altered information includes the name change from Maria Smith to Marie Dolores Smith, the father's name Joseph Anthony Smith (instead of Joseph Smith) whose birthplace is now listed as Wilmerding, PA, and not Italy, and the mother's name Clara Alice Masters whose birthplace is listed as Monongahela City, PA. and not Italy. The Notary Public who worked at a bank and in Chicago Heights signed this certificate, and her name was Margaret Gansbergen of 1648 Halsted, Chicago Heights, IL. The copy of this delayed birth certificate follows.

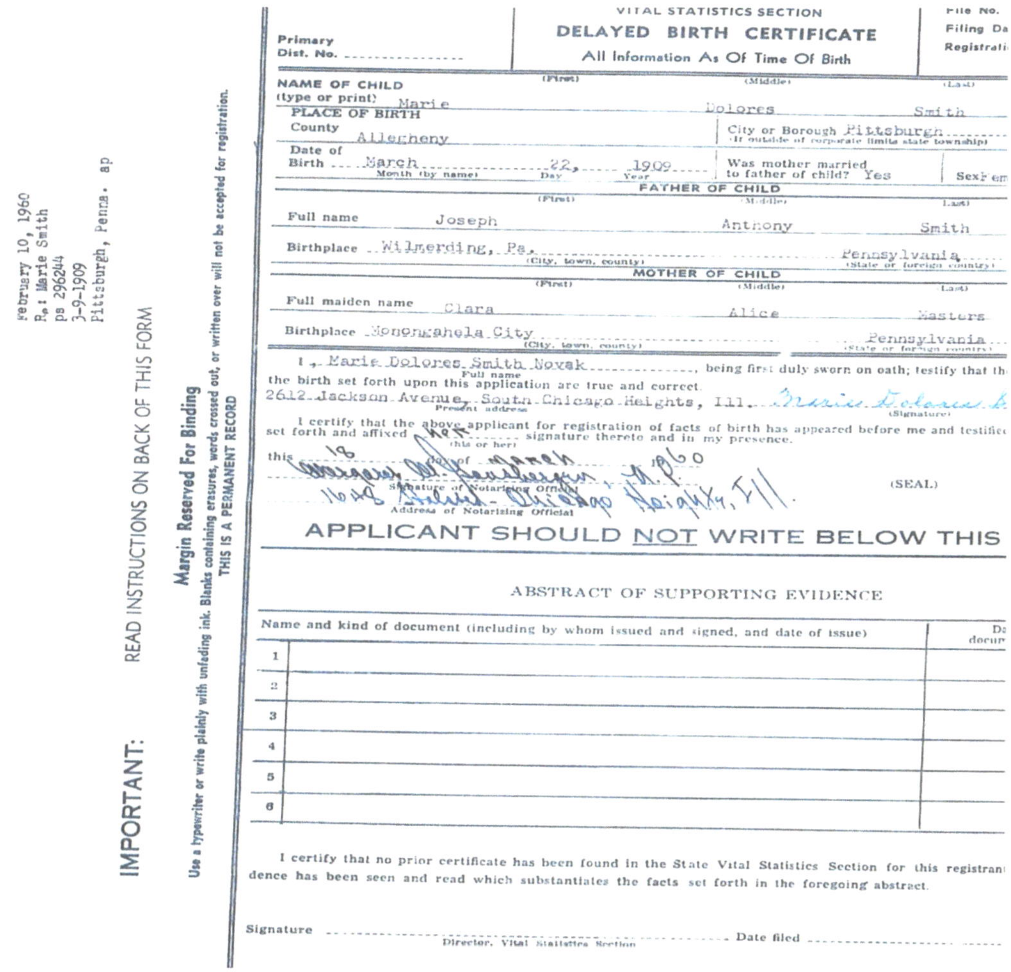
February 10, 1960
Re: Marie Smith
ps 296244
3-9-1909
Pittsburgh, Penna. ap

IMPORTANT: READ INSTRUCTIONS ON BACK OF THIS FORM

Margin Reserved For Binding

Use a typewriter or write plainly with unfading ink. Blanks containing erasures, words crossed out, or written over will not be accepted for registration. THIS IS A PERMANENT RECORD

Primary Dist. No.

VITAL STATISTICS SECTION
DELAYED BIRTH CERTIFICATE
All Information As Of Time Of Birth

File No.
Filing Da
Registrati

NAME OF CHILD (type or print) (First) Marie (Middle) Dolores (Last) Smith

PLACE OF BIRTH
County Allegheny
City or Borough Pittsburgh (If outside of corporate limits state township)

Date of Birth March (Month (by name)) 22, (Day) 1909 (Year)
Was mother married to father of child? Yes
Sex F em

FATHER OF CHILD
Full name (First) Joseph (Middle) Anthony (Last) Smith
Birthplace Wilmerding, Pa. (City, town, county) Pennsylvania (State or foreign country)

MOTHER OF CHILD
Full maiden name (First) Clara (Middle) Alice (Last) Masters
Birthplace Monongahela City (City, town, county) Pennsylvania (State or foreign country)

I, Marie Dolores Smith Novak (Full name), being first duly sworn on oath; testify that th the birth set forth upon this application are true and correct.
2612 Jackson Avenue, South Chicago Heights, Ill. (Present address) Marie Dolores S (Signature)

I certify that the above applicant for registration of facts of birth has appeared before me and testifie set forth and affixed her (his or her) signature thereto and in my presence.
this 18 day of March 1960
(Signature of Notarizing Official)
(SEAL)
(Address of Notarizing Official)

APPLICANT SHOULD NOT WRITE BELOW THIS

ABSTRACT OF SUPPORTING EVIDENCE

Name and kind of document (including by whom issued and signed, and date of issue)	Da docur
1	
2	
3	
4	
5	
6	

I certify that no prior certificate has been found in the State Vital Statistics Section for this registrant dence has been seen and read which substantiates the facts set forth in the foregoing abstract.

Signature ______ (Director, Vital Statistics Section) Date filed ______

Figure 61. **Copy of Delayed Birth Certificate for Maria Smith with Changed Information**

A slightly different copy, a typed version, of the birth certificate for Maria Smith, was issued on 3 November 1992 as per a request for genealogical information. The name on the certificate is Maria Smith, and it shows the birthdate as 22 March 1909. It does not have the street address but does have the county as being Allegheny, the parents' names are the same as are their ages and birthplaces. It is signed by Charles Hardester, the state registrar at the time this was issued in 1992. It has the official seal of the Commonwealth of Pennsylvania on it. This copy of the birth certificate of Maria Smith follows.

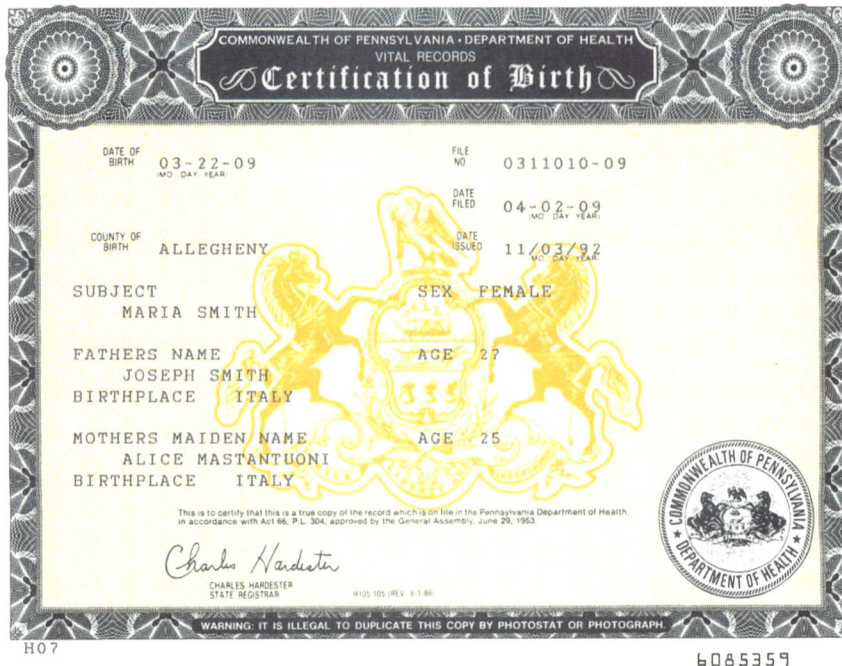

Figure 62. **Copy of Birth Certificate Requested on 3 November 1992 for Maria Smith**

About two years and 5 months later, Giuseppe, age 28, and now going by Joe A. Smith, and Cleonice, age 26, and going by Ales Mastantuoni gave birth to their second daughter whose name appears on the original handwritten birth certificate as **Elesabth Smith**, born in Allegheny County in the Township of Wilkins on 30 August 1910. Both parents are listed as having the birthplace of Italy and now living in **Wilkinsburg/ Wilkinstownship**. Joe is an electrician, and Ales is a housewife. Sofia Panalta (sp?) was the attending midwife, and the registrar Walter Elder filed the certificate on 7 September 1910. The typed version of the birth certificate was issued on 16 October 1992 for the purpose of genealogical health research. The registrar in 1992 was Charles Hardester. See the copies of the birth certificates of Elesabth Smith in the next two images below.

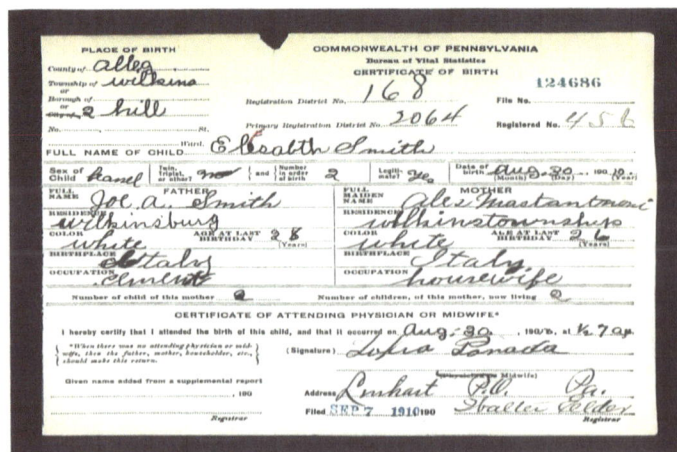

Figure 63. **Original birth certificate of Elesabth Smith**

Elizabeth Agnes Smith Birth Certificate

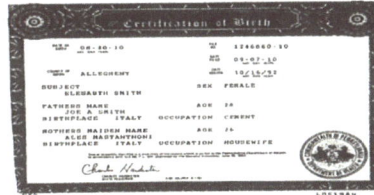

Date: 30 Aug 1910
Description: Birth Certificate

Figure 64. Birth certificate of Elesabth Smith issued in 1992.

The Joseph A. Smith family was living in Allegheny County, PA on 30 August 1910 at the time Elesabth Smith was born. They should have been listed in the 1910 Federal Census for PA for Allegheny County; however, various combinations for their first and last names were searched with no success. A map is provided below which shows the Pennsylvania locations where Joe Smith lived before his marriage, where both he and Alice lived in PA after their 1907 marriage, and where some of their friends lived. These locations include **Braddock, Clairton, Monongahela City, East Pittsburgh, Wilmerding, Turtle Creek, Duquesne, and Wilkins Township**.

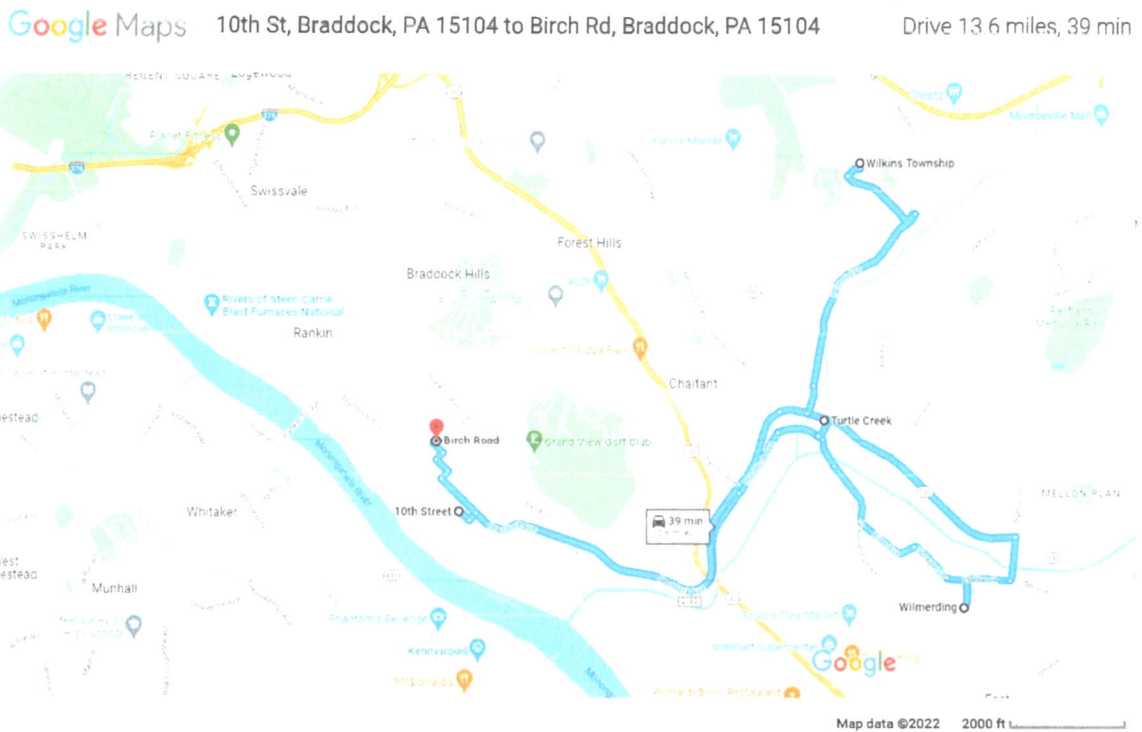

Figure 65. Google Map showing Braddock (Tenth Street), Turtle Creek, Wilmerding, Wilkins Township, Birch Road—Places Mentioned in Joseph Smith's Documents.

Journey from Braddock, PA to Chicago Heights, IL

Mention is now made of the McGranes, a family who was very important to the Joseph A. Smith family. Peter Joseph McGrane was born on 4 October 1876 and resided in Braddock, PA. He was 23 years old when he married Julia Gertrude Kane on 30 November 1899. She was 22 and was born 10 December 1876. The city directory for 1901 shows him working as a mill worker and living on Priscilla Avenue and 7th in McKeesport, Pa. In 1906 he lived at 210 3rd Street, Braddock, PA. The 1910 Federal Census shows that Peter and Julia were living in PA with his father-in-law and his mother-in-law on Priscilla Street in Duquesne, Allegheny, PA. The in-laws' names were John and Mary Kane. Peter was doing work in the steel industry and was an electrician. Peter and Julia's children were Eleanor (age 7, born in 1902), Marcella (age 3, born in 1907), and Joseph (a newborn, born 1910). It is thought that the McGranes and Smiths had met in Allegheny County. They did not live far from each other (less than a mile apart—see map below, and both possibly attended the same Catholic Church or even worked at the same place, both Peter and Joe being electricians.

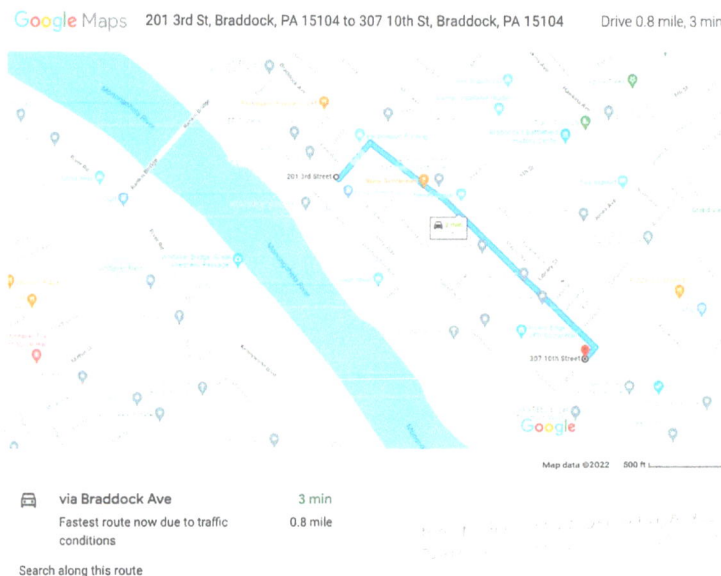

Figure 66. Google Maps: Less Than a Mile Apart: Residences of McGrane and Smith Around 1911 in Braddock, PA

Regardless of the first place of meeting, the story has it that Joe Smith met Peter and Julia McGrane on a train heading west to look for new work opportunities. Their stopping place was Chicago Heights, IL.

Chicago Heights, IL

Chicago Heights is in northeast Illinois, in the County of Cook. It has a long history of native American tribes such as the Illini and the Pottawattomi tribes. (This can be further researched at the Britannica.com website.) The area was first called Thorn Grove in 1833, then the Village of Bloom in 1849, and it was incorporated as Chicago Heights in 1901. In 1892 a group of entrepreneurs from Chicago decided to develop the area as an industrial suburb, namely a steel-making town. In the late nineteen century there was a great influx of Italian immigrants to this town. Workers in the steel-making towns of Pennsylvania would have been aware of the great employment opportunities of the Chicago Heights area at that time.

Granddaughter of Joe Smith, Clenise Stonitsch White, interviewed the son of Peter whose name was Joseph Julian McGrane (a lawyer) sometime in the early 1990's. (He died in 2002 at the age of 93.) See picture of Joseph Julian McGrane below.

1305

FICHA DE TURISTA CIDADÃO DE PAIS AMERICANO PARA UMA ESTADA DE TRINTA DIAS NO BRASIL

(Tourist Card for Citizens of American Countries for A Thirty-Day Stay in Brazil)

Desta ficha, expedida em duplicata, uma via será entregue ao passageiro, para uso da autoridade competente por ocasião de desembarque, e uma via sera enviada pela transportadora à Repartição consular brasileira a qual couber o despacho do navio ou aeronave.
This card will be issued in duplicate; one copy will be delivered to the passenger for use by the competent authority at the time he disembarks, and one copy will be sent by the carrier to the Brazilian Consular Office clearing the ship or aircraft.

Nome por extenso / Name in full: Joseph Julian Mc Grane

Admitido no Brasil em caráter de TURISMO Nos têrmos da Lei No. 2526, de 5 de Julho de 1955
Admitted to Brazil under tourist status Under the terms of Law No. 2.526 of July 5, 1955

Lugar e data de nascimento / Place and date of birth: Duquesne, Pennsylvania January 10, 1910

Estado civil / Civil status: Single — Nacionalidade / Nationality: U.S.A.

Filiação (nome do Pai e da Mãe) / Filiation (name of the Father and Mother): Peter J. Mc Grane, Julia G.Kane

Profissão / Profession: Lawyer

Residência no país de origem / Residence in the country of origin: 468 W. 15th Street, Chicago Heights, Illinois

FILHOS MENORES DE 18 ANOS / CHILDREN UNDER 18 YEARS — Nome (Name) — Idade (Age) — Sexo (Sex)

CHICAGO

FEB-2-64

Passaporte No. / Passport No.: E111211 — expedido pelas autoridades de / issued by the authorities of: U. S. Dept of State

na data / on (date): January 24, 1964

Remitida ao Consulado do Brasil em / Sent to the Consulate of Brazil in: MVD por / by: RG em / on: FEB-28 de 19 64

ASSINATURA DO PORTADOR (SIGNATURE OF HOLDER)

Joseph Julian McGrane

NOTA—Esta ficha deve ser preenchida à máquina pela companhia transportadora, sendo as duas vias em original.
NOTE—This card should be filled out in the typewriter by the carrier and the two copies should be original.

FORM 9213-6167

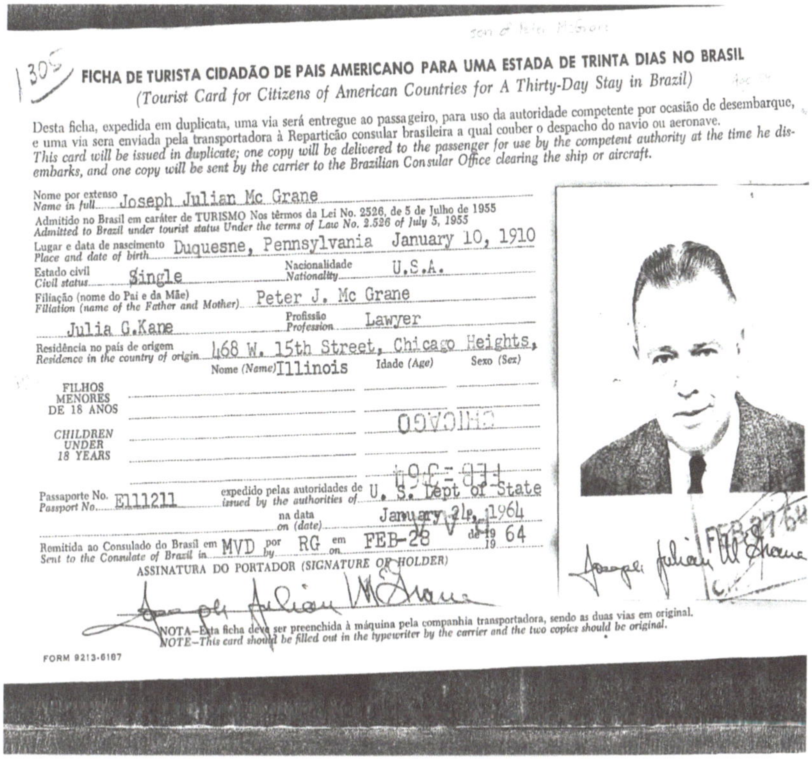

Figure 67. **Joseph Julian McGrane, Son of Peter McGrane**

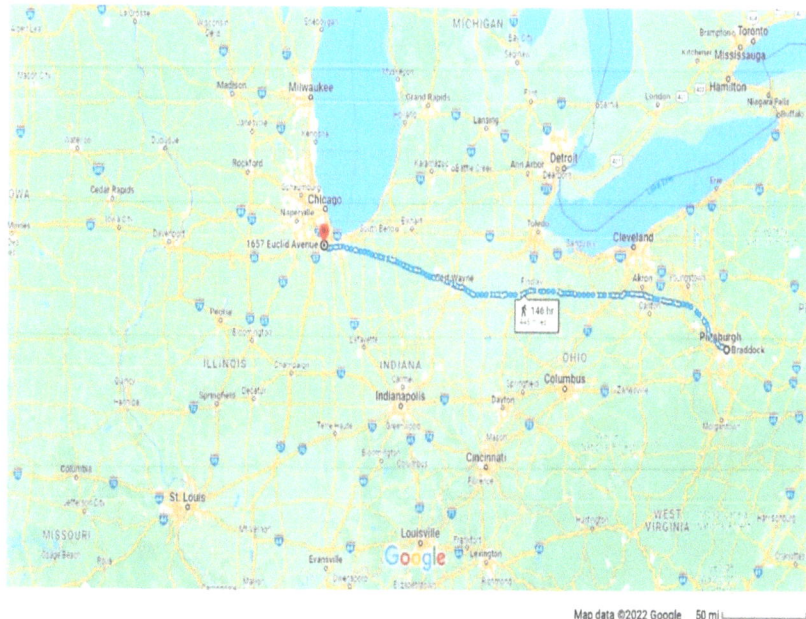

Figure 68. **Google Map Showing Distance Between Braddock, PA and Chicago Heights, IL (445 miles)**

In the telephone conversation, Joseph McGrane confirmed that his dad Peter had helped Joe Smith get a job in Chicago Heights around 1911 (after Elesabeth's birth in August 1910). He also mentioned what good friends they were. Peter may also have helped Joe Smith find a house to rent near their new place of employment. Both Peter McGrane and Joe Smith first worked for Railway Steel Spring Company. And both families lived close to each other in Chicago Heights. An early residence of the McGrane family was 1916 Circle Street in Chicago Heights. This is mentioned on Peter's 1917 WWI Draft Registration card along with his occupation as a chief engineer at a steel mill, namely Railway Steel Spring Company. See below.

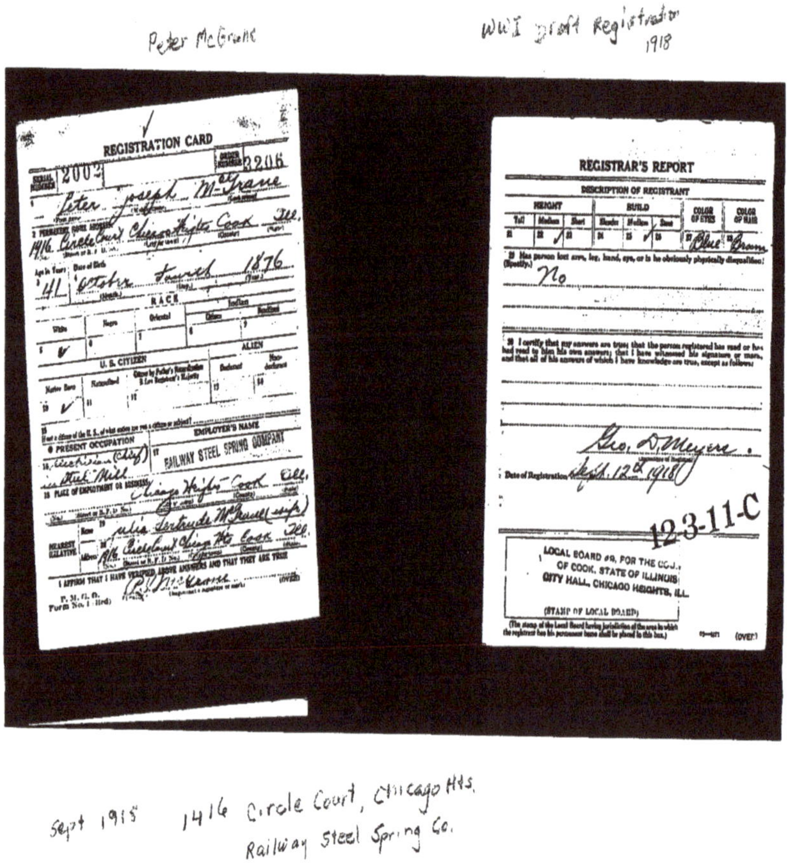

Figure 69. **Peter McGrane's 1918 WWI Draft Registration showing Chicago Heights Address**

The McGrane residence was close to **1657 Euclid Avenue in Chicago Heights, IL,** the residence that Joseph and Ales (Cleonice) Smith rented. The distance from Joseph's house to the Railway Steel Spring Company was .6 miles (or a thirteen-minute walk). That house is shown below in a photo that is marked "1657 Euclid Avenue, Chgo. Hghts. Ill" on the back.

Figure 70. **House at 1657 Euclid Avenue, Chicago Heights, Illinois with Joseph Smith standing on the porch with his two small girls (possibly Marie and Elizabeth) around 1912. Under magnification, Joseph has a mustache and is wearing a type of work outfit.**

Next is a Google map that shows the locations of the Smith and McGrane residences. Walking time from one house to the other was about 13 minutes (.6 miles). Both Joe and Peter were within walking distance of their employment at Railway Steel Spring Company (about six-tenths of a mile for each of them). (Josephine Stonitsch confirmed that her dad walked to work each day with his tin lunch pail from their Euclid Avenue house.)

Figure 71. **Distance between Smith and McGrane Chicago Heights homes.**

From 1911 to 1914 Joseph worked at the Chicago Rail Steel Spring Company in Chicago Heights. The company was first organized as International Steel Company in 1909 and was acquired by Railway Steel in August of 1911 and became known as Railway Steel Springs, a unit of American Locomotive. It is now ALCO Spring Industries, Inc. It was (and still is) located at 23rd and Euclid Avenue, and it manufactured springs for the railroads as one important product. More information can be obtained about this company by going to the website cs.trains.com. It's shown on the map as Alco Spring Industries today. This was the same place that Peter McGrane was working. During this time from 1911 to 1914, Joseph and Clara lived in Chicago Heights at the rental house at 1657 Euclid Avenue.

It is interesting to note that the home that the Smiths rented at 1657 Euclid Avenue was still in existence in 2022. It was built in 1898 and the two houses on each side of that house were built in 1901 and are still standing. The picture of the 1657 Euclid house as it currently looks is seen below (from the Zillow.com website.) The photo was shown to Josephine Stonitsch a few years ago in 2020, and she commented that the closed-in porch was added much later when the Smith family no longer was living there.

Figure 72. **Euclid Avenue house that was first rented and later purchased by the Smiths.**

The Euclid Avenue household included Maria and Elesabeth who had been born in Pennsylvania. After that, Lucia Ann was born on 3 March 1912 to Joseph Giancola and Cleonice Mastrantuoni, and Diamentina Antoinette was born 13 March 1913. (Giuseppe Giancola's father was Diamante Giancola, so this fourth child was initially going to be named after the grandfather of the infant. The name eventually evolved to be Amanda Delores Smith, "Mandy."). The fifth of the daughters (Josephina) was born at the Euclid house in 1914.

Lucia's birth certificate was issued several times. The first one, which wasn't located in the records, most probably had her name as Lucia Ann Giancola. This was the one presented to the church upon baptism. There is another one that was issued after that which has her name as Lucia A. Smith from Canada with Joseph and Lice Smith as her parents (LDS Microfilm 1287756), and yet another with Lucia Any Smith with her ethnicity as American, her father's name as Joseph Smith and her mother's name as Alice (LDS Microfilm 1288241).

The Cook County birth certificate for Amanda who was born 13 March 1913 was not readily found in the records. It can be assumed that the first was issued as Diamentina Antoinetta Giancola, and the second as Amanda Smith with the parents' names changing as in a similar pattern with Lucy's birth certificate.

Both Luciam Annam (Latin for Lucy Ann) and Diamentina Antoinetta Giancola (called Amanda) were baptized at St. Ann Catholic Church on 3010 Ridge Road in Lansing, Illinois on 12 July 1913, with parents listed as Joseph Giancola and Cleonice Mastantuoni. (Note that Amanda was initially named after Joseph Smith's father who was Diamante Giancola.) The record indicates that the two infant girls are twins (this is not so) with the same information, and the godparents are Petrus and Emilia Cozazza. The source of this information is from FamilySearch Catholic Church Records for St. Ann, Baptism, 1907-1915. See below.

Film # 004332259

ST. ANN

CHICAGO HEIGHTS

BAPTISM

1907-1915

'Illinois, Chicago, Catholic Church Records, 1833-1925," database with images, FamilySearch
https://familysearch.org/ark:/61903/3:1:S3HY-X2M7-H1J?cc=1452409&wc=M66L-DNY%3A39681201%2C39681202 : 20
May 2014), St Ann Parish (Chicago Heights) > Baptisms, marriages, deaths, communions 1907-1916 > image 1 of 60; Catholic
Church parishes, Chicago Diocese, Chicago.

Figure 73. Information from FamilySearch Catholic Church Records for St. Ann, Baptism, 1907-1915

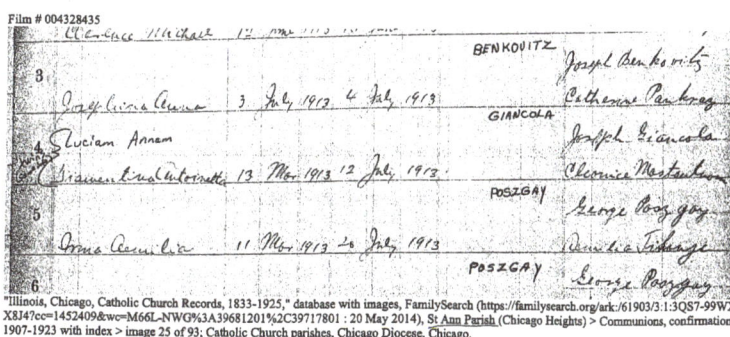

Film # 004328435

"Illinois, Chicago, Catholic Church Records, 1833-1925," database with images, FamilySearch (https://familysearch.org/ark:/61903/3:1:3QS7-99WX-
X8J4?cc=1452409&wc=M66L-NWG%3A39681201%2C39717801 : 20 May 2014), St Ann Parish (Chicago Heights) > Communions, confirmations
1907-1923 with index > image 25 of 93; Catholic Church parishes, Chicago Diocese, Chicago.

Figure 74. Church Record of Baptisms of Lucy and Amanda Smith

In another part of the records, displayed in Latin, the same information is listed and is signed by Otto C. Nabholz who was the pastor of St. Ann Church from December 1910 to 1917. Both birthdays are correct on these two records.

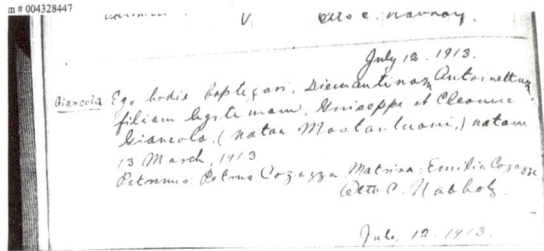

Figure 75. **Latin Version of Baptism Records for Diemantinam Antoinettam (Mandy) and Luciam Annam (Lucy) Smith**

In two other records the information is different. Lucy and Amanda are the new names, the birthday for Lucy is correct as 3 March 1912 (and not 1913), and Amanda's is listed as 3 March 1913 (and it should be 13 March 1913), the parents are now given as Joseph A. Smith and Clara Masters with the sponsors now Michael Rich and Mrs. Michael Rich. The baptism is shown as May---1913. There is a letter "C" next to the parents' names to show this is a correction. Those two records follow:

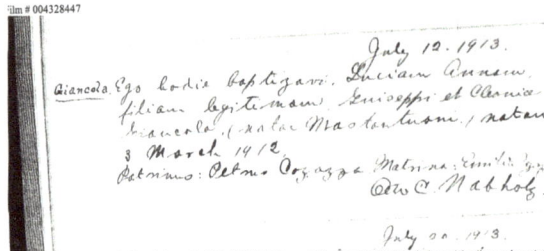

Figure 76. **Partially Corrected Baptism Records for Lucy and Amanda Smith**

Amanda Smith's Certificate of Baptism was later reissued on 6 November 1974 and sent to her at her home in Chicago, 6202 S. Troy Apt 2E on 17 November 1974 by her sister Marie Novak who was living at 2612 Jackson Avenue, So. Chicago Heights, Illinois.

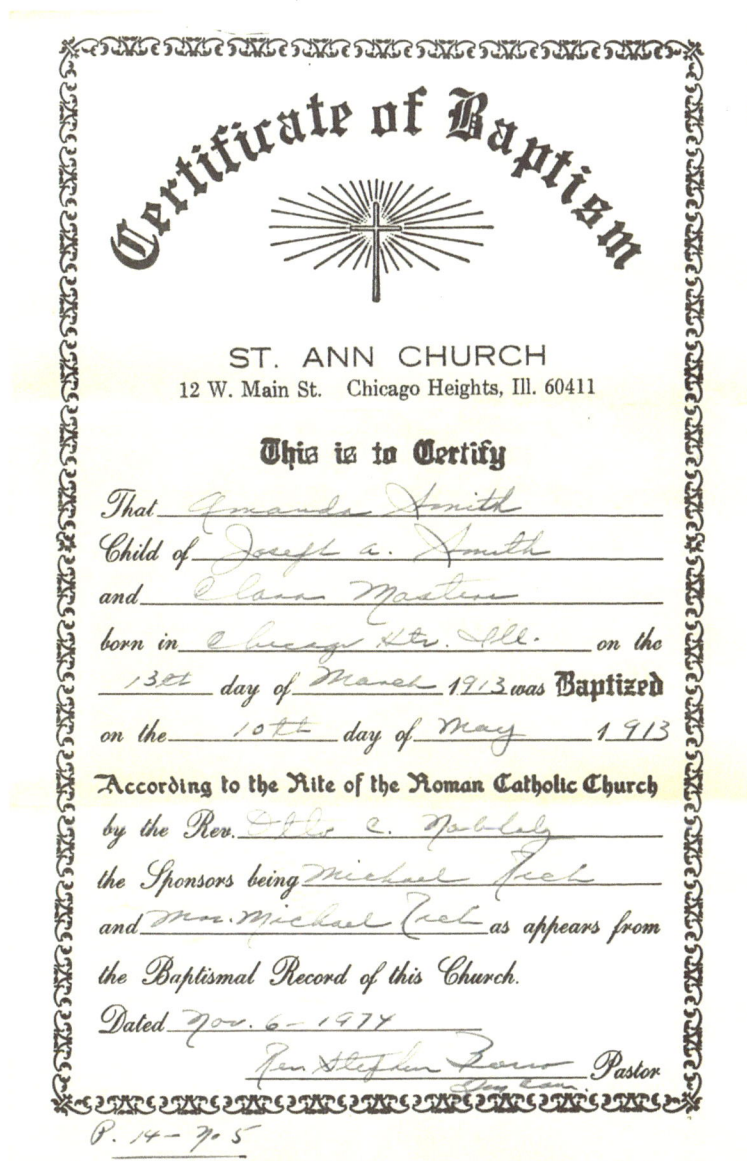

Figure 77. **Amanda Smith Baptism Certificate Reissued on 6 November 1974**

St. Ann Church was not the closest Catholic Church to the Smiths in 1913, but they were probably influenced by Peter and Julia McGrane whose daughter, Phillis Clara, was born 5 November 1911, and was baptized on 4 March 1912 at St. Ann Catholic Church. The church was founded in 1907 as a German parish, and the church still exists today; however, it has "unified" with two other parishes—St. John's in Greenwood and St. James in Sauk Village in July 2021, and it is now called All Souls Catholic Parish. The St. Ann Church in its early days looked like that pictured on the website www. allsoulscatholicparish.org/about/parish-history/st-ann below in Figure 78. Figure 79 is a photo from 2021 Google Maps, and Figure 80 is another Google Map showing the distance between the Smith Euclid Avenue house and St. Ann Church. That distance was 9.6 miles.

St. Ann - All Souls Catholic Parish

Figure 78. **St. Ann-All Souls Catholic Parish as it Appeared in Early Days**

Google Maps   All Souls Catholic Parish at St. Ann Church

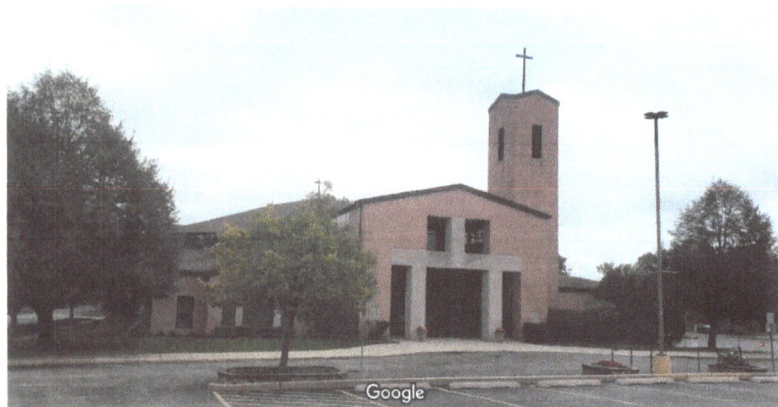

Figure 79. **Google Maps Image of St. Ann-All Souls Church in 2021**

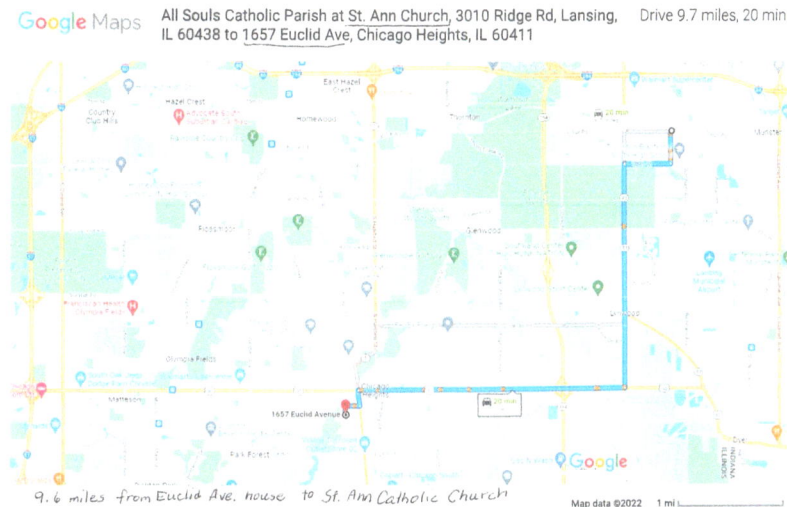

Figure 80. **Google Map Showing Distance Between Euclid Avenue House and St. Ann Church**

After Lucy and Amanda, the next daughter number 5, **Josephina Giancola**, was born on 11 December 1914 and baptized on 8 October 1916, her parents being listed as Joseph Giancola and Cleonice Mastantuoni, and godparents Thomas and Valentina D'Amico. The church where Josephina was baptized was St. Rocco in Chicago Heights and was founded in 1906 by Father Pasquale Renzullo, who was the first pastor of St. Rocco. (He remained pastor there until 1922 when he resigned from the priesthood and got married.) This was known as the Italian Catholic Church of the area. The church was meant to serve those who spoke Italian as their first language. The Smith family did not choose this as its regular church of worship, although it was only 1.6 miles from their home on Euclid Avenue. Selecting it for the baptism of Josephine in 1916 might have had something to do with the D'Amicos' influence and suggestion since they were the godparents of Josephine, and they were friends of the family. This was the parish of the D'Amico family, not the Smith family. (More on the D'Amico family later.)

The original birth certificate for Josephina Giancola was not found in the records, but the one that was issued on 29 May 1942 shows her name as Josephine Smith, her father Joseph Anthony Smith from Wilmerding, PA, and her mother as Clara Alice Masters from Buenos Aires, SA. Her dad was 32, and her mom was 30. This was explained to Clenise (Lindy) by Josephine around 2020. Josephine was planning on joining the Army around 1942, and when she went to get a copy of her birth certificate, she was horrified to see a name that she had never used before. She made her dad go down to the courthouse and get it reissued with the name she had been using her whole life—Josephine T. Smith-- along with the names she knew her parents as.

Here is a copy of the Baptismal Registry page for Josephina Giancola.

Film # 005251863

"Illinois, Chicago, Catholic Church Records, 1833-1925," database with images, FamilySearch
https://familysearch.org/ark:/61903/3:1:33S7-91HV-JD1?cc=1452409&wc=M66P-829%3A40340501%2C40448501 : 20 May
2014), St Rocco Parish (Chicago Heights) > Baptisms 1916-1919 with index > image 43 of 127; Catholic Church parishes,
Chicago Diocese, Chicago.

Figure 81. **Baptismal Registry Page for Josephina Giancola**

Below is a map showing the relative positions of the Euclid Avenue house, All Souls
Catholic Parish at St. Ann Church, and San Rocco. Recall that Lucy and Amanda were
baptized at St. Ann, the further location in Lansing in 1913; and Josephine was baptized
in 1916 at Saint Rocco's. Josephine was born when the family rented the Euclid house. It's
not clear whether her baptism, which took place about two years after her birth, occurred
while the Smiths were still living in Chicago Heights or whether they had moved by then
to their next rental house in **Glenwood, IL on Main Street.**

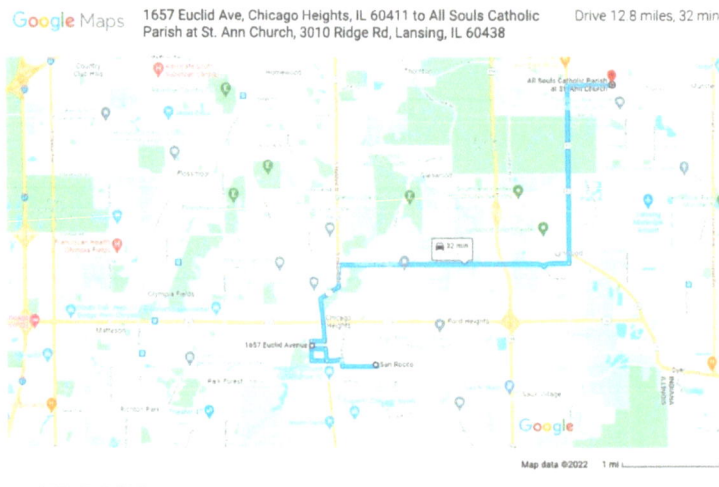

Figure 82. **Google Map Showing Relative Positions of Euclid Avenue House and Local Catholic Churches**

Glenwood, IL

After the birth of Josephine in December 1914, it is likely that the Smiths moved to
Glenwood, because Joseph no longer needed to be close to Chicago Rail Spring Company.
On 4 January 1915, he applied for employment at Victor Chemical Works and began
work there right away. The company was located at 11th and Arnold Street. Sometime
around 1915, Joseph acquired an old Ford crank-car and was able to travel from his new
Glenwood rented house to his new place of work.

Additionally, the move to Glenwood was likely to have been motivated by the need to
save money to prepare eventually to buy, rather than rent, a home. The Glenwood area
was rural and rents there would have been much less than what they were for the Euclid

Avenue rent. By contrast, the Glenwood rental house had fewer conveniences than the Euclid Avenue house: i.e., there was no indoor plumbing and no bathroom—only an outhouse. While the Smiths were increasing their family size, the move to Glenwood allowed them to save their money to eventually buy their future home.

Evidence of this relocation to Glenwood is from the WWI Registration Card dated 12 September 1918. Joseph Alfonso Smith lists Main Street, P.O. Box 42, Glenwood, Cook Country, Illinois as his address, his age as 36, his birthday as 19 May 1882, his occupation as chief electrician at Victor Chemical Works located at 11th and Arnold Street, Chicago Heights, Illinois. He is of medium height and build, and he has gray eyes and dark hair. He signed his name as Joseph Alfonso Smith. See the Registration Card below.

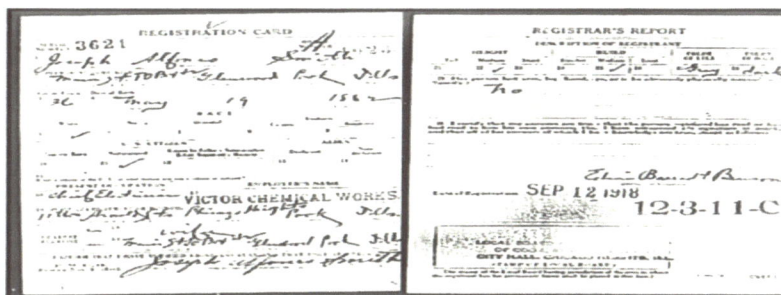

Figure 83. **World War Registration Draft for Joseph Smith September 1918**

Glenwood, Illinois was first known as Hickory Bend in 1838, and was renamed Glenwood in 1871. It is described as a quiet community with forested areas and a railroad that was established in 1872. An inn named Hottinger's was built there in 1847 and was known to be a stop on the Underground Railroad. The slaves and conductors often used the Glenwood Railroad, called the Chicago and Eastern Illinois Railroad, to escape. For the Smith family in the several years that they rented and lived in a house on Main Street in Glenwood, the railroad would have given them easy access to the Chicago Heights area where Joseph's new place of employment was—Victor Chemical Company.

In the early 1990's Clenise (Lindy) White interviewed the keeper of records for the Victor Chemical Works Company which was Rhone-Poulenc Rorer. The representative retrieved Joseph A. Smith's application which said that he was born in "Wilmerding, Pansilvania." (His penmanship was said to be good, but his spelling had some problems!) He had difficulty spelling his wife's last name and wrote it first as Mastant crossed out, then Maston, and finally Masters. He was very well thought of by the others in the company according to the records. His application also mentioned E. Pittsburgh and Turtle Creek. He said that his wife was from Buenos Aires, Argentina.

Victor Chemical Works was founded by a German-born man named August Kochs in 1902. According to the website encyclopedia.chicagohistory.org, Kochs had been experimenting with manufacturing baking powder. He directed the production of monocalcium phosphate. Victor Chemical Works was making ammonium phosphate and sulfuric acid by the 1910s.

From the **Journal of Agricultural and Food Chemistry**, some of the accomplishments of Victor Chemical Works included the following: "...Victor initiated research resulting in perfection of this country's first process to eliminate arsenic from food grade phosphates.

Soon after, a new process for concentrating phosphoric acid was developed, with lead troughs replacing uneconomical porcelain lined kettles, required in large numbers. To rid the finished products of objectionable lead thus introduced, sulfuric acid was added to the concentrated phosphoric, precipitating lead sulfate, and permitting production of high-grade food products." Victor chemicals were used in self-rising and pancake flours, prepared biscuit and cake mixes, processed cheese, evaporated milk, instant pudding, and yeast.

Joseph continued to work at the company for 32 years. His job was to maintain the boilers. The company was sold in 1958 to Stauffer Chemical.

Here's a Google Map showing the approximate location of the Glenwood house relative to the Victor Chemical Works plant.

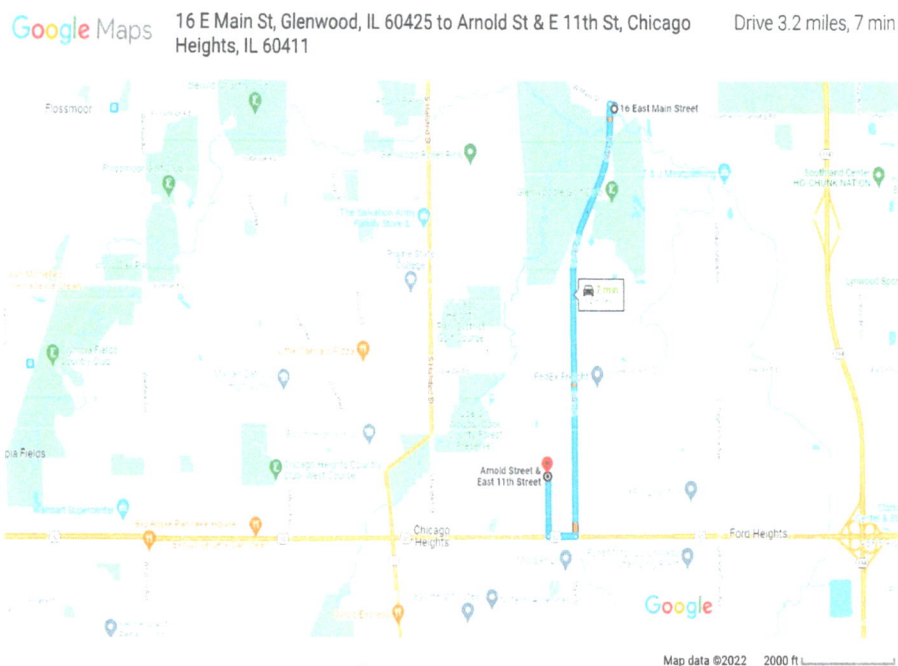

Figure 84. **Locations of home in Glenwood and Victor Chemical Works Company**

August Kochs founded Victor Chemical Works in 1902. The plant produced phosphate for the baking industry. It is still doing business as Rhodia, producing chemical compounds for baking, food processing, and tooth paste.

my dad worked here

Figure 85. <u>Images of America Chicago Heights Revisited</u> by Dominic Candelro and Barbara Paul: picture of Victor Chemical Works where Joseph Smith worked from 1915 to 1947.

And here's a picture of the site of Victor Chemical Works from 2020.

Figure 86. Google Maps Photo of Victor Chemical Works in 2020

March 1916 saw the birth of the next child of Joseph and Cleonice: Julia Giancola. The date was 31 March, although her baptismal record incorrectly lists her birthday as 30 March 1916. The original birth certificate must have had Julia Giancola as the infant's name, the parents as Joseph Giancola and Cleonice Mastantuoni. The baptism records of San Rocco show that information and the date of baptism of her sister Josephine who was almost two years old. The godparents' names were the same as Josephine's, namely Thomas D'Amico and Valentina D'Amico. The index for that year shows a misspelled last name of Grancolo, Giulia. See the San Rocco records below along with the index with the misspelled last name.

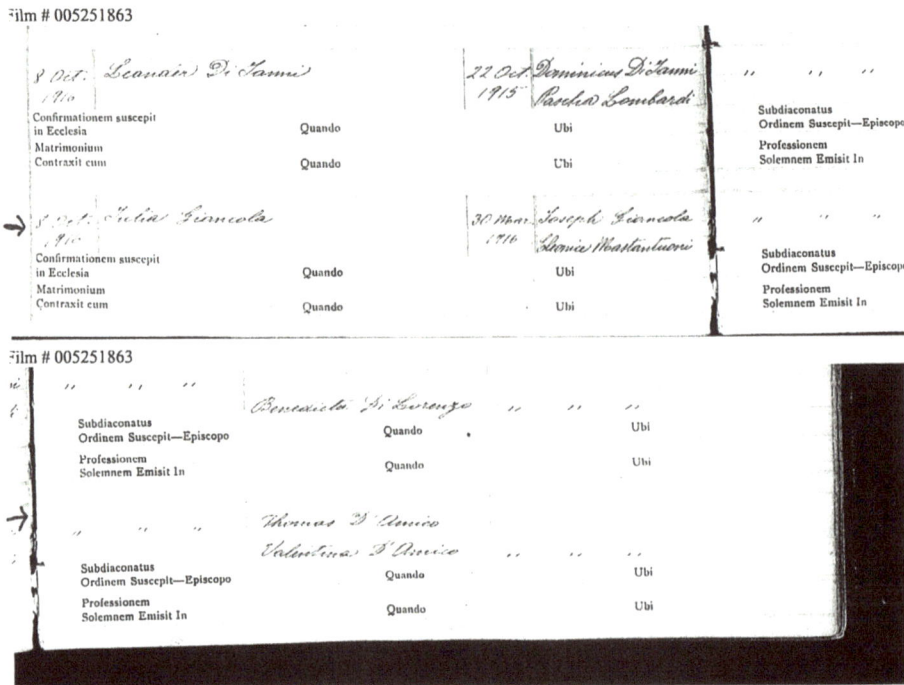

"Illinois, Chicago, Catholic Church Records, 1833-1925," database with images, FamilySearch
https://familysearch.org/ark:/61903/3:1:33SQ-G1HV-JTJ?cc=1452409&wc=M66P-829%3A40340501%2C40448501 : 20 May
2014), St Rocco Parish (Chicago Heights) > Baptisms 1916-1919 with index > image 42 of 127; Catholic Church parishes,
Chicago Diocese, Chicago.

Figure 87. San Rocco Church Records for Baptism of Julia Giancola

"Illinois, Chicago, Catholic Church Records, 1833-1925," database with images, FamilySearch
https://familysearch.org/ark:/61903/3:1:33SQ-G1HV-VXH?cc=1452409&wc=M66P-829%3A40340501%2C40448501 : 20
May 2014), St Rocco Parish (Chicago Heights) > Baptisms 1916-1919 with index > image 9 of 127; Catholic Church parishes,
Chicago Diocese, Chicago.

Figure 88. Index of San Rocco Baptism Records of Julia Showing Misspelled Last Name Grancolo

Julia's registration date for her revised birth certificate was 16 August 1944. This was issued in preparation for her license for marriage on 4 February 1945. The information on that reissued certificate shows her name as Julia Smith, her father Joseph Anthony Smith (age 33) from Wilmerdine, Pennsylvania, and her mother Clara Masters (age 31), from Buenos Aires, South America. (Josephine Stonitsch told daughter Clenise (Lindy) that Julia was named after Julia Gertrude McGrane.)

Here is a family photo taken 4 July 1917 with Marie (8 years old standing between her dad and mom), Elizabeth (6 years old to the very left), Lucy (5 years old next to Elizabeth), Amanda(4 years old at the right side), Jo (2 1/2 years old sitting next to mom Clara), Julia (1 year 4 months old sitting on her dad's lap), and Joseph and Clara. Clara Alice is about 3 or 4 months pregnant with Ellie.

Figure 89. **Smith Family Photo Taken 4 July 1917**

The first birth certificate for Eleanor Smith shows her name as Adelina Smith, born 16 December 1917 with Joseph Smith as her father (age 35) and Cleonice Montrantoni as her mother (age 33). (FHL microfilm 1,308, 564.) The reissued registration date is 7 October 1948 with the name now Eleanore Smith. The father is Joseph Anthony Smith from Wilmerding, PA and the mother is Clara Masters from Buenos Aires, South America.

The baptism of Eleanor took place at San Rocco Church on 18 August 1918. The name in the register is Magdalena Giandicola with birthdate 16 December 1917; the father Joseph Giandicola and the mother Cleonicis Mastantonio; and godparents Thomas D'Amico and Valentina D'Amico. The index shows the selected name of Magdalena Giandicola.

The records are shown below in Figures 90 and 91.

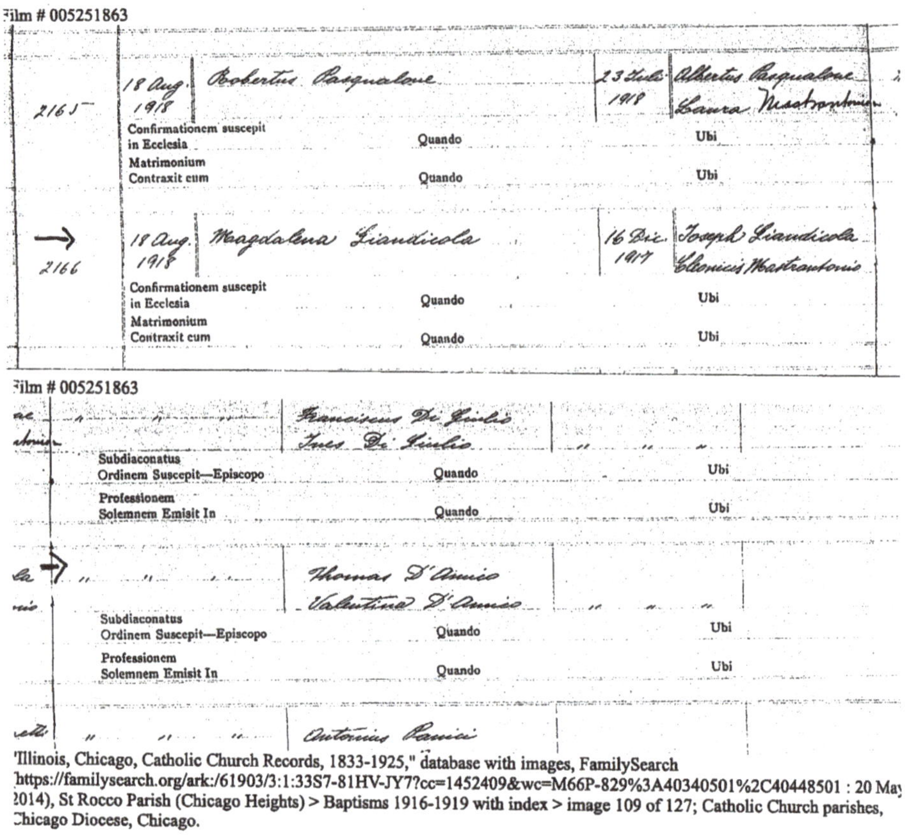
Film # 005251863

2165 | 18 Aug. 1918 | Robertus Pasqualone | 23 Iulii 1918 | Albertus Pasqualone / Laura Mastrantonio

Confirmationem suscepit in Ecclesia Quando Ubi
Matrimonium Contraxit cum Quando Ubi

2166 | 18 Aug. 1918 | Magdalena Giandicola | 16 Dic. 1917 | Joseph Giandicola / Eleonicis Mastrantonio

Confirmationem suscepit in Ecclesia Quando Ubi
Matrimonium Contraxit cum Quando Ubi

Film # 005251863

Franciscus Di Giulio / Ines Di Giulio

Subdiaconatus Ordinem Suscepit—Episcopo Quando Ubi
Professionem Solemnem Emisit In Quando Ubi

Thomas D'Amico / Valentina D'Amico

Subdiaconatus Ordinem Suscepit—Episcopo Quando Ubi
Professionem Solemnem Emisit In Quando Ubi

Antonius Ramici

"Illinois, Chicago, Catholic Church Records, 1833-1925," database with images, FamilySearch https://familysearch.org/ark:/61903/3:1:33S7-81HV-JY7?cc=1452409&wc=M66P-829%3A40340501%2C40448501 : 20 May 2014), St Rocco Parish (Chicago Heights) > Baptisms 1916-1919 with index > image 109 of 127; Catholic Church parishes, Chicago Diocese, Chicago.

Figure 90. **Baptism Record for Eleanore Giancola, Showing Name as Magdalena Giandicola**

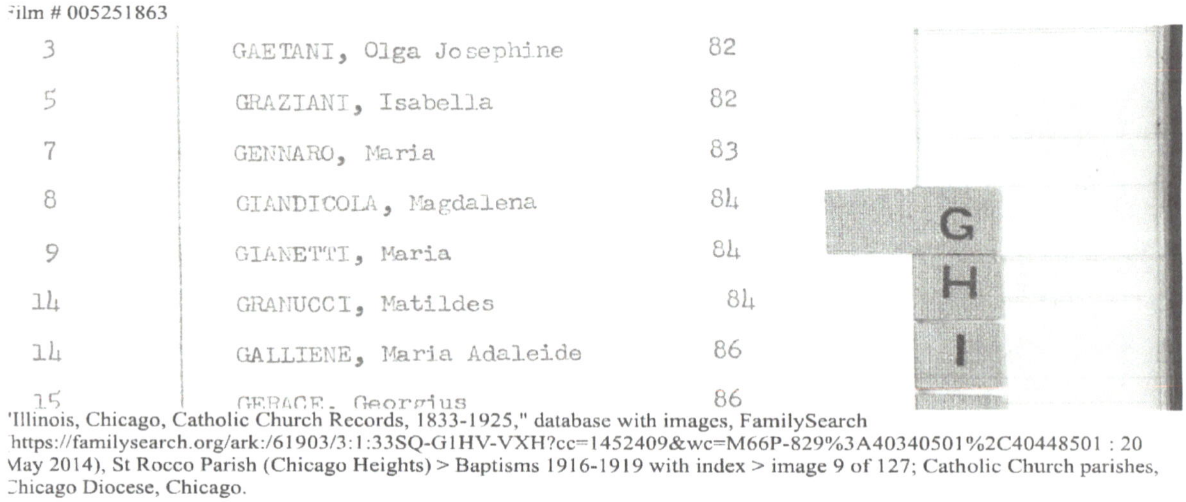
Film # 005251863

3	GAETANI, Olga Josephine	82
5	GRAZIANI, Isabella	82
7	GENNARO, Maria	83
8	GIANDICOLA, Magdalena	84
9	GIANETTI, Maria	84
14	GRANUCCI, Matildes	84
14	GALLIENE, Maria Adaleide	86
15	GERACE, Georgius	86

"Illinois, Chicago, Catholic Church Records, 1833-1925," database with images, FamilySearch https://familysearch.org/ark:/61903/3:1:33SQ-G1HV-VXH?cc=1452409&wc=M66P-829%3A40340501%2C40448501 : 20 May 2014), St Rocco Parish (Chicago Heights) > Baptisms 1916-1919 with index > image 9 of 127; Catholic Church parishes, Chicago Diocese, Chicago.

Figure 91. **Baptism Record Index, Showing Name as Magdalena Giandicola**

When Adelina/Magdalena/Eleanor was almost a year old, there was an incident that occurred in Glenwood that left a lasting impression on her almost four-year-old sister Josephine.

Here is a rendition of a 1994 journal entry written by **Josephine Stonitsch** about one of her first memories of an incident that occurred when she was almost four years old and was living in the rented house in **Glenwood** with her family:

It was my mother's 36th birthday on Armistice Day, November 11, 1918. World War I ended. I was only 3 years old at the time but would be 4 years old one month to the date. The reason I can remember is that my father had a "talk of the town" car accident that day. But let me go back some. At the time, my parents rented a home in Glenwood, Illinois. There were 5 of us then. With Julie, the 6th on the way. I remember the old black iron stove, mom used to cook, bake, heat water for our baths, and to keep warm on cold nights, as we would huddle near the stove, as well as another coal burning stove in another room. Basically, the kitchen, as I recall, was our mainstay. We had a pump outdoors for all our needs, and an outhouse. Running water in houses was unheard of in that small town, though a few may have had it. To get back to Armistice Day and mom's birthday: Birthdays were special days in our family, but this day wasn't special to mom as far as happiness for her went. Dad worked 4 or 5 miles away at Victor Chemical Works in Chicago Heights, IL. He drove his friend Mr. Tattersall in our crank-started Ford which wasn't always reliable to say the least. But it took us to church, St. John's where Fr. Burke, a kindly and jolly priest, as I remember, was pastor. Mom and dad were always fervent church goers. On that day of days, my dad and Mr. Tattersall were returning from work, and we were all waiting eagerly for mom's birthday celebration to begin. Mealtimes were always happy times in our household. Dad always came home with jokes—not always ones we should hear. Though we little ones didn't understand them, we joined in the laughter. This night was different. Mom had supper all prepared. We never ate a meal without dad being there, so we were all hungry as time went by and no dad. As it was, dad's Ford stopped directly on the railroad tracks. Dad saw no trains coming. There were no signal gates there, so dad got out, started to crank the engine, when he heard, in the distance, a train whistle to clear all rails. Thinking quickly, he told Mr. Tattersall to get out of the car, and as they stopped far enough for safety, they watched the car being hit to smithereens, both safe. There was a tavern close by, called Hottinger's place (see picture on a later page), where dad and Mr. Tattersall went to call the police about the accident. While they waited, it being the end of the war, Mr. Tattersall, who imbibed and enjoyed his drinks, talked my dad into having a beer, which was far out of line in practice for my dad, but he was always a good sport, and this day he probably felt a drink was the thing to do. Anyway, by the time the police came and the celebration at the tavern was done, dad came home singing as though not a thing was wrong. All I was told was that mom certainly didn't enjoy that episode of either kind, she quickly fed the family and off to bed we went. Mom was justifiably angry to end her birthday this way. The only remaining parts of the Ford were the little leather curtains from the side windows, which blew a distance away. Needless to say, the car was demolished. As small as I was, the events of that day were my first recollection. Glenwood, as probably still is today, was a quaint little town. People were very neighborly. Everyone had a garden, small homes, outhouses, pumps outdoors, and wood/coal-burning stoves. Milk wagons, drawn by horses came down the dusty roads. We were well fed, prayed daily, had our "Saturday baths." Mom would heat the water, put it in a large tub in the kitchen, and one by one each would take a bath in the same water. I remember that! But it was the thing of the day, and we accepted it as a blessing to get cleaned. We washed our feet in tubs of water outdoors as we played in dirt. We lived in Glenwood for two years.

Hottinger's Gardens Main Street

Figure 92. **Hottinger's Gardens Inn: Old Fashion Lager Draught**

At the time of Joseph's car/train incident, the Smiths lived on Main Street in Glenwood, and the empty field to the left of the Google Maps photo below is the approximate location of their rented residence. See the railroad crossing sign in the picture.

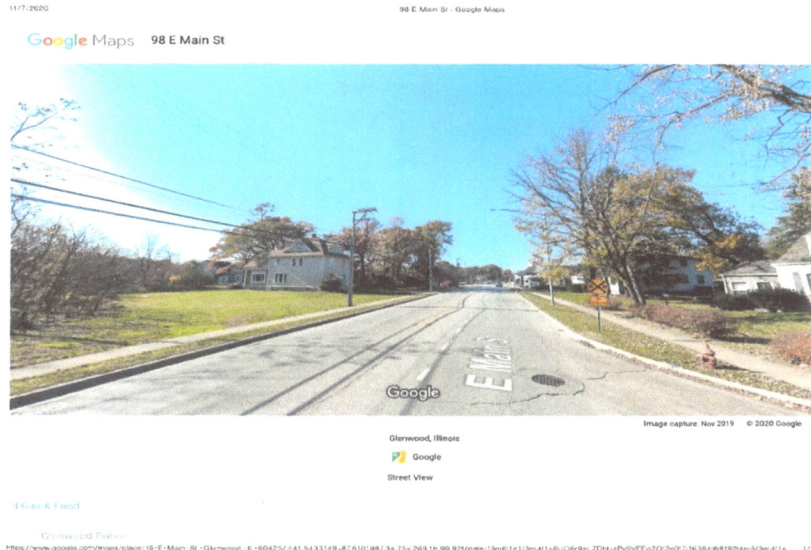

Figure 93. **Approximate Location of Smith House on Main Street in Glenwood**

Here is some information about George Tattersall, the man that was accompanying Joseph Smith in the car at the time of the car/train accident. Joseph used to give George a ride to work each day while they were neighbors in Glenwood, and when Joseph still had a usable car. George was born 10 September 1884 in Pennsylvania. In the 1910 Federal Census, his address was 1306 5th Avenue, Chicago Heights, and he was a glass blower who worked for the Chicago Heights Bottle Company on 12th Arnold Street (as his 1918 Draft Registration card showed). This company was very close to Victor Chemical Works which made it quite easy for Joseph Smith to drive George to and from his work, both living on the same street in Glenwood, and both working at jobs on the same street in Chicago Heights. The Tattersalls had five children by the time of the 1920 census. There are several records at St. Ann Church in Lansing, IL that mention baptisms of Tattersall infants. This is where Lucy and Mandy were baptized in 1913. (Mr. Tattersall died in 1954 and was buried in the Holy Name Catholic Cemetery in Indiana.)

As mentioned above in Josephine's journal entry, the church that the Smith family regularly attended was St. John's where Father Burke was pastor in Glenwood. Here is a prayer card entitled "To a Friend" which was given to the Smith family from Father Burke with a personal note on the back. The picture of Father Burke is from e-churchbulletins.com/bulletins which has a detailed history of St. John's Church.

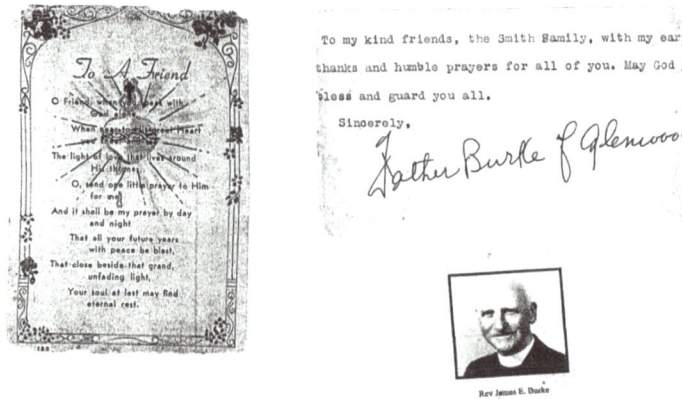

Figure 94. **Items Relating to Father Burke of St. John's Church in Glenwood**

After the car/train accident, Joseph Smith wanted to get closer to his place of work because he no longer had his car. The family moved to a small house on **Main Street close to Chicago Road in Chicago Heights**. They rented that house for a short time and finally purchased the **1657 Euclid Avenue** house that they had rented when they had first arrived in Chicago Heights. The house had a big, fenced backyard and indoor plumbing and bathrooms, unlike their rented Glenwood house. Their neighbors were the Noxins at 1661 Euclid, and the Hoels at 1655 Euclid.

This second move to the Euclid Avenue house took place most likely in 1919, and the 1920 Federal Census confirms that the family was living at the **1657 Euclid Avenue** house in that year. Joseph and Alice (Clara) were listed with the children Marie, Elizabeth, Lucy, Magdella, Josephine, Julie, Elenor, and Anthony. The census shows they claimed Argentina for the birthplace of both Joseph and Alice, and that Joseph was working as an electrician at a factory.

The first son born to the Smith family arrived on 11 November 1919. (Clara, his mom, was also born on 11 November but in 1884.) His birth certificate shows his name as **Anthony Smith**, and his father Joseph A. Smith (age 37), born in Argentine, South America, and his mother Clara Senas (age 34), born in Argentine, South America also. The following is a copy of the Illinois Cook County Birth Certificate for Anthony Smith.

Anthony Smith

FamilySearch   Family Tree   Search   Memories   Get Involved   Activities   ⦿ 🌐 ⓘ 💬 🔔 C CWhite3

Records   Images   Family Tree   Genealogies   Catalog   Books   Wiki

⬛ SAVE   ⦸ SHARE

Name	**Anthony Smith**
Sex	**Male**
Birth Date	**11 Nov 1919**
Birthplace	**Chicago Heights, Cook, Illinois, United States**
Birthplace (Original)	**Chicago Heights**
Father's Name	Joseph A Smith
Father's Age	37
Father's Birth Year (Estimated)	1882
Father's Birthplace	**Argentine, S A**
Mother's Name	Clara Senas
Mother's Age	34
Mother's Birth Year (Estimated)	1885
Mother's Birthplace	**Argentine, S A**
Event Type	**Birth**
Certificate Number	**360**
Registration Place	**, Cook, Illinois**

Family Tree

Similar Records

No similar records were found.

Document Information ⌄

Collection Information

Illinois, Cook County, Birth Certificates, 1871-1949 ⓘ

Cite This Record

"Illinois, Cook County, Birth Certificates, 1871-1949," database, *FamilySearch* (https://familysearch.org/ark:/61903/1:1:N7QB-1V3 : 18 May 2016), Anthony Smith, 11 Nov 1919; Chicago Heights, Cook, Illinois, United States, reference/certificate 360, Cook County Clerk, Cook County Courthouse, Chicago; FHL microfilm 1,308,626.

Anthony Smith's Parents and Siblings   OPEN ALL

Joseph A Smith	Father	M	37	Argentine, S A ⌄
Clara Senas	Mother	F	34	Argentine, S A ⌄

Figure 95. Birth Certificate for Anthony Smith

Here is an entry in **Josephine Smith Stonitsch's journal** that she wrote around 1994 about her memories of her little brother Anthony who was born in 1919:

I remember when my little brother Anthony was born on my mom's birthday, November 11th. He seemed to have been sick ever since he was born. He would have convulsions, so mom had quite a time since she herself wasn't that well.

We had a maid come to help whenever mom was sick or had a baby. Women had midwives during birthing, so she would stay on as maid until mom felt better. We must have been a handful. I can remember one incident when she had a broom to scare us to being good. In my mind, she was not taking my mom's place. But little Anthony and mom pretty much stayed upstairs.

I remember the night well. Anthony was in his crib, really suffering, so mom called the priest to come baptize him. This was the following February. Mom cooked our supper. I can still see the table set. We were all hungry, waiting for dad to come home. When he came home around 5 or 5:30 p.m. he picked Anthony from his crib, and I can still remember standing very close at dad's side, holding Anthony as he breathed heavily. He died in dad's arms as we watched. Needless to say we were too sad to eat after that.

I remember the day of the funeral. Julie and I and maybe Lucy, who took care of us as we watched them pass our house once more. In those days, on funeral days, the hearse would drive past the house of the deceased as a last tribute. Doors would have a purple wreath on them, to indicate a death had occurred. I remember the big brown leather rocker we sat in together, by the window. We pulled back the curtains to say goodbye to our brother Anthony.

Here is a copy of the certified death certificate for Anthony Joseph Smith, infant of Joseph Smith of the Argentine Republic and Alice Mason also of the Argentine Republic. Date of death is listed as 3 February 1920 with burial on 4 February 1920 at Evergreen Hill Cemetery. Cause of death was broncho pneumonia, secondary enteritis. Dr. Cornet was the attending physician. (Josephine remembers the doctor coming to the house.)

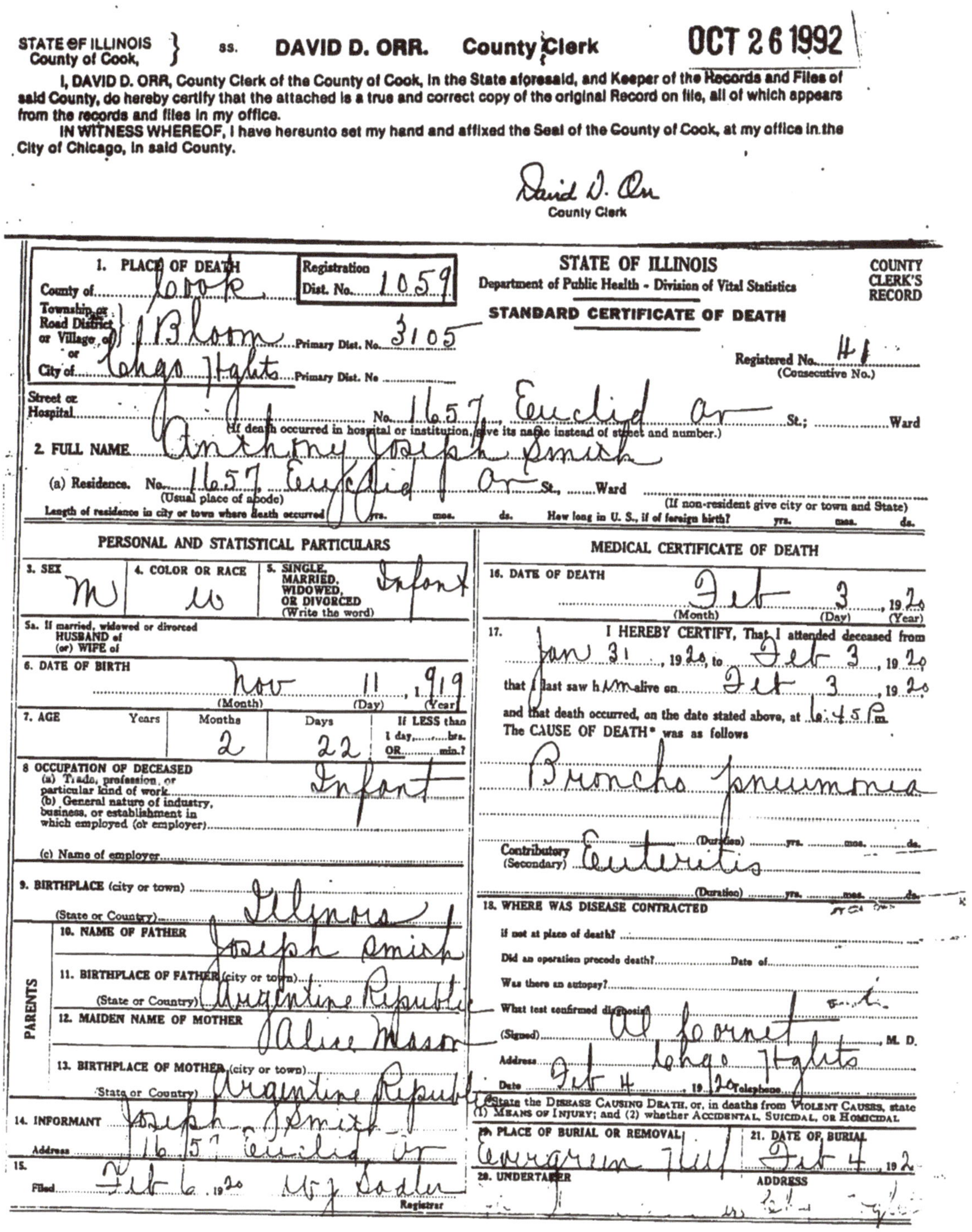

STATE OF ILLINOIS } ss. DAVID D. ORR. County Clerk OCT 26 1992
County of Cook,

I, DAVID D. ORR, County Clerk of the County of Cook, in the State aforesaid, and Keeper of the Records and Files of said County, do hereby certify that the attached is a true and correct copy of the original Record on file, all of which appears from the records and files in my office.

IN WITNESS WHEREOF, I have hereunto set my hand and affixed the Seal of the County of Cook, at my office in the City of Chicago, in said County.

David D. Orr
County Clerk

STATE OF ILLINOIS
Department of Public Health - Division of Vital Statistics
STANDARD CERTIFICATE OF DEATH
COUNTY CLERK'S RECORD

1. PLACE OF DEATH — County of Cook — Registration Dist. No. 1059
Township or Road District or Village of Bloom — Primary Dist. No. 3105
or City of Chgo Hghts — Primary Dist. No.
Registered No. 41 (Consecutive No.)
Street or Hospital — No. 1657 Euclid Av St.; Ward (If death occurred in hospital or institution, give its name instead of street and number.)

2. FULL NAME Anthony Joseph Smith
(a) Residence. No. 1657 Euclid Av St., Ward (Usual place of abode) (If non-resident give city or town and State)
Length of residence in city or town where death occurred yrs. mos. ds. How long in U. S., if of foreign birth? yrs. mos. ds.

PERSONAL AND STATISTICAL PARTICULARS

3. SEX: M
4. COLOR OR RACE: W
5. SINGLE, MARRIED, WIDOWED, OR DIVORCED (Write the word): Infant
5a. If married, widowed or divorced HUSBAND of (or) WIFE of
6. DATE OF BIRTH: Nov (Month) 11 (Day), 1919 (Year)
7. AGE: Years — Months 2 — Days 22 — If LESS than 1 day, hrs. OR min.?
8. OCCUPATION OF DECEASED (a) Trade, profession, or particular kind of work: Infant
(b) General nature of industry, business, or establishment in which employed (or employer)
(c) Name of employer
9. BIRTHPLACE (city or town) (State or Country): Illinois
10. NAME OF FATHER: Joseph Smith
11. BIRTHPLACE OF FATHER (city or town) (State or Country): Argentine Republic
12. MAIDEN NAME OF MOTHER: Alice Mason
13. BIRTHPLACE OF MOTHER (city or town) (State or Country): Argentine Republic
14. INFORMANT: Joseph Smith — Address: 1657 Euclid Av
15. Filed Feb 6, 1920 — M. J. Sadler, Registrar

MEDICAL CERTIFICATE OF DEATH

16. DATE OF DEATH: Feb (Month) 3 (Day), 1920 (Year)
17. I HEREBY CERTIFY, That I attended deceased from Jan 31, 1920, to Feb 3, 1920
that I last saw him alive on Feb 3, 1920
and that death occurred, on the date stated above, at 6:45 Pm.
The CAUSE OF DEATH* was as follows: Broncho Pneumonia (Duration) yrs. mos. ds.
Contributory (Secondary): Enteritis (Duration) yrs. mos. ds.
18. WHERE WAS DISEASE CONTRACTED if not at place of death?
Did an operation precede death? Date of
Was there an autopsy?
What test confirmed diagnosis?
(Signed) A. Fornet, M. D.
Address: Chgo Hghts
Date Feb 4, 1920 Telephone
*State the DISEASE CAUSING DEATH, or, in deaths from VIOLENT CAUSES, state (1) MEANS OF INJURY; and (2) whether ACCIDENTAL, SUICIDAL, OR HOMICIDAL
19. PLACE OF BURIAL OR REMOVAL: Evergreen Hill — 21. DATE OF BURIAL: Feb 4, 192
20. UNDERTAKER — ADDRESS

Figure 96. **Death Certificate of Anthony Joseph Smith 3 February 1920**

The Smith family was still living at 1657 Euclid Avenue at this time in 1920. The 1920 Federal Census shows this to be the case. See the page below of the Fourteenth Census of the United States: 1920.

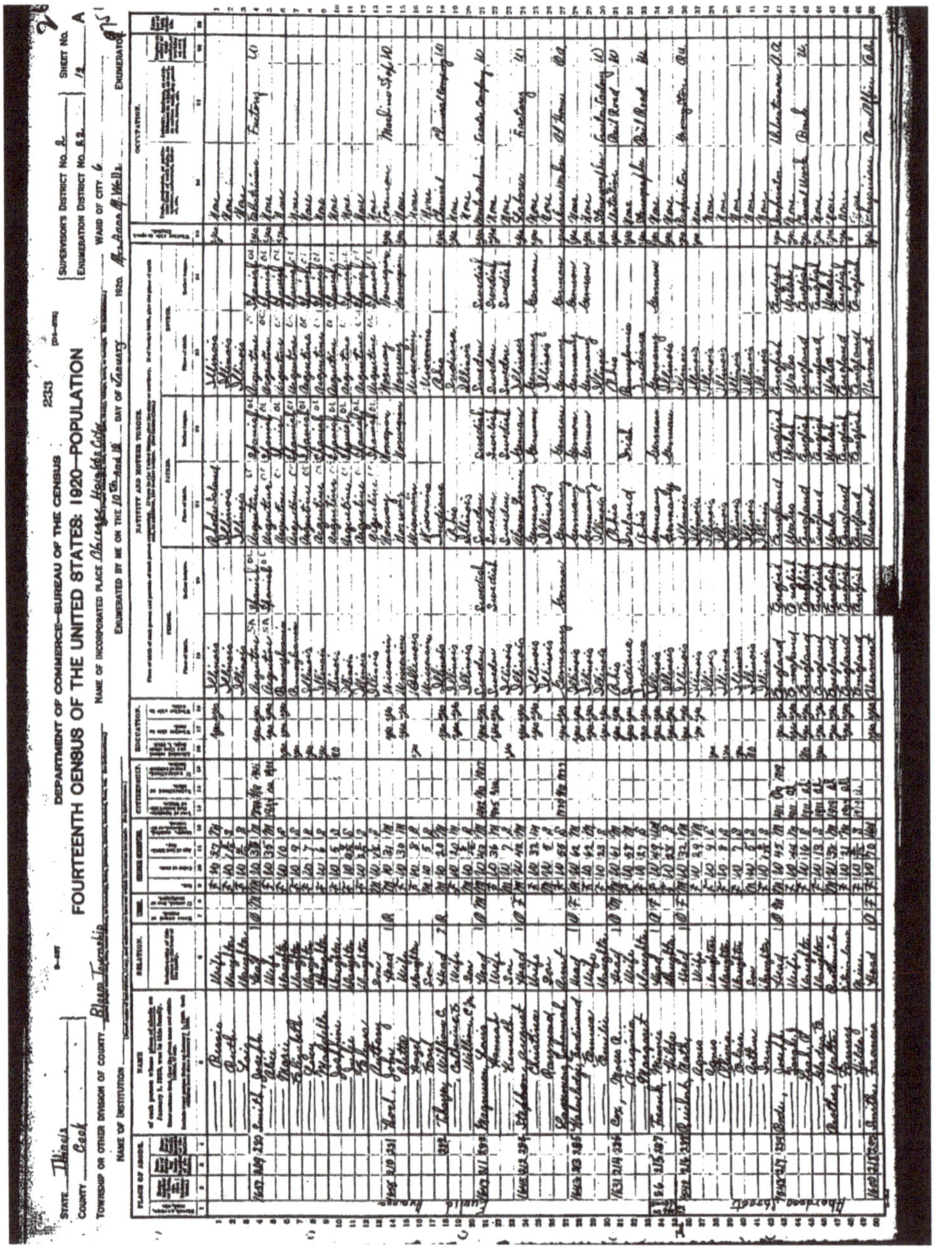
DEPARTMENT OF COMMERCE—BUREAU OF THE CENSUS

FOURTEENTH CENSUS OF THE UNITED STATES: 1920—POPULATION

Figure 97. **1920 Federal Census Showing Smith Family at 1657 Euclid Avenue**

Here is the typed-up version of the 1920 census information for Joseph Smith on the ancestry.com website.

Joseph Smith
in the 1920 United States Federal Census

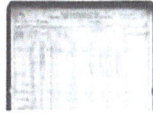

View

View blank form

Add or update information

Report a problem

Name:	Joseph Smith
Age:	37
Birth Year:	abt 1883
Birthplace:	Argentina
Home in 1920:	Chicago Ward 1, Cook (Chicago), Illinois
Street:	Euclid Avenue
House Number:	1657
Residence Date:	1920
Race:	White
Gender:	Male
Immigration Year:	1894
Relation to Head of House:	Head
Marital status:	Married
Spouse's Name:	Alice Smith
Father's Birthplace:	Argentina
Mother's Birthplace:	Argentina
Native Tongue:	Spanish
Able to Speak English:	Yes

Figure 98. Information About Smith Family from 1920 Census Shown at Ancestry.com, Part 1

Occupation:	Electrician
Industry:	Factory
Employment Field:	Wage or Salary
Home Owned or Rented:	Owned
Home Free or Mortgaged:	Mortgaged
Naturalization Status:	Naturalized
Able to Read:	Yes
Able to Write:	Yes
Neighbors:	View others on page

Household Members:

Name	Age
Joseph Smith	37
Alice Smith	35
Marie Smith	10
Elizabeth Smith	9
Lucy Smith	7
Magdella Smith	6
Josphine Smith	5
Julie Smith	3
Elenor Smith	2
Anthony Smith	0

[Save & create tree ∨]   Cancel

Source Citation
Year: *1920*; Census Place: *Chicago Ward 1, Cook (Chicago), Illinois*; Roll: *T625_358*; Page: *12A*; Enumeration District: *22*

Source Information
Ancestry.com. *1920 United States Federal Census* [database on-line]. Provo, UT, USA: Ancestry.com Operations, Inc., 2010. Images reproduced by FamilySearch.

Original data: Fourteenth Census of the United States, 1920. (NARA microfilm publication T625, 2076 rolls). Records of the Bureau of the Census, Record Group 29. National Archives, Washington, D.C. For details on the contents of the film numbers, visit the following NARA web page: NARA. Note: Enumeration Districts 819-839 are on roll 323 (Chicago City).

Description

Figure 99. Information About Smith Family from 1920 Census Shown at Ancestry.com, Part 2

The 1920 census has incorrect information in it regarding the birth places of Joseph and Alice Smith. It shows that they were both born in Argentina and have Spanish as their native language. They are listed as immigrating in 1894 which is not correct, nor is the date of naturalization correct.

Daughter Number 8, **Claratine Smith**, was born on 6 May 1921 to Joseph Anthony Smith (age 39) at Wilmerdina, PA and Clara Alice Masters (age 37) of Buenos Aires, Argentina (Certificate #176 Cook County Courthouse, Microfilm 1308634).

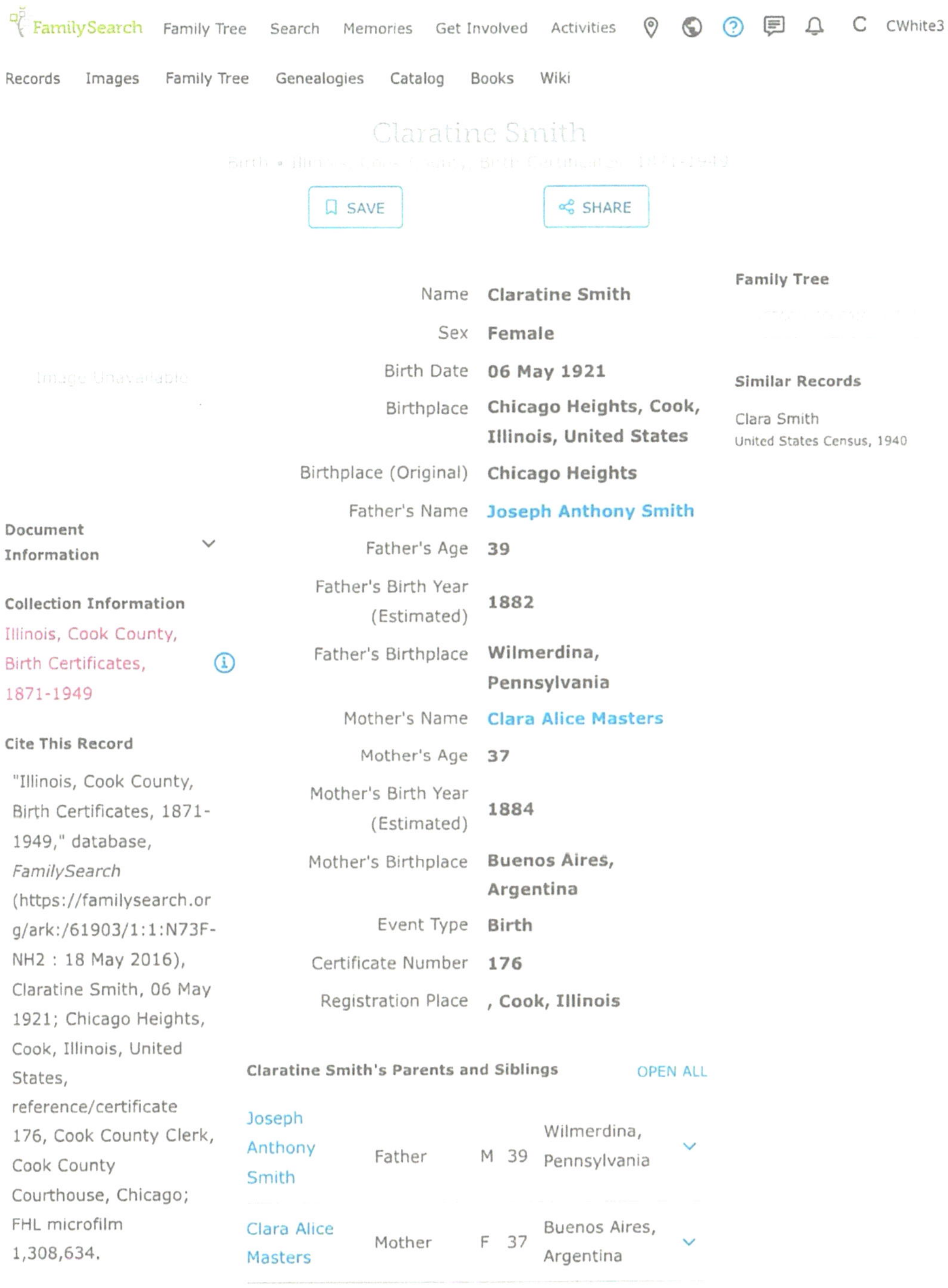

Figure 100. **Birth Certificate of Claratine Smith, Certificate #176 Cook County Courthouse, Microfilm 1308634**

Certificate #254 shows the name as Clara Smith; father Joseph Smith (age 38) from Buenos Aires, Argentina; mother Alice De Maso (age 36) from Buenos Aires, Argentina. Here is that birth certificate that has slightly different information.

ancestry

Clara Smith in the Cook County, Illinois, Birth
Certificates Index, 1871-1922

Name:	Clara Smith
Birth Date:	6 May 1921
Birth Place:	Chicago Heights, Cook, Illinois
Gender:	Female
Father Name:	Joseph Smith
Father's Birth Place:	Buenos Aires, Argentina
Father's Age:	38
Mother Name:	Alice De Maso
Mother's Birth Place:	Buenos Aires, Argentina
Mother's Age:	36
FHL Film Number:	1308634

Source Information

Ancestry.com. *Cook County, Illinois, Birth Certificates Index, 1871-1922* [database on-line]. Provo, UT, USA: Ancestry.com Operations, Inc., 2011.

Original data:

"Illinois, Cook County Birth Certificates, 1878–1922." Index. FamilySearch, Salt Lake City, Utah, 2009. Illinois. Cook County Birth Certificates, 1878–1922. Illinois Department of Public Health. Division of Vital Records. Springfield.

"Illinois. Cook County Birth Registers, 1871–1915." Index. FamilySearch, Salt Lake City, Utah. Illinois. Cook County Birth Registers, 1871–1915. Illinois Department of Public Health. Division of Vital Records, Springfield.

Description

This database contains an index of details extracted from Cook County, Illinois, birth records. Learn more...

© 2015, Ancestry.com

Figure 101. Clara Smith Birth Certificate from Ancestry.com

Daughter Clara's baptism took place at San Rocco Parish in Chicago Heights. The date was 19 June 1921, and the godparents were again Thomas D'Amico and Valentina D'Amico. Clara's name was recorded as Clara Valentina Antoinetta Giancola, with parents Joseph Giancola and Cleonices Mastrantoni. The index has the infant's name as Clara Giancolla. See copy of records below.

Film # 005251864

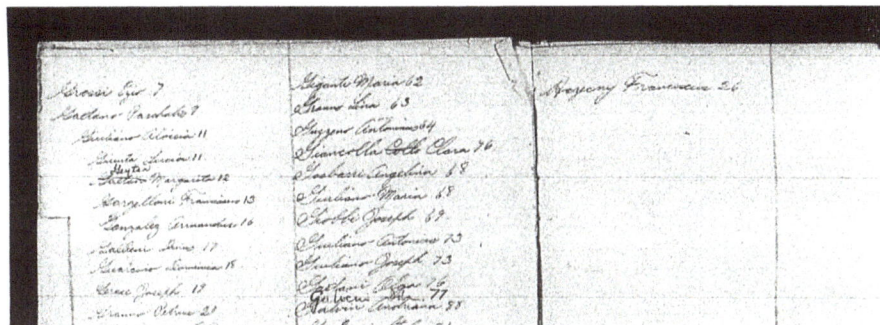

"Illinois, Chicago, Catholic Church Records, 1833-1925," database with images, FamilySearch
https://familysearch.org/ark:/61903/3:1:33S7-81HV-JMQ?cc=1452409&wc=M66P-XZ3%3A40340501%2C40475301 : 20 Ma
2014), St Rocco Parish (Chicago Heights) > Baptisms 1919-1922 with index > image 7 of 117; Catholic Church parishes,
Chicago Diocese, Chicago.

Film # 005251864

"Illinois, Chicago, Catholic Church Records, 1833-1925," database with images, FamilySearch
https://familysearch.org/ark:/61903/3:1:33S7-L1HV-JT6?cc=1452409&wc=M66P-XZ3%3A40340501%2C40475301 : 20 May
2014), St Rocco Parish (Chicago Heights) > Baptisms 1919-1922 with index > image 92 of 117; Catholic Church parishes,
Chicago Diocese, Chicago.

Figure 102. San Rocco Baptismal Records for Clara Giancola

At the time of Clara's birth in 1921, her sister Josephine was in first grade at St. Agnes
School. Here is a class picture of Josephine standing next to Sister Esther in front of the
school building in 1921.

Figure 103. First Grade Class 1920-21 Saint Agnes School. Josephine Back Row on left next to Sister Esther

In 1922, the last of the Smith children was born: **Joseph Anthony (Smitty)**. His birth date was 21 October. There are two birth certificates that have slightly different information. One shows his father's name as Jos A. Smith from Buenos Aires, Argentina, and his mother as Clara Miseneo, also from Buenos Aires, Argentina. The other certificate shows his mother's name as unknown, and she was born in Wilmerding, Pennsylvania. A thorough search of the records of San Rocco and Saint Agnes did not result in locating the baptismal certificate of infant Joseph Anthony.

Below is a picture of the inside of San Rocco Catholic Church from the pinterest.com website, taken around 1930. Josephine, Julie, Eleanor, and Clara were baptized in this church. Joseph (Smitty) Anthony Smith Jr. was most likely also baptized at San Rocco Church or St. Agnes Church which were the two closest Catholic Churches to their Euclid Avenue house in Chicago Heights.

Figure 104. **San Rocco Catholic Church, Chicago Heights, IL from Pinterest.com website (about 1930).**

St. Agnes Church and Catholic School were .4 miles from the Euclid Avenue house (see Google Maps below), and it was the church and school the family attended on a regular basis.

Figure 105. **Google Maps walking path from Euclid to St. Agnes (Our Lady of the Heights)**

Here is a picture from facebook.com/HistoricChicagoHeights/photos showing the Catholic Church at the turn of the 20th century with trolley tracks in the foreground.

Figure 106. **St. Agnes Catholic Church in Chicago Heights, Illinois**

The church was founded in 1895. Father Lanigan was the pastor from 1920 to 1925, and Father A. C. Martin was the pastor in 1926 who built the yellow brick structure in Roman architecture. Here is a picture of the interior of St. Agnes from an original postcard with handwriting on the back that says "St. Agnes Church at Chicago Heights, Ill."

Figure 107. **Interior of St. Agnes Catholic Church from Postcard**

As noted in the discussions of the baptisms of the last 4 or 5 Smith children, the D'Amicos served as godparents for Josephine, Julie, Ellie, and Clara (and possibly Smitty) at San Rocco Catholic Church and were an important part of the family's life. The D'Amicos were well-established in the Chicago Heights area. They had arrived in America sometime around 1895 (at least fifteen years before the Smith family moved there). Gaetano and Giacinta D'Amico were born in Castel Di Sangro in the middle of the Italian peninsula between Rome and Naples, and they immigrated to the United States in 1889 with their infant son Thomas to seek a better life.

Here is a current Google Map of the location of the birthplace of Gaetano, Giacinta, and Thomas D'Amico in Italy. It was only 27.3 miles away from Castelpetroso where Joseph was born; however, it is unlikely that the D'Amico and Smith families met in their home country of Italy.

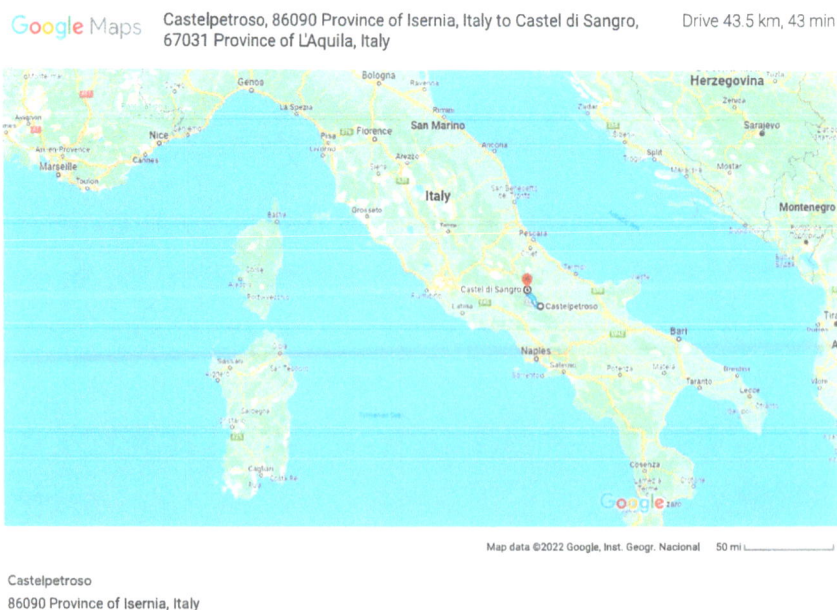

Figure 108. **Google Map Showing Birthplace of Gaetano, Giacinta, and Thomas D'Amico and Giuseppe Giancola**

In 1902 the D'Amico family purchased and operated a grocery store on 188 East 22nd Street, and they lived above the store and expanded the building over time. (The death certificate of Gaetano in 1955 mentions his residence at that time as this same East 22nd Street address.) Their children (including Thomas) worked in the grocery store. Thomas and his wife Valentina were very good friends with the Smith family. In 1914 Thomas and his father established the G. D'Amico Macaroni Company in Chicago Heights, selling the "Mama Mia" pasta brand nation-wide. See the advertisement in the <u>Chicago Heights Star</u> on 19 July 1938 for the G. D'Amico Macaroni Company.

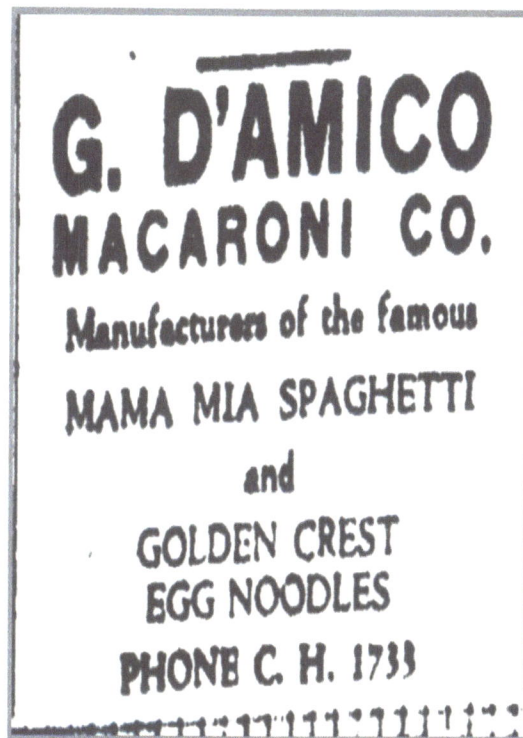

Figure 109. **Newspaper Advertisement in 1939 for the G. D'Amico Macaroni Company**

It is likely that the Smiths met the D'Amicos at the grocery store. (Josephine Stonitsch mentioned to Clenise (Lindy) that the D'Amicos used to give them food, and that the D'Amicos owned a grocery store and a restaurant that sold pasta. Josephine said that her mom Clara would walk to whatever grocery store had the cheapest prices to save money. There probably was another store closer to the Smiths' house, but the prices may have been better at the D'Amico grocery store, and Clara would have walked the extra miles to save a few pennies. Mrs. D'Amico would visit with Clara to teach her how to bake biscotti. The newspapers often mention that Valentina D'Amico would host a number of social events including bridge, pinochle, and bunco.

Here's a map showing the distance from the home/grocery store of the D'Amicos to the house of the Smiths at Euclid Avenue. It is a 5-minute drive and about 1.2 miles apart.

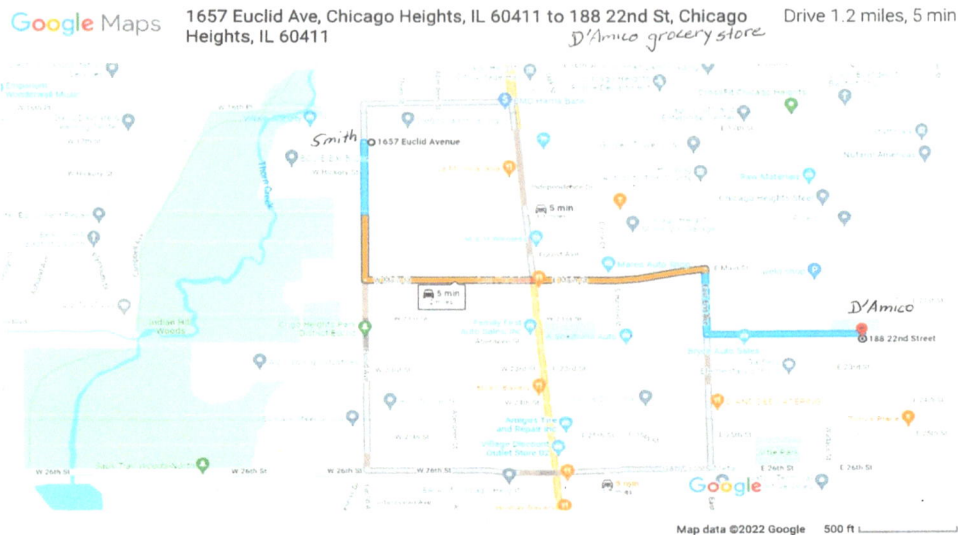

Figure 110. **Google Map Showing Distance from D'Amico Grocery Store to Smith House on Euclid Avenue**

The D'Amicos were frequently in the **<u>Chicago Heights Star</u>** newspaper. One unfortunate story appeared in the 4 January 1923 issue which mentioned that someone had placed a bomb in the front of the grocery store at 188 22nd Street on 28 June 1922 that did a lot of damage to the front of the building. There were no injuries, and no arrests were made. In 1928 the D'Amicos found a larger building in close-by Steger for the business which was off Chicago Road. The D'Amico family, however, continued living in the house at 188 E. 22nd St., Chicago Heights at least until Gaetano's death in 1955 at age 94. Gaetano and Giacinta did not try to hide their Italian heritage, nor would it have been possible with their business and "Mama Mia" brand. They went to the Italian Saint Rocco's Church and had Gaetano's funeral Mass held there.

It was a different story with two of the D'Amico sons who took over the business after Gaetano retired. A newspaper article mentioned that two sons (but not Thomas who died in 1943) changed or contemplated changing their name from D'Amico to D'Emic to avoid discrimination in the business due to their Italian heritage. (In 1951 the business had been vandalized again with the safe being smashed, and cash and other items stolen.) Later records do not show that they changed their names.

As mentioned above, Joseph and Clara Smith were close friends with the son Thomas and his wife Valentina D'Amico as evidenced by their choosing them as godparents for several of their children. In 1930 Thomas and Valentina were living at 362 West 14th Street. That was just 1.2 miles distant from each other's house.

Joseph Smith had his own ideas about his Italian heritage, and he was determined to leave his hometown behind him. No records were found to indicate that he ever travelled back to Castelpetroso after his marriage to Clara. In addition, he never lived in a town where all his neighbors were Italian—no "little American Italy" towns. He chose places to live that were filled with a variety of nationalities. (The family attended church in Lansing (St. Ann) and in Saint John in Glenwood early on when they rented the Euclid house, and eventually St. Agnes in Chicago Heights more exclusively when they lived closer to that church and the children attended that school.) It was said that those who preferred the English language went to St. Agnes, although there were plenty of Italian members at St. Agnes also. St. Agnes was considered the "Irish-American" church, staffed by Irish priests, while St. Rocco was known as the Italian church, staffed by Italian priests. That is another indication of Joseph's desire to "integrate" into the American society. That was of the utmost importance to him.

Based on Joe Smith's plans for the rearing of his family, he never had the intention of keeping his Italian background in the forefront of his life in America nor to pass on the Italian ways or language to his children. (In her later life, Josephine recalled that when she was a young girl, her dad had all the children join hands in a circle and made them promise to never mention their heritage to others. At that time, they did not even know what heritage that was. It was to be a family secret to which they were bound. Joe and Clara never spoke Italian in front of the children, only between the two of them.) Joe had worked hard since he was fourteen years old to carve out his path for a successful blending into the American culture, and he wanted his family to be truly American. He did not hide his Italian identity on the early baptismal records of his children. (Some of his offspring changed those (or tried to change them) later in life when they were changing their marital status or entering the military service during World War II and wanted to use the name they had grown up to know.)

Joseph did not subscribe to "campanilismo" which is the practice of living near others from the same home village or region, as many Italians at that time chose to do when they came to America. He had no special loyalty to his hometown of Castelpetroso or his province of Molise once he moved to the United States. And he did not want his Italian heritage to be something that would hold him back in achieving his goals. He therefore began using an Americanized version of his name—Joseph Smith on his official documents including his job application to Victor Chemical Works. He used Wilmerding, PA as his birthplace and Buenos Aires, Argentina for Clara's birthplace to blend in better. After a while, it became sort of a joke with Joseph; however, this was not something that Clara appreciated. She would feel quite guilty about the use of this incorrect information throughout her life and would say to Joseph "A lie has (or is) a short tail/tale." (This was told to Clenise (Lindy) by her mom Josephine.) In early 1990s conversations with most of the Smith aunts, Clenise learned that each of the Smith sisters still held firmly to this promise and admitted that their lives would have been so much different if they had not had to keep that promise. In fact, Josephine did not find out what that heritage was until she was told by her Forte relatives when the family went for a visit to Ohio. She was seventeen years old and was very sad, cried her heart out, and was very angry with her dad to find out the truth. The Smith family bond was so strong that the children even as adults kept to the promise of only telling their spouses if they married. It was a life-long regret for each of them, and it gave them great pain to hide the information from the ensuing generations. It seemed to be as strong a commandment as the Biblical ten commandments! The subject would be changed, or a clever response would be given if one of the offspring or any of the acquaintances ever brought up the topic of family backgrounds.

There are plenty of documentaries, books, and articles on the discrimination against the Italians at the turn of the 20th century when both padrones and others took advantage of and harmed Italians just for being Italian. Joseph's strong desire was to protect his family from this discrimination and get a chance to truly blend into the American life. In fact, he and Clara did not speak Italian in front of their children, only amongst themselves. They never chose to live in an Italian neighborhood nor attend an Italian Church. That is not to say that the Smiths had no Italian friends; some of their best friends were Italians such as the D'Amicos (discussed previously), but they also had many friends of various nationalities. Joseph did such a good job of keeping his Italian background in the past that even his own children were unaware of their heritage, and they only found out when visiting a cousin in Ohio during their teenage years.

In an article published in the <u>Journal of Contemporary Criminal Justice</u> relating to crime in Chicago Heights in the 1920's and onwards, the author mentioned that Italians experienced a great amount of discrimination because of their nationality. The Chicago Heights Boys were involved in organized crime such as slot machines, bootlegging, prostitution, and other crimes. Chicago Heights was said to be "the pickup department for illicit alcohol trade in middle west." Organized crime was embedded in Chicago Heights; however, the author of the article makes it clear that many Italians were far removed from those criminal ventures. The worst areas were Wards 3, 4, and 5 and the Hill, where almost 90% of the Italians in Chicago Heights lived. The neighborhoods west of the railroad tracks were generally the places less likely to be involved in those criminal activities, and Joseph Smith always tried to choose the safer areas for his family to live.

Euclid Avenue was on the west side of the tracks, but the Smiths had outgrown the current house with their expanding family, and some of the children were now in high school. A move to a bigger house was in order where they would have a nearby high school for the older children and an elementary school for the younger children. Joseph wanted to be within walking distance of his job at Victor Chemical Works also, and the family wanted to be near a Catholic Church. Choosing another safe "west of the tracks" house, they found 1144 Emerald Avenue to fit their specifications. They were still close to St. Agnes Catholic Church and the St. Agnes Elementary School, but now Bloom High School would be walkable for the older children, and the new house was easily within walking distance for Joseph. Figure 111 shows a photo of 1144 Emerald Avenue in Chicago Heights shortly after the Smiths purchased the house, and Figure 112 shows the house on Google Maps from 2022.

Figure 111. **1144 Emerald Avenue, Chicago Heights House**

The house still stands today and is pictured in the Google Maps photo below.

1144 Emerald Ave

Figure 112. **1144 Emerald Avenue, Chicago Heights 2022 Picture**

Figure 113. **Smiths: Clara, (friend Harriet), Amanda, Josephine, Julia, Baby Smitty, Lucy at Emerald Avenue around 1923**

Figure 114. **Amanda, Josephine, friend, and Julie at Emerald Avenue**

Figure 115. **Smith Family Photo in Chicago Heights around 1924. From left to right: Clara, Julie, Amanda, Clara Alice, Joseph J. (Smitty), Joseph Sr., Marie (behind Smitty), Elisabeth, Lucy, Josephine, Ellie**

In her journal of recollections written in 1994, Josephine Stonitsch says of the house: "…it was exciting to move to the big 2-story house at **1144 Emerald Avenue**. It was on a huge corner lot, black iron fence all around, our own fruit trees—2 apple, 2 cherry trees, one date, one peach and a huge grape arbor which Dad added later." In the attic there was an old player piano and all the wartime (WWI) sheet music. There also was a huge trunk in the attic filled with many of the treasures of her mom Clara including old pictures and pretty clothes.

Some of the nostalgic moments included:

...sitting midst the rows and rows of dad's most delicious tomatoes, saltshaker in hand and really feasting on the juicy fruit on a hot summer's day. Going to open air band concerts on a Sunday evening, feeling the sound of each drum beat as the Star-Spangled Banner was played. Nestling quietly on a comfortable chair in the living room with a mystery book, an apple, and soda crackers to munch on. My idea of pleasure on a summer day. Running outdoors, barefooted, to splash in the water, as the city opened hydrants to flush out the debris in the water pipes. We waited till the orange rust was cleared. Smelling mom's delicious homemade jellies, tomato preserves and home-baked breads and pies as we came home from school. Waiting for the "Ice Man" to stop to bring ice when mom had her "25 lbs" sign in the window for our non-electric refrigerator. As he chopped away to weigh 25#s, our eyes widened, knowing we'd get to take the large pieces which we put in layers of newspaper, to hold and suck on a hot day. Hearing and watching the Jewish vendor, with his rickety wagon drawn by a horse, calling out, "Rags, Rags. I take rags." He later sold his collection to earn his living. Remembering the bakery truck driving by to sell fresh bread and goodies, and we'd get a sample from the baker whom we knew. The "milk man" on his funny cart, driven by an old horse, who used to "drop" his "road apples" right in front of our house. The birds were there before we knew it to have a feast. The cream on the bottles of milk that rose above the neck of the bottle as it froze, lifting the little paper cap, so that I, for one, cut off the top cream and put the little cap on. I'm not sure that my mom ever discovered less cream. Those days, there was almost half cream and half pure milk. No vitamins added in those days. Watching the "coal man" shooting tons of black coal through a small window in the coal bin in our basement to last the winter to keep our house warm. Oil or electricity were not heard of for heating homes back in those days.

Josephine recalls in her 1994 journal that:

In the cold snowy winters on Emerald Avenue, we would huddle near the kitchen vent to keep warm. We would have tons and tons of coal in our coal bin for it to last all winter, so dad would shovel it in the big furnace before he went off to work, and again at night, but it was never that warm in our house, so the kitchen was where we stayed after supper. We had a large house, 4 bedrooms upstairs, a stairway both back and front halls, a huge octagon shaped dining room with an archway into the parlor as we called it, a side room off the dining room as a playroom for all our toys.

Here are some pictures of Smith family members during the mid to late 1920's at Emerald Avenue.

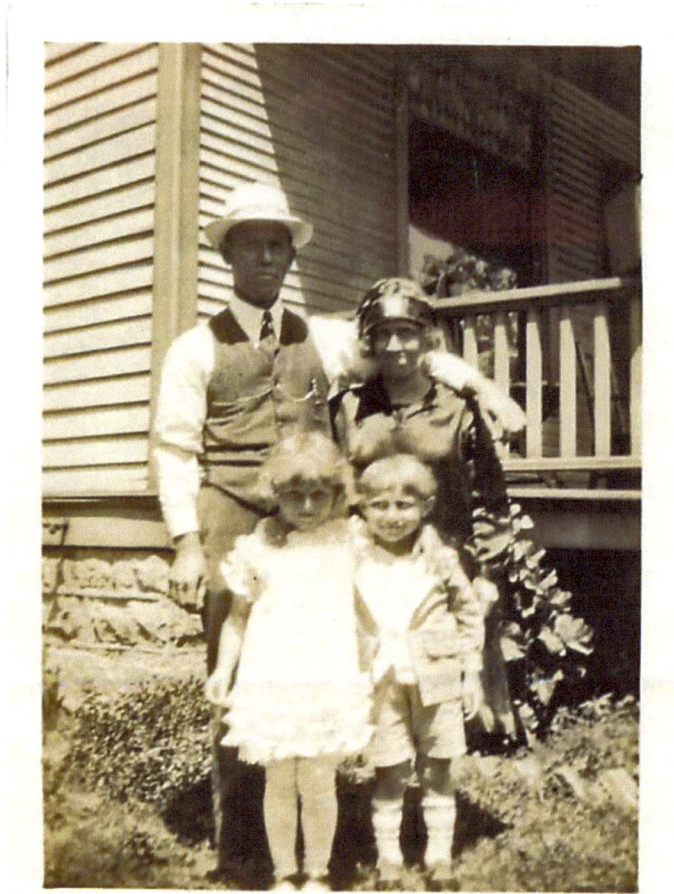

Figure 116. Joseph and Clara, with children Clara and Smitty at Emerald Avenue around 1925

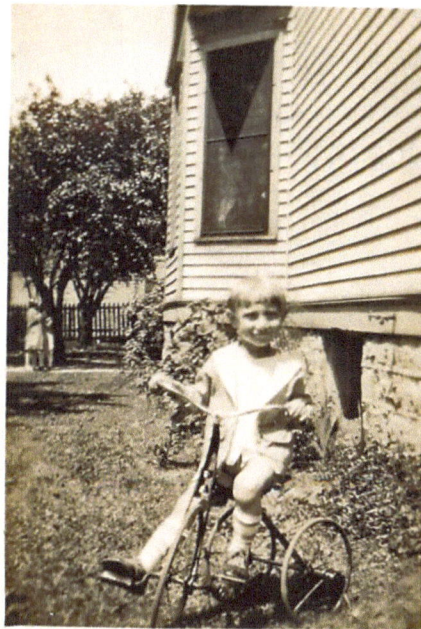

Figure 117. Photo of Smitty riding tricycle at Emerald Avenue

Figure 118. Josephine (age 13), friend Mabel, Marie, Ellie (age 9), Clara (age 6), and Julie (age 11) at house on Emerald Avenue. Picture taken 27 August 1927.

Figure 119. **Clara, Ellie, Smitty, Josephine, Julia, and friend Loretta King at Emerald Avenue.**

Figure 120. **Joseph Smith sitting in rocker near his grape vines at Emerald Avenue**

In a conversation with Lindy around 2020, Josephine mentioned her childhood memory of a male relative of her dad (a brother or cousin?) who came to visit their family sometime in the 1920's who brought a large bag of Hershey Kisses, to the great delight of the Smith children. Evidently, Joseph and Clara also visited that or other cousins from time to time in Pittsburgh and elsewhere. Several postcards are stamped from Pittsburgh, PA in 1924 from Papa and Momma Smith; one was directed to Amanda and Josephine, and the other addressed to Marie. **Marie** was the oldest daughter and had been put "in charge" of the younger children at home in Chicago Heights while the Smith parents were in Pittsburgh visiting a cousin. The 1924 date is another indication that the Smiths had certainly moved from Euclid Avenue to Emerald Avenue by that time. Here are the two postcards from 1924. (These were found by Jim Novak, 3rd son of Marie and Walter Novak, among papers found in Marie Novak's attic in recent years.)

Figure 121. **Postcards from Papa and Momma Smith, 1924**

During the mid to late 1920's and the 1930's, the newspapers covered a number of stories that mentioned some of the achievements of the Smith children. Marie was mentioned as receiving Honors for the Semester as a freshman at Bloom High School in 1924, and as taking part in a piano recital. Lucy was in a Christmas play in 1927, and she received an award in 1926 for perfect attendance. Ellie received awards for athleticism. Josephine was given an award for best efforts and also for perfect aattendance. There were undoubtedly many other awards given to family members: most of the children were competitive, high achievers, and hard-working. In 1938, Joseph Smith Sr. was selected to be the financial secretary of Victor Club of Victor Chemical Works and this appeared in an article in the **Chicago Heights Star**. They were engaged in family, church, school, neighborhood, and social functions and activities. After all, they were on the "right side of the tracks" where it was safe.

That is not to say that no crimes took place in these western wards. On the contrary. The newspapers of the time have a major story in January 1929 detailing the Chicago Heights Boys' criminal activities--one of which occurred only .2 miles from the former residence of the Smiths on Euclid Avenue. (Recall that the Smith family had already moved about 5 years earlier from Euclid Avenue to Emerald Avenue.) The headline for 7 January 1929 <u>Chicago Daily Tribune</u> final edition reads: CHGO. HEIGHTS RAIDED BY U. S.: 100 DRYS TAKE CITY HALL; NAB RICH RUM RING. The article says that all of Chicago Heights was under the control of federal agents and police as they raided booze rings, seized city hall, and arrested members of the corrupt police force. The series of raids resulted in the capture of 25 men who were accused of bootlegging, racketeering, and killings. Over 20 homes were broken into to curb the illegal activities of the syndicate which had amassed millions of dollars through illegal means. Books and articles on the topic do give names and those associated with the crimes.

Joseph Smith was someone who was far removed from any such activities. It was not in his nature to get involved in anything of this sort. It was never a secret that Joseph Smith had a small grape arbor at his Emerald Avenue house, and he also had a chicken coop. Wine is a common beverage in Italian households, and it is reasonable to assume that Joseph made his own wine from the grapes in his arbor for personal use and possibly for some of his friends, but there is no evidence that this was anything but for personal consumption. (His home was large enough for his family, but not large enough to store slot machines or a distillery.) The Smith family was quite frugal and made ends meet through resourceful hard work. Joseph was too busy working at his job at Victor Chemical Works where he had a fine reputation for diligent and excellent work. (See letter from 1947 Victor Chemical Works written upon the occasion of Joseph's retirement.)

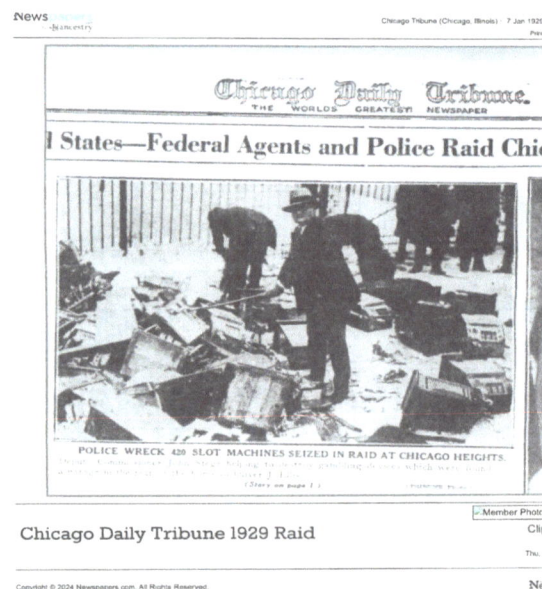

Figure 122. **Newspaper Article about Law Enforcement Raid in 1929**

The news-breaking raid is mentioned in this narrative to show the challenges that honest, law-abiding citizens had to face during these difficult times with the start of the Great Depression.

Italian immigrants were in general not looked upon highly for many reasons including because they were suspected of being involved with the criminal element or because they were successful and were taken advantage of by the Italian padrones or people who exploited immigrants. The Criminal Justice article mentioned that Italians were held back just because they were Italians. One Chicago Heights resident who was interviewed in 1979 said that "When you went to apply for a job as soon as you put down your name. What nationality are you? Italian? We have no use for you...I've had that said to me several times." In another interview an Italian man was asked if he had ever considered changing his name and that he would have less trouble getting a job if he changed his name.

The Criminal Justice article says that some of the Chicago Heights Boys saw great advantage to putting their slot machines in legitimate venues in society such as a garage in St. Agnes. Other places that were favored for the slot machines included the Fraternal Order of Eagles, the American Legion posts, the CIO Steel Workers Club, the Catholic War Veterans, and the Loyal Order of Moose. Joe Smith was a member of St. Agnes Catholic Church and the Loyal Order of Moose, but there was no evidence found that he participated in those ventures.

The Great Depression which began in 1929 started to have a noticeable effect on the lives of the citizens in Chicago Heights. Josephine remembers

> ...when banks closed, and my father's savings were withheld. Many businesses closed. Jobs were lost. I was in high school at the time and the future looked glum. My dad never lost his job through the entire depression (which lasted until 1939). Being from a sizeable family he was able to buy staple groceries in bulk to save money. His place of business provided this for their employees. We were one of the lucky families; many of our neighbors would receive bags of groceries to provide for their families like on welfare." The Smiths filled their time "... with family gatherings and friends visiting all the time. Close relationships were the norm since no one had much money to spend. People found time to make a go of it...We would go "barn dancing" at a small town near us. We acted in plays given at church, went to parties on birthdays. My mom sewed all our clothes. Shoes could be bought cheap--$1 a pair, which didn't last long as we liked to play jump rope, hopscotch, ball-and-jacks, and take long walks.

> Even during the depression years, we were never without food, although many were who received bags of free food regularly. I remember the time dad bought a half pig with another man at his work. But we had no freezers then, so dad par-cooked pork patties, and put them in a large crock with the grease to seal the meat. We had a pantry to store foods in our basement so hams were hung there. I remember, needless to say, we were sick of pork as we couldn't keep it too long. One time, dad thought he got a bargain with a barrel of flour. They sold groceries in large quantities for the employees to buy cheaper then. With eleven mouths to feed, dad was able to buy good food for us. But the flour was something I'll never forget. It got damp and tasted like the wooden barrel. Mom used it every which way, bread, pie, pasta, gravy, etc. That's a lot of flour even for our large family. It didn't make us sick at all, but the taste was something I will never forget, and we more or less got used to the taste as mom added things to disguise it.

Bloom Township High School was the school that most of the Smith children attended. The first building was built in 1902, and the new Bloom High School was built in 1934. The school was about a mile from their house.

Here's a picture of the old Bloom High School, where **Lucy** was a member of the Class of 1930.

Figure 123. **Old Bloom High School where the three oldest daughters went to high school. Picture from <u>The Bloom 1930</u> yearbook.**

Lucy's activities included Girls Athletic Association, Shorthand Certificate, Glee Club, and Bookstore.

This is a picture of the new Bloom High School from <u>Images of America Chicago Heights</u> by Dominic Candeloro and Barbara Paul.

On February 6, 1934, students moved their desks and other equipment to the new Bloom High School. In 1982, this handsome art deco structure was included in the National Register of Historic Places as a national landmark.

Figure 124. **New Bloom High School, Chicago Heights, Illinois**

The oldest daughter **Marie** was graduated from Bloom High School around 1927 or 1928 and shortly thereafter, on 19 September 1929, she married Walter ("Wally") Thomas Novak. She was 20 and he was 24. **Elizabeth**, the 2nd daughter, graduated the following year, and next came the graduation of **Lucy,** the third daughter, in 1930.

The 1930 United States Federal Census

The 1930 United States Federal Census shows the Smith family (Joseph, Clara, Elizabeth, Leysie, Amanda, Josephine, Julia, Lalorna, Clara, and Joseph) living at 1144 Emerald Avenue. Maria was no longer living at 1144 Emerald Avenue, because she was now living with her new husband who lived close by the Smith family. Elizabeth was an office worker at a tile and flooring company and had completed four years of high school. Amanda, age 17, had completed two years of high school and was working as a clerk for a chair store.

The census also shows that the value of the home owned by Joseph Smith Sr. at 1144 Emerald Avenue house was $6,000, and it had a radio set. He worked as an electrician in the chemical works industry, and the census listed that he and Clara were from South America. A copy of the relevant page of the 1930 Federal Census follows.

Figure 125. **1930 Federal Census showing house numbers and families on Emerald Avenue. Smith family is near the bottom of the page.**

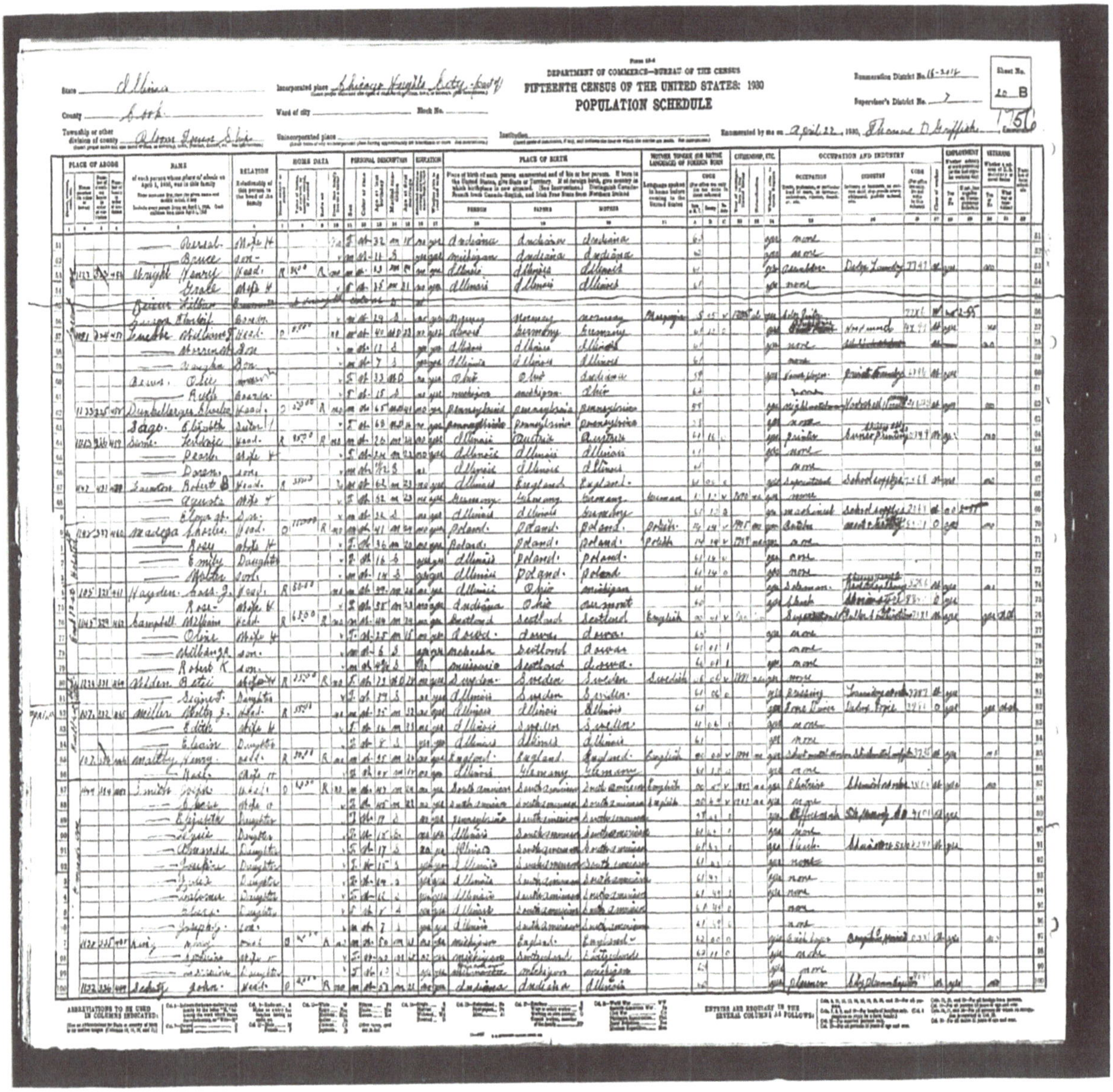

Ancestry.com - Print Image http://search.ancestry.com/Browse/print_u.aspx?dbid=6224&iid=4584340_00731&pid=24913732

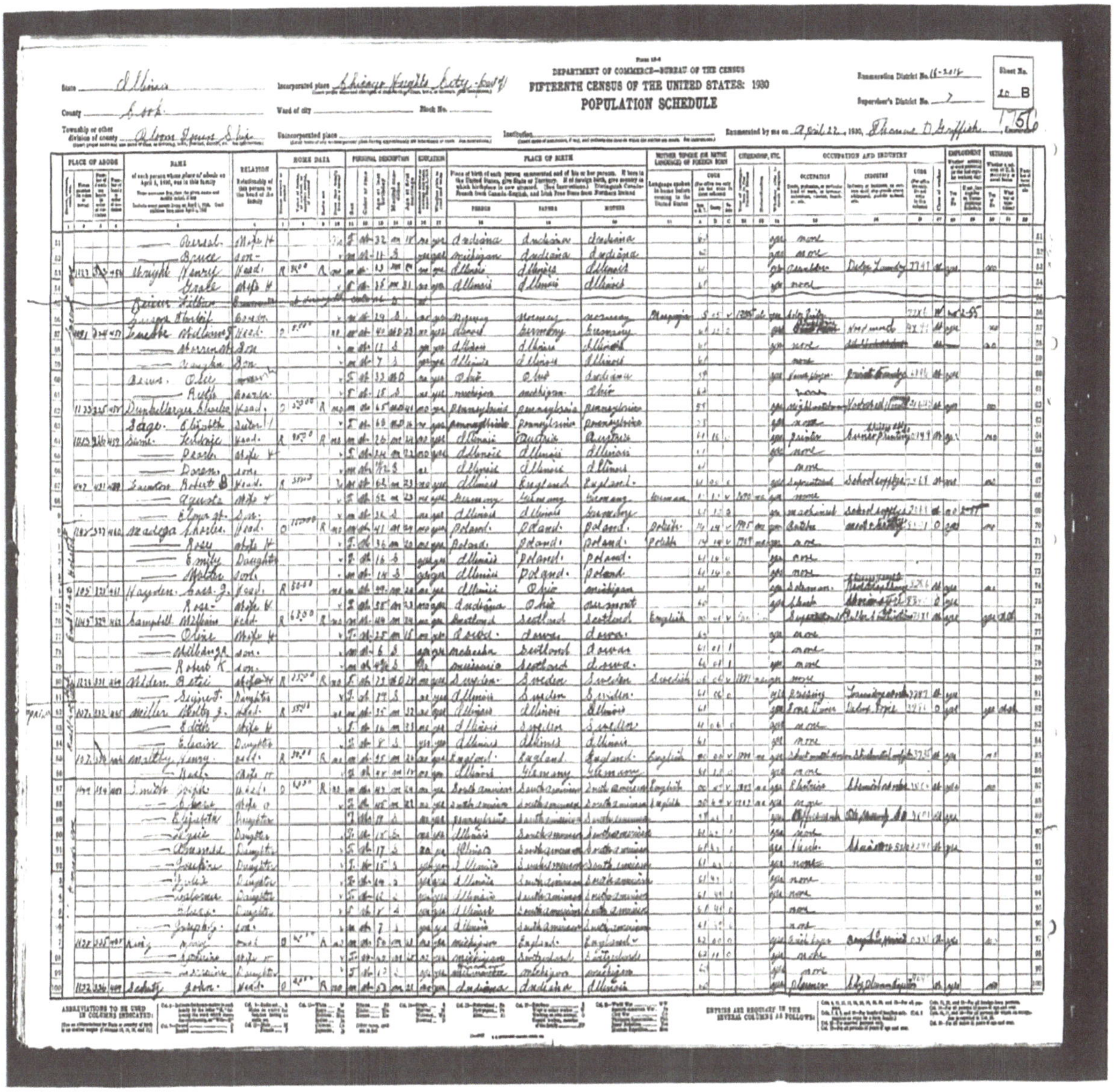
DEPARTMENT OF COMMERCE—BUREAU OF THE CENSUS
FIFTEENTH CENSUS OF THE UNITED STATES: 1930
POPULATION SCHEDULE

1 of 1 4/3/2012 12:22 AM

Figure 126. **1930 Federal Census showing house numbers and families on Emerald Avenue. Smith family is near the bottom of the page.**

At times, Joseph would take some of the children with him on trips to visit relatives, and Clara would stay home with the smaller children. Josephine remembered one of those occasions in one of her journals. She wrote the following:

> I remember a trip to Cincinnati, Ohio. Dad, Luce, and two others. My mom stayed home with the smaller ones. We packed lunch and drove all day. There were no motels then. We slept on the side of the road all night, huddled together. We had a flat tire, so spent much time getting that repaired. One had to do those things alone. No such services as today. We went the "cheap" way, but oh what joy when we reached our destination. A feast was waiting for us. We

met people we didn't know, tho (sic) dad did. It didn't matter having to double up each nite (sic). We laughed and enjoyed whatever we did—mostly playing, eating, and talking was the norm those days. People shared and it was enough. We loved visiting. Dad was fun to be with. He loved to tell us jokes every night at table.

The relatives that those Smith family members were visiting on that trip to Cincinnati around 1931 were the Fortes. Recall that when the newly-wed couple Joseph and Clara Giancola back in 1907 traveled from Italy to Pennsylvania with a stop in New York, they met up with Aunt Rosina Armenti in New York who was the wife of Michele Arcangelo Giancola. Erminia was one of their three children. Erminia and Nick Forte in Cincinnati were the parents of Margaret, Mary Dean, Dominick, Nicholas, and Rosina Forte--the cousins of the Smith children who informed the Smith children of their Italian heritage.

Although many hours of research were spent on the Italian records for the births, weddings, and deaths of the various relatives of the Forte, Armenti, and Giancola families going back to the early 1800's, with an attempt to find a direct linkup between those families and the Smith Giancola family, none was found. Based on the ship manifesto of 1907, mentioning Aunt Rosina, and later mentions of the cousins who moved from Ohio to Kentucky, and the conversation with the Forte family in 1993, a conclusion can be drawn that these individuals were relatives, but the exact relationship is unknown without a great deal more research. The families both had quite a few Giancola and Armenti relatives. Here is the letter from Nick Forte to Clenise White dated 10 August 1993 discussing the Forte/Giancola relationship.

August 10,1993

Dear Clenise

First off let me admit that my typing is not the greatest, but
its better than my handwriting, so if you note errors like just
now, please disregard and forgive.

Sorry to be responding so late, but it took ¥¥/ awhile to gather
some /information. Last week my sisters Dean, Fan, Marg /and/ and
I met to discuss the family structure to clarify (where possible)
the various connections and lines. I've attempted to illustrate
the family connections on the enclosed diagram. I hope it is
sufficiently clear.

The photographs I mentioned to you are not identified at all; we¢
don't know who are represented except for our parents. We're
hoping that we can get some help in identifying these unknowns
by showing them to the two remaining family elders, namely our
aunt Angie (Angela) Giancola and cousin Benny Forde. Benny is
actually a Forte, but her husband Mike changed it to 'Forde' when
he was in the army in the first world war. Aunt Angie is ≠89 years
old; Benny is 90. I¦ll send¥ to you whatever pictures are relevant.

An interesting thing occurred when Marg spoke to Aunt Angie
about you. Aunt Angie /¥/ believes she knows your family or at
least some members of it. If you want to speak to her for /details,
her number is 606-441-6845.

Figure 127. **Letter from Nick Forte to Clenise White Re Forte/Giancola Relationship, Page 1**

We are not sure if the Congietta (sp?) Giancola is the one you speak of,nor are we sure how she fits in what we know of family structure. So /we've made some assumptions. Our relativ in Indeprete are cousins, so it seems logical to assume as she is a cousin. We stay in contact with them from time to t mainly at Christmas and Easter. We visited them most recently in 1981, so its been a while since we say them. You may wish to write to them. If so, write to Alfredo Giancola, the son of Augustine and Congietta Giancola; see the chart as to where th

fit in. Alfredo can speak some English, but if you want detail you probably should write to him in Italian.

His address is: 86090 Indeprete
                (Isernia),Italia

I hope all this is of some help to you.

Best Regards,

Nick

Nick Forte
1005 Central Ave
Newport,Ky 41071

Figure 128. Letter from Nick Forte, Page 2

Here's a narrative from the Forte family which details some of their family history. They included this with the letter written by Nick Forte in 1993.

Nicholas and Erminia Giancola Forte—Samuel Salvatore and Marguerite Forte Russo

Nicholas came to the United States when he was 19 years old and Erminia came over when she was 14 years old. Nicholas Forte and Erminia Giancola got married October 6, 1902 in Cincinnati, Ohio. They had 5 children—Marguerite, Dominic, Dean, Fannie and Nick. Nicholas worked for Pennsylvania RR. Erminia was a house wife. She liked to crochet many things. Nicholas liked to play cards. Nicholas also liked to grow grapes in his backyard and he would make wine out of them.

When Erminia was a little girl in Italy, the people in the town started building a church in Castilapatrosa Italy. Dean—the third born child—went to Italy in 1980 and found out that the church, started long ago, had just been finished. Before coming to the United States, Archangelo Giancola—Erminia's father—helped lay the foundation of that church. The church took so long to build because of World War I and World War II. The church was named Mother of Sorrows. It was built on a hill and the Blessed Virgin appeared there. Water that flows from a stream near the church has performed miraculous cures.

The Forte family lived in Cincinnati, and later moved to Kentucky. Marguerite—the first born child —went to a dance and met Salvatore (Samuel) Russo. They got married on June 21, 1930. They had 8 children—all of which were boys—Jack, Sonny, Richard, Robert, Danny, Michael, Jerry and Ronny—who was born on February 24, 1938 and died March 24, 1940. Marguerite and Salvatore (Samuel) Russo lived in 3 1/2 room house on Clay St. in Cincinnati. They had a kitchen, living room, large bedroom, small bedroom and a bath. Marguerite and Salvatore had the big bedroom, Jack and Sonny had the 1 /2 bedroom and the rest of the boys slept on 2 couches that opened up.

Salvatore worked at Proctor and Gamble for 15 years, then he worked in a spaghetti factory. After he quit the spachetti factory he worked for the Cincinnati Board of Education as a custodian. Marguerite worked at Western Southern LifeInsurance. The boys all went to St. Mary's school and church on Clay St.

Salvatore loved to go to the horse races, and Marguerite loved to go to Bingo. Together they made Ravioli—everybodies facorite. Marguerite also made the best cookies in the world and homemade Banana Creme Pie and Custard Pie.

In the year 1931, Julia was attending Bloom High School and was a sophomore there. Here's a picture of **Julia.**

Figure 129. **Julia, age 15 in 1931**

Julia's high school activities included Semester Honors, GAA, Volleyball, May Festival, Basketball, Baseball, Councilman, Monitor, Girls Club, and Senior Class Play. Julia also participated in the 1933 Chicago Heights Centennial Celebration.

Finding it difficult to find employment after **Josephine**'s graduation from Bloom High School in 1932, "Teenie" accepted her dad's offer to send her to the Wilfred Academy of Hair and Beauty Culture in New York to increase her chances of getting a job during the Depression. There were three or four beauty shops on the south side of town that were hiring. She did indeed get a job giving manicures and cutting hair. Her high school activities had included Volleyball, May Festival, GAA, Basketball, Broadcaster Typist, Hall Guard, Girls Club, Audubon Society, and Travel Club. She had a part in the 1933 Chicago Heights Centennial Celebration also.

Figure 130. **From** <u>**Images of America: Chicago Heights Revisited**</u> **by Dominic Candelero and Barbara Paul**

The **Chicago Heights Centennial Celebration** took place in 1933, and many of the Smith sisters had parts in the historical pageant and plays. The souvenir program includes a brief history of Thorn Grove, the Town of Bloom, and Chicago Heights from 1833 to 1933. **Amanda** Smith is listed as having a part in the Wednesday, 30 August 1933 Pageant Queen Day at the Kiwanis Club as a member of the Court of Honor. **Marie** and **Josephine** were each cast as one of the 48 states. **Julia** was listed as a Spirit of Land and Sky as was Eleanor. Daughter **Clara** was cast as a member of the French and Italian group.

A production company was hired to train and direct the hundreds of people who took part in the drama that was held on September 2nd, 3rd, and 4th at the Baseball Park of the Chicago Heights Athletic Association. Companies from around the town submitted advertisements for their associations (including Victor Chemical Works) to support the celebration.

Figure 131. **Souvenir Program for Centennial Celebration for Chicago Heights 1933**

Several months after this celebration, there was another grand occasion for the Smith family. On 9 November 1933, **Elizabeth** (daughter #2 of Clara and Joseph) married Gerald Baker at St. Agnes Church with Father Fitzgerald presiding at the ceremony.

Figure 132. **Elizabeth and Gerry Baker are Standing in Front of the Grape Arbor and Chicken Coop at the Smith's Emerald Avenue House.**

Around 1935, the names of Clara (Mrs. Joseph Smith) and Miss Lucy Smith began appearing in the **Chicago Heights Star** newspaper on a regular basis. These articles were about their association with the St. James Hospital Auxiliary activities. In the 19 February 1935 edition, the St. James Sewing Circle was being reorganized under the name of the St. James Hospital Auxiliary, and Lucy was named the new secretary. The organization's meetings were to be on the second Tuesday of each month in the hospital. In the 17 May 1935 edition of the paper, twenty-seven members met for a business and social hour, and Lucy Smith was one of the hostesses who served refreshments. It was announced that Clara Smith was to be one of the four hostesses at the 11 June meeting. The 14 June 1935 newspaper edition mentions that the women sewed and held their business meeting, with Clara (Mrs. Smith) as a hostess at the social hour. Plans were being made for a large benefit card party for the benefit of the St. James Hospital.

Here is a picture of Mrs. Joseph Smith standing at the Emerald Avenue house, photo dated 6 June 1938, possibly getting prepared for one of her St. James Hospital Auxiliary activities.

Figure 133. **Clara Smith at Emerald Avenue 6 June 1938**

Here is a picture of the St. James Hospital as it looked in the 1930s. It is still in existence to this day in 2024.

Figure 134. St. James Hospital, Chicago Heights in the 1930's . From <u>Images of America Chicago Heights Revisited</u> by Dominic and Barbara Paul

There is a three-year gap in the appearance of news articles for the auxiliary, but seven more articles appear in 1938 that mention Lucy Smith. The 24 June 1938 edition talked about the upcoming annual ice cream social and the annual card party on 18 August. Lucy Smith was selected to be the general chairman of this event. Then there is the 19 July 1938 article mentioning the St. James benefit with tables for bridge, pinochle, and bunco. Lucy Smith was the refreshment chairman at this event. The 26 July 1938 edition announces that the event would take place at the old Bloom building, and that Lucy Smith is the chairman of the benefit event. The 2 August 1938 newspaper has an article about the upcoming event again, listing Lucy as the head of the committee in charge. This is followed by a 16 August 1938 article mentioning that Lucy is heading a committee to arrange the organization's annual affair, with contract bridge, pinochle, and bunco. Local merchants were to provide prizes for the event. The next article on 23 August 1938 announced how successful the event was, and it had one of the largest crowds to attend such an event—approximately 250 people were there. Again, Lucy is mentioned as the organizer. The 16 September 1938 article has both **Lucy Smith** and **Mrs. Walter Novak (Marie)** as hostesses at the annual "pink tea" of the auxiliary.

Besides sewing activities and organizing benefits on behalf of St. James Hospital, **Lucy** helped with household duties at the Emerald Avenue household. At some time, she decided to enter the religious life and joined The Servants of the Holy Heart of Mary; however, she developed pleurisy while in the convent. This is a condition in which the tissues that separate the lungs from the chest become inflamed, and her health became quite a problem. She eventually left the convent life. (Dates are unknown.)

Shortly after the 16 September 1938 article about Lucy and Marie's involvement as hostesses for the St. James Hospital Auxiliary, another Smith family member appeared in a 23 September Chicago Heights newspaper article. **Joseph Smith Sr.** finished third place at the Victor Chemical Works club outing horseshoe tournament. The article appears below.

Figure 135. **Chicago Heights Newspaper Article, 23 September 1938**

Meanwhile, **Elizabeth and Gerry Baker** were busy with raising their new baby girl **Loral Beth** who had been born 20 September 1935. She is grandchild #1 of the Smith family.

Figure 136. **Elizabeth Smith Baker 1936**

Figure 137. **Elizabeth Smith Baker with Husband Gerry and Baby Loral Beth**

Figure 138. **First Grandchild of Joseph and Clara Smith. Baby Loral Beth Baker**

Loral Beth is pictured above and is the first grandchild of Joseph and Clara Smith. It is likely that the handmade pink sweater and bonnet were crafted by Clara Smith (Cleonice Mastrantuoni) who was an expert in tatting, crocheting, knitting, and sewing. (The mother of Clara (**Elisabetta Martelli Mastrantuoni**) was a seamstress and a lacemaker living in Italy as mentioned on the birth certificate of Cleonice.)

Below is a photo of **Loral Beth** and **Pat** (daughters #1 and #2 of Elizabeth and Jerry Baker. **Patricia Lynette Baker** was born on 19 June 1939. They are standing with Josephine. (Josephine was nicknamed "Teenie" by her brother Smitty because he could not pronounce the name "Josephine" as a young toddler. It came out as "Teenie.") They are at Emerald Avenue, and the date of the photo is 8 July 1941.

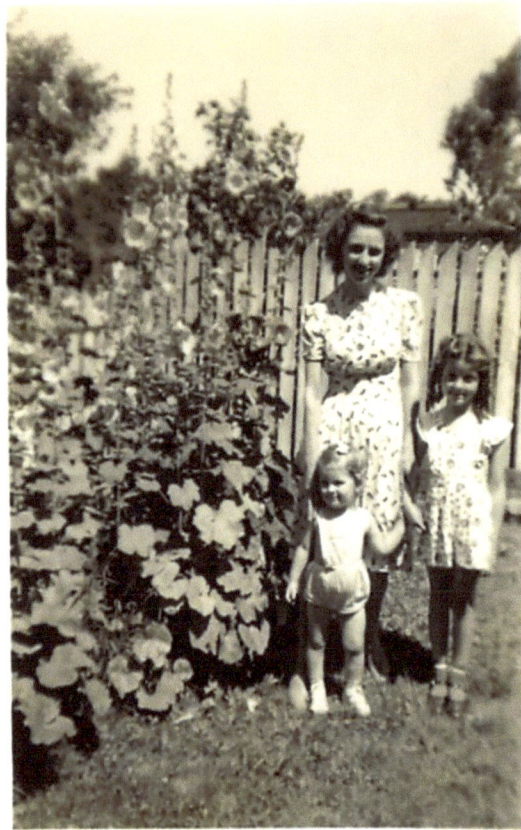

Figure 139. Josephine, Loral Beth Baker (Grandchild #1) and Patricia (Pat) Lynette Baker (Grandchild #3)

In 2020, **Loral Beth** wrote about her childhood memories of a visit to the Smith's Emerald Avenue house. Those memories are presented below.

The House on Emerald Avenue

Many years ago there was a big white frame house surrounded by a black iron fence on a corner lot of Emerald Ave. in Chicago Heights, IL. It was the Smith Family home. Grandma & Grandpa & a bevy of aunts & one uncle lived there.

Since my family always lived long distances away, when we came to visit this wonderful home & my Dad pulled up in his merry Oldsmobile, it was a thrill!

The excitement started when everyone came spilling out of that house, squealing with delight, lavishing hugs & kisses, scooping me up & whisking me away to be entertained inside that house for the remainder of the visit.

The house itself seemed large to me at the time. We always went in the back door through a porch to the kitchen with a separate eating area & a back stairway. Grandma Smith was always baking bread. A dining room centered the house & to its side was a room adapted as a bedroom for Uncle Smitty. The living room was bordered by a solarium where I remember a big electric train taking up the space one Christmas. The front entrance on the other edge of the living room included a spot for a piano. (My mother & Clara, for sure, played the piano. "Le Secret" by Gautier was one of my Mom's specialties.) At the bottom landing of the front stairway was a statue of Mary & there was always a votive burning. Upstairs were 4 bedrooms & a bath. An oft told story was about when I came to visit as a little girl after living in Nashville, TN & I exclaimed in a southern accent "who done painted that toilet seat?" They all seemed to think that was funny. Ha! Ha! (They were big on Ha!Ha!s!) Grandma& Grandpa's front bedroom was like an inner sanctum. We didn't hang out there much. Lucy & Clara shared the other large bedroom where we usually stayed. Jo had the room across the hall that had access to the attic. Julie & Ellie had a bedroom at the end of the hall & that is where I liked to hang out with them, laughing & talking & going through their jewelry box & stuff.

Laughing! That is what I remember most about visiting the Smiths on Emerald Ave.! Most of the aunts were very silly & I was a good audience.

Grandma Smith was usually in the background. I don't remember any direct conversations with her but I do remember her accent. Grandpa Smith was very congenial & kind of silly too! It sounds irreverent but he'd "play Communion" with my sister & me by having us kneel in the dining room, fold our hands, stick out our tongue & he'd place a Necco Candy wafer on it! He'd occasionally give us a sip of wine. He made wine out of anything he could get his hands on – grapes from the arbor out in back, elderberries or even dandelions! He had a little shed in back of the arbor that was his special retreat! After all, he lived in a house filled with a lot of little women! (everyone, starting with little Grandma, was short. I think my Mom was the tallest at close to 5'2 / 5 ft 2 , eyes of blue.... They all had blue eyes!)

I just loved the Smith Family! In general, they were a happy, lively, good humored group with deeply religious roots. Individually, they had distinction in their personalities, interests & ways of life. Marie, as the oldest sister, is the only member of the family to settle & stay in the Hts. She was quick in movement and matters of speech, very expressive & a good cook. Both Marie & Lucy could sew beautifully. Since Lucy was my Godmother she always doted on me & made me a

Figure 140. Memories of Loral Beth Baker, Part 1

beautiful blue velvet coat trimmed with white fur & a coordinated bonnet when I was a few years old. She later made a delicate baptismal gown that all my children wore. She was a tenacious, very generous, self sacrificing and yes! funny person!

I didn't see as much of Amanda & Jo growing up, though I do remember Jo's room & that later she became a WAC during WWII (coincidentally trained in Des Moines at Camp Dodge) & sent us Heath Bars, a treasured delicacy at that time. Though I don't remember Amanda at the house, (I know she took off for Chicago at a young age.) I became fast friends with her when I moved to Chicago in the late fifties. Much later when my son-in-law Donny was in baseball, Bob & I with Katie & Donny had some great & hilarious experiences with her! She was gruff on the outside but inside had a heart of gold!

I always associate Julie with Ellie. They were roommates & best buddies. Julie was always pretty & sweet with a big smile & a good sense of humor. Ellie was petite, with a husky voice & very animated. She particularly fascinated me because she was a ballroom dancer. She danced at the Trianon & Aragon Ballrooms in Chicago & made her own perky little hats that matched her outfits so that she'd stand out in the crowd. Clara was the baby girl. She was so much fun & loved to clown around. My sister Pat & I were in Clara's wedding & she walked around like Groucho Marx in her wedding gown before being escorted down the aisle.

Good old Uncle Smitty! He was a tease & silly as his sisters though both he & Lucy spent a lot of time at the Church. (I still think of Lucy when I smell candle wax at Church. She used to take me with her to clean the melted candle wax from the votives at St. Agnes.) Lucy & Smitty used to run a Karmelcorn shop next to the movie theater. I liked keeping company with them!

Though my Mom was the 2nd oldest, & a visitor rather than a resident at the house on Emerald from my perspective, she had her uniqueness in the family. She moved away from the Hts. with my Dad as he pursued his career with Montgomery Ward with frequent transfers throughout the Midwest. She could talk plenty & had a sense of humor but comparatively in the company of her sisters seemed more reserved. She always seemed to be treated with a special respect.

The cast of characters that grew up in the house on Emerald Avenue were vast & varied. If there was a mystery that pervaded their lives, it was never apparent to me growing up. Were there secrets behind those walls?

This is certainly not the epic tale of The Emerald City & the Wizard! Or was there a wizard within that house on Emerald Avenue???

Love to all from the first cousin of the family,
Loral Baker Kirke

PostScript: My Mom told my sister and me that it was "the sorrow of her life" to have to deny her ancestry. In response partially, I said to her & and I say to you, ancestry is interesting but should not make us different persons than who we are here & now. The past should not negate the valuable assets we have had in our lives. The essence of our being, our minds & hearts should prevail! Amen!

Figure 141. Memories of Loral Beth Baker, Part 2

In the <u>Chicago Heights Star</u> newspaper dated 26 April 1935, Joseph Smith was mentioned as being installed as one of the new officers in the Chicago Heights Loyal Order of the Moose. The Moose Lodge was a fraternal and service organization. Joseph was being installed as the successor to the former dictator of Lodge No. 828. He held that position from April 1935 to April 1936. He was first initiated into the organization in 1918. That article is shown below.

Moose Lodge Installs New Officers Tonight

Chicago Heights lodge No. 828 Loyal Order of the Moose, has made elaborate plans for installation of officers and a general social hour to be held at eight o'clock this evening in the Moose hall on Illinois street.

Joseph Smith succeeds F. W. Logan as dictator who has served the lodge through several successful terms of office. The new corps of officers will be inducted by a staff headed by Fred Landsea, past dictator, as installing officer assisted by Frank Martin as marshall.

At the conclusion of the installation rites there will be entertainment, dancing and refreshments. Members are invited to bring their families and friends to the affair. Representatives of several lodges in the South Cook district are to be in attendance.

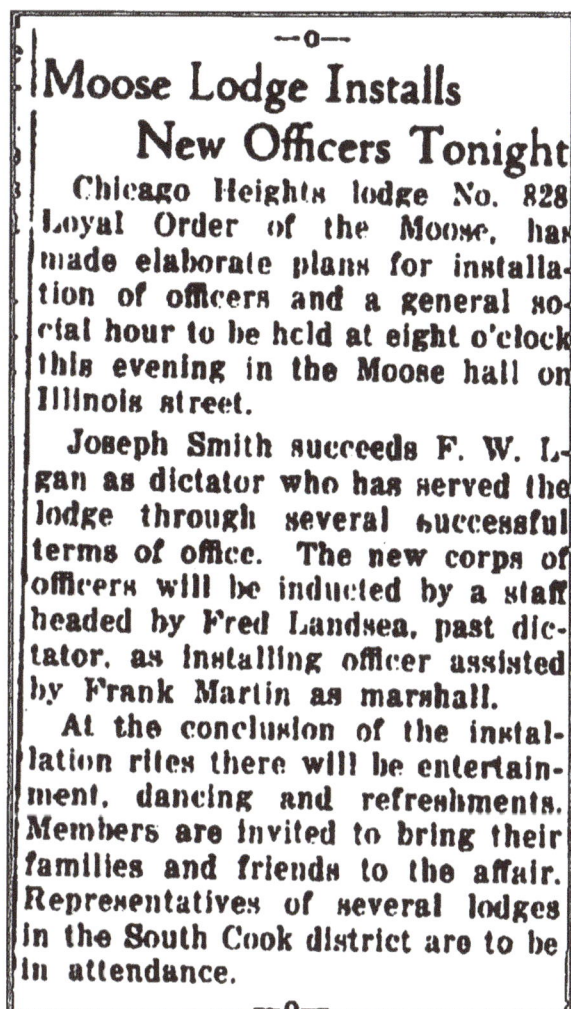

Figure 142. **Newspaper Article of 25 April, 1935, re Joseph Smith Installation as Moose Lodge Officer**

Donald Louis Novak, the second grandchild of Joseph and Clara Smith, (born 12 October 1935 to Marie and Walter Novak) remembered going to the Moose Lodge when he was a young child with his Grandpa Joseph. The Lodge is still in existence today.

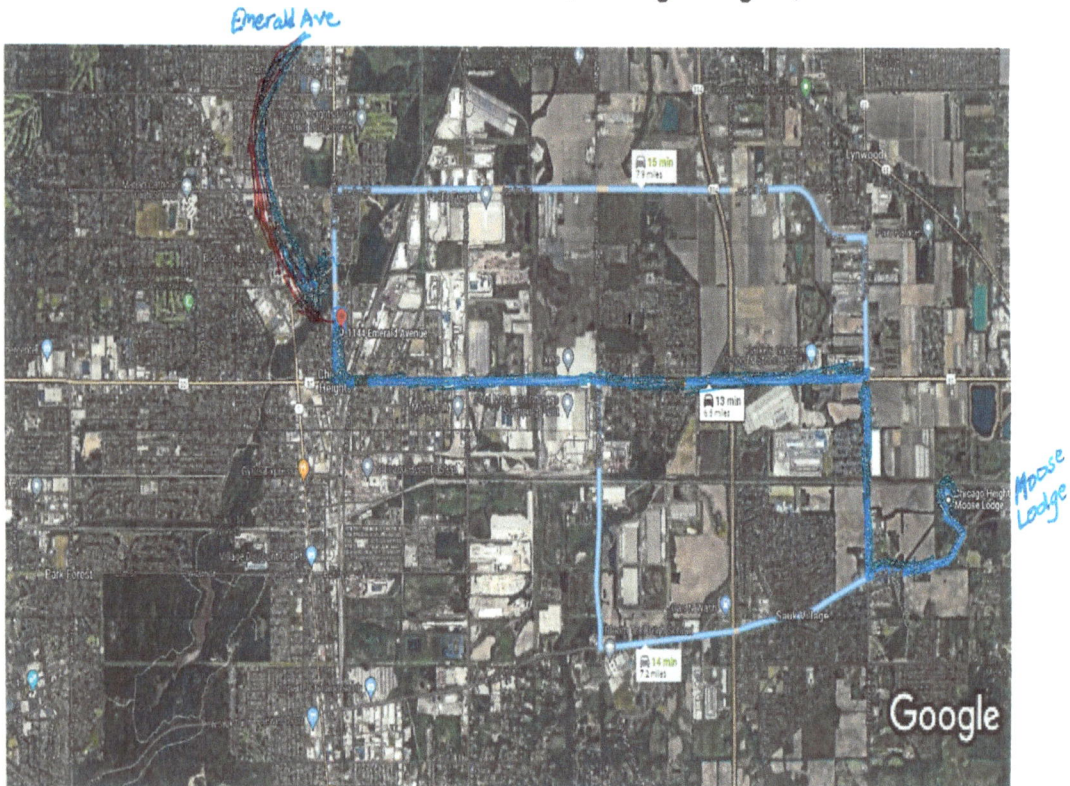

Figure 143. **Google Maps Image Showing Location of Moose Lodge in Present Times**

Figure 144. **Marie and Wally Novak and son Donald Louis (Grandchild #2 of Joseph and Clara Smith). Photo Taken 20 Sept. 1935**

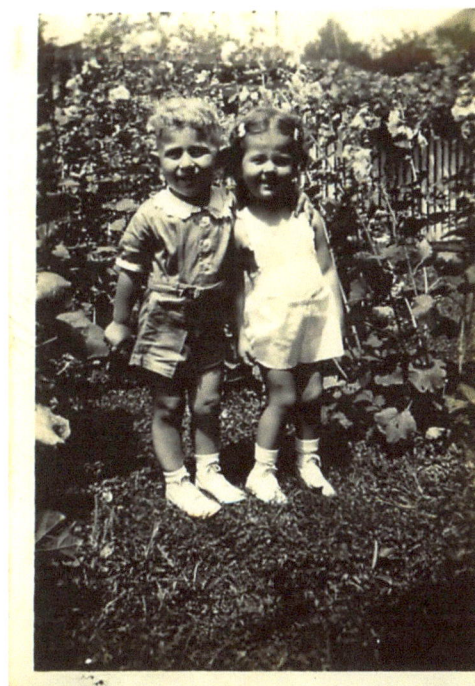

Figure 145. **Don Novak (Grandchild #2) and Loral Beth Baker (Grandchild #1) 4 July 1938 at Emerald Avenue**

Sometime in mid-1936 U. S. Social Security numbers first started to be issued. On 21 November 1936 Joseph applied to obtain his U. S. Social Security number. He listed his name as Joseph Alphonso Smith, his address as 1144 Emerald Avenue, his place of employment as Victor Chemical Works, his birthdate as 19 May 1882, born in Wilmerding, Alleghany Co., PA, his father's name as Joseph Smith, and his mother's name as Mary (?). He signed his name as Joseph A. Smith. Here is a copy of the request for information and the microprint copy of the application.

DEPARTMENT OF HEALTH & HUMAN SERVICES　　Social Security Administration

Refer to:
S5EP3　　Baltimore MD 21235

SEP 2 1 1993

Mrs. Clenise A. White
9931 South Park Circle
Fairfax Station, Virginia 22039

RE: Joseph A. Smith

Dear Mrs. White:

Enclosed in response to your request of June 22 is a microprint copy of Joseph A. Smith's application for a Social Security number (Form SS-5).

Thank for your $7.00 check as payment for searching our records.

Sincerely,

Deborah Piazza
for Delmar D. Dowling
Freedom of Information Officer

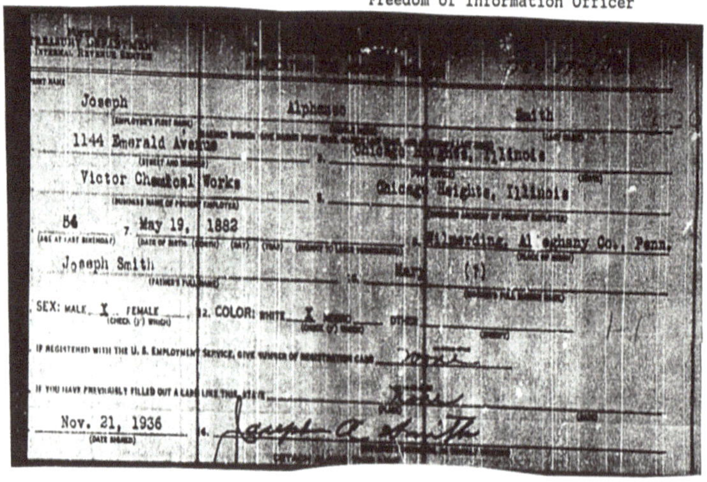
Joseph　Alphonso　Smith
1144 Emerald Avenue　Chicago Heights, Illinois
Victor Chemical Works　Chicago Heights, Illinois
54　May 19, 1882　Wilmerding, Alleghany Co., Penn.
Joseph Smith　Mary (?)
SEX: MALE X FEMALE　12. COLOR: WHITE X
Nov. 21, 1936　Joseph A. Smith

Figure 146. **Application for Social Security Number for Joseph Alphonso Smith**

Below is a picture of Marie Smith Novak in 1937 at Emerald Avenue. The caption says "Our Car" referring to the auto parked at the street.

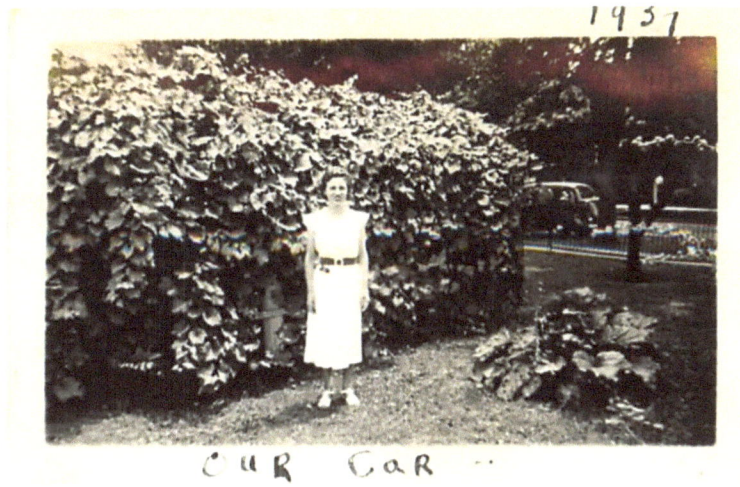

Figure 147. **Marie Novak 1937 at Emerald Avenue**

Figure 148. **Smitty and His Mom Clara 1937**

Figure 149. **Daughter Clara at Grape Arbor Emerald Avenue 1937**

Figure 150. **Daughter Clara on 6 June 1938 in High School Graduation**

Figure 151. **Joseph Smith Sr. and Joseph (Smitty) Smith Jr. 1938**

Figure 152. **Lucy in late 1930's**

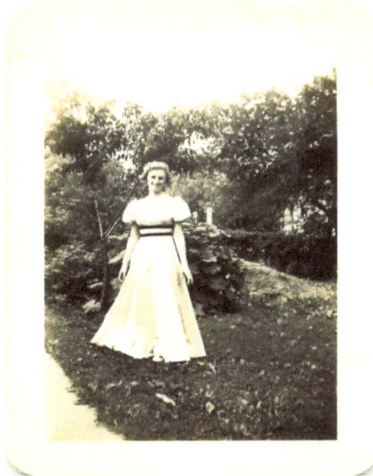

Figure 153. **Daughter Clara at Emerald Avenue**

Figure 154. **Ellie**

Figure 155. **Lucy**

Figure 156. **Josephine and Her Mom**

Figure 157. **Julie and Ellie on Back Porch at Emerald Avenue**

A vacation destination for the Smith family was a beach community developed in the 1930's called **Michiana Shores in Indiana**. It was a log cabin town for vacationers which was on the shore of Lake Michigan. Pictures show activities such as horseback riding, canoeing, rowing, and relaxing on the pier near the cottage. The cottage was about

56 miles from their home on Emerald Avenue. Below is a picture of Ellie in her jodhpurs sitting on a log fence near the cottage. A Google Map shows the distance from Emerald Avenue to Michiana Shores.

Figure 158. **Ellie at Michiana Shores Cottage**

Figure 159. **Google Map Showing Distance from Emerald Avenue to Michiana Shores, Indiana**

Figure 160. **Julie at cottage at Michiana Shores, Michigan City, Indiana**

Figure 161. Michiana Shores, Indiana—Julie, Clara, Ellie

Figure 162. Josephine at Michiana Shores Catching a Fish.

Figure 163. Smith siblings Josephine, Julie, Clara, Smitty, and Unknown Person at Michiana Shores, Indiana

Figure 164. Michiana Shores Cottage with Joseph Smith Sitting on Wooden Post Next to Father Fitzgerald in Navy Commission Suit

Growing Up in the Smith Family in Chicago Heights, Illinois by Josephine Smith Stonitsch, Written at age 104.

(These words of Josephine were taken down via iPad by Rita Stonitsch Lepinskie during a visit in 2019 to see her mom Josephine who was living with Clenise (Lindy) Stonitsch White and Alex White in Virginia.)

Luce stood for what she believed in. She loved the nuns. Marie too worked really hard. Julie was #6, closest to me. She was so easy to be with, always easy going, very smart, but she did her own thing. She stuck with what she believed in.

I used to do my own thing, too. Nobody else seemed to care. I did a lot of reading and was by myself a lot. I didn't depend on others that much. I spent a lot of time with my mom, when I was home. Mom was kind of lonesome. Dad loved her a lot but I don't think she had anyone she could confide in. Mary Kyleman, a big woman, rough and tough lady, my mom liked her a lot. She'd open her mouth and say "Pa-owl." (Paul was her husband.) Mom didn't have a lot of friends like that.

I didn't have a life where I did anything outstanding. I fought everybody. Nobody stood up for me, but we were just normal kids. I remember Mandy, poor Mandy. She was really pretty. She'd get mad at me because I'd tell her, but she was good to me.

I took care of Clara a lot, like her big sister. I treated Clara like a little girl. Lucy took over Smitty. She was really good to Smitty, and they ended up living together. Lucy was bossy because my mom used to leave everything to her. Lu went to the convent but got out because of pleurisy and stayed in bed for over a year. Then Lucy got a job three days a week. Lucy was very good with sewing, everything was perfect. Lindy reminds me of Lucy. Everything she did was just perfect. She worked for Dr. Howarth for many years, took care of his kids and loved those kids. She never got married. She knew lots of people, doctors, went to parties, loved traveling. She knew how to swear too. Momma went and told sister at school, 7th and 8th grade. My mom loved the nuns, brought them something like cakes every week. Lucy would swear and Mandy was involved somehow. Sister called all of us in and told that Momma told on us. Mandy was so mad that she pounded on the desk and said all the words that Lucy said. I think we all got punished for it.

Mandy had a lot of nerve too. Mom shouldn't have told on us. I didn't have anything to say— the nuns had a lot of nerve butting in our business. I bet the nuns talked about us over their mealtime.

Sister Apelonia, the 8ᵗʰ grade teacher, was fat and would lean on me as little as she was, going down the stairs. We laughed about the nuns. I couldn't have been a nun. Lucy liked the nuns. My dad let Lucy go to a boarding school. Maybe my mom lost a child in there in between Beth and Lucy, besides her little Anthony. There was only a year between all the kids. Lucy had to take over, did the work so she was the boss.

Once Mom locked the door on Luce so she tried to come in through the window. We played tricks on each other.

Loral Beth (daughter of Elizabeth Smith Baker and Jerry Baker) did know that house on Emerald Avenue, and everything she said about it was right. We used to run up the front stairs, also the back stairs when we were mad at each other. We were all afraid of the dark. The lights at that time weren't very bright anyway, maybe they didn't have much power.

Every Sunday we'd gather in our living room, the Olivieris used to come over. There were people lying on the sofa, sitting in chairs. Someone would come over. 9:30 or 10:00 everyone would order ice cream or caramel corn, everyone pitched in. Dad would take us for a ride a lot, pile in the car, just ride, maybe stop at a farm and pick up a bushel of apples or peaches. We always ended up getting an ice cream, not every week, but on Sundays.

We used to see the Dolans in Glenwood. Mr. Dolan had a mustache. He'd pour coffee in a saucer to cool off his coffee. We'd be lying on the living room floor and would read the comics. I don't think they had any children. We liked the fact that we went together as a family.

We had to go to Mass on Sunday. We took up a whole seat. St. Agnes Church. I don't remember the story about St. Agnes. It's still there. Don Novak went there too. The school was a block long with the church in the middle. On each side was the school, so it was easy to make a little visit at church or light a vigil light. I think it's still there like that.

St. James Hospital used to be right there. Lucy used to help at the hospital.

We walked to school; sometimes my dad would get off work early and would give us a ride. We roller skated. We were only 6 to 7 blocks away. Halsted Street/Chicago Road. We went all the way down Emerald Avenue, straight down, nothing there. That's where the guy pulled down his pants. He said what street was this, then pulled down his pants. We ran all the way home. My dad was so mad: he was very careful about us kids.

****

As mentioned earlier, the Smiths were good friends with a lot of priests and nuns. Clara Smith used to bake pies and goodies for the nuns frequently and made altar linens for St.

Agnes Church. They had invited Father Fitzgerald to the Michiana Shores cottage for a visit, and they often invited the priests to their house for dinner.

Following is a picture of a dinner party at 1144 Emerald Avenue with Joseph (with suspenders) and Clara at the head of the table, Father Walter E. Croarkin (who became the Pastor of St. Agnes Church in 1941) to the left of Joseph, Father Joseph Petro, daughter Clara, and Father Croarkin's father. To the right of Joseph and Clara is Smitty, Father William Horan, Aunt Lucy, Wally and Marie Novak, and toddler **Don** Novak. (Incidentally, Don Novak recently in September 2022 mentioned that he remembered going to the Michiana Shores cabin as a child.)

Figure 165. **Smith family Emerald Avenue dinner and priest friends about 1937**

Clara did not always travel along with Joseph on his visits to see relatives. An example of this is Joseph's trip from the 24th through the 27th of August 1937 to Pittsburgh when several of the children traveled with him. Joseph wrote a postcard on 24 August 1937 to his oldest daughter Marie (now Novak) living in Chicago Heights with husband Walter on Hickory Street.

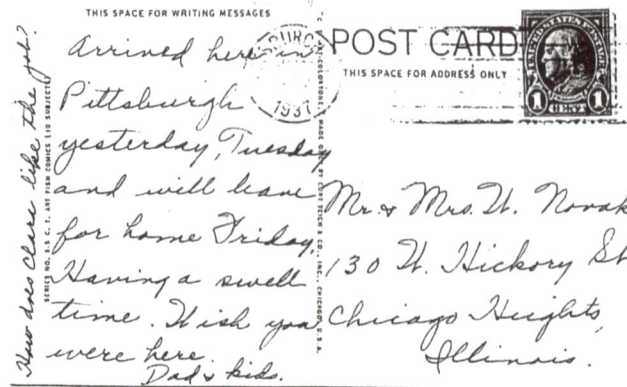

Figure 166. **Postcard from Joseph Smith and kids to Marie and Wally (Walter) Novak Dated 25 August 1937**

In the records, there is a letter written by mom Clara while visiting Elisabeth, Jerry, and Loral Beth Baker who were living in Nashville, Tennessee. The letter is dated 2 November 1937 and is addressed to Marie in Chicago Heights. A photo was taken on 19 September 1937 of Loral Beth, age 2, at Centennial Park in Nashville, Tennessee, which may have been a favorite place to take visitors.

Figure 167. **Loral Beth, Centennial Park, Nashville, TN 19 September 1937**

Another Smith family member who went to visit the Bakers in Tennessee was Josephine. The Chicago Heights Star newspaper 22 July 1938 edition has a brief article noting that Miss Josephine Smith of Emerald Avenue had traveled to Nashville, Tennessee to visit her sister, Mrs. Gerald A. Baker.

A letter in the files written by mom Clara while she was visiting Elizabeth, Gerry, and Loral Beth on 11 December 1938 this time in Greenville, Ohio is addressed to the "Bunch" in Chicago Heights. Clara mentions that she hopes Lucy will be free to go visit Elizabeth in the summer of 1939 when Elizabeth and Gerry's next child is due to be born. Clara wants Lucy to help Elizabeth in Greenville, Ohio for several months when the baby arrives, and so she tries to encourage Marie to discourage Lucy from accepting a job as secretary at the hospital in Chicago Heights. In the letter, Clara also mentions that she is bothered by "the darn headaches." She says, "I like here very well, and the people so friendly, better than all Chicago Heights stuck up people." Clara also says that Elizabeth is working on making an afghan and that when Elizabeth is finished, Clara will crochet around it to finish it off. She is delighted by Loral Beth's many kisses and dancing and thinks that Loral and Donnie are both so smart.

Figure 168. **Clara Smith crocheting or tatting sitting on porch.**

Clara signs her letter as "Well lots of love and kisses to you all. I remain as ever your Mother Mrs. J. A. Smith"

Teenie's Additional Memories in Her Last Years

These are other comments made by Teenie to Clenise White about her recollections of the past. Teenie seemed very much to enjoy relating these memories, and Clenise used to carry around sticky-notes to be sure to remember them for her future writing. Teenie was well aware of Lindy's intentions and was eager to share.

****

Grandpa was well-liked and was a member of various clubs. He did not write English well, nor did he spell well.

Grandma was a very lonely lady. She did not speak English well, but really wanted someone to teach her. No one did. She had never worked before and was not a good cook at all. She had many hardships including going blind several times. She named Lucy for St. Lucy as a thank-you for the return of her sight. Peter McGrane was a good friend of Grandpa's who helped him get a job in Chicago.

The D'Amico family owned a pasta restaurant in Chicago and were always offering food to the Smith family. Grandpa was a good cook and always wanted to be a chef. Mrs. D'Amico was the godmother to Julie and Teenie.

Food in those days would come in big crates.

****

Names that were frequently mentioned in conversations were the following: Mary Rohe—one of Jo's best friends in high school; Helen Stua—Julie's friend who lived down the street; Glen Eberly, Klyczek, Hinkley family; Gladys Crowe; Fitzgerald family; Joe Lupiun—very smart classmate; Helen Conway—said "Another day, another dollar"; Frank Spencer; Terese Turcanny—friend of Mandy; Mrs. Spahn—said "If you don't have time, at least read the headlines"; Dolan family--Glenwood; D'Amico family; Amanda Bucey; Sister Claratine; Clarissa Widing; Mable Kubliak; McGrane family; Forte family; Battaglia—produce; Mary Kyleman; Klein jewelry; Freelanders; Hartman; Marge Maloney; Hoels.

Joseph Smith Sr. sayings: "God will provide. There's always room for one more."

Figure 169. **Clara at Emerald Avenue with Dog Queenie**

Figure 170. **Grandchild #3: Patricia Lynette Baker (Born 19 June 1939)**

The 1940 United States Federal Census

The 1940 United States Federal Census shows the Smith family still residing at 1144 Emerald Street with both Joseph and mom Clara born in Pennsylvania, owning the house which was now valued at $7,000. Joseph is shown as having completed the 5th grade of school as his highest grade, and Clara as completing 8th grade. Joseph worked full-time as an electrician for Victor Chemical Works and received $2,400 as his annual salary. The household also consisted of Lucy (houseworker), Josephine (beautician for Beauty Shop), Julia (bookkeeper for national bank), Eleanor (stenographer for brewery), daughter Clara (saleslady at retail store), and Joseph Jr.

Beth and Marie were on their own living with their husbands at other locations, and Amanda was living in Chicago at this time, renting her living space with Mary Row Hamlett (listed as a cousin?). She was working as a cashier and, at another time, as a beauty culturist, specializing in shaping, styling, tinting, and permanent waving of hair. Later in life, at age 82, Amanda wrote a note that said:

> Reminising (sic) about my younger days with my sisters: I worked in Chgo. and came home on weekends. I couldn't wait to see all the open arms to greet me. I always hoped that it wasn't because of all the goodies I'd bring and the anticipation of buying them ice cream cones. But today I know it was because of their love for me and not what I gave as they have proved it all thru the years.

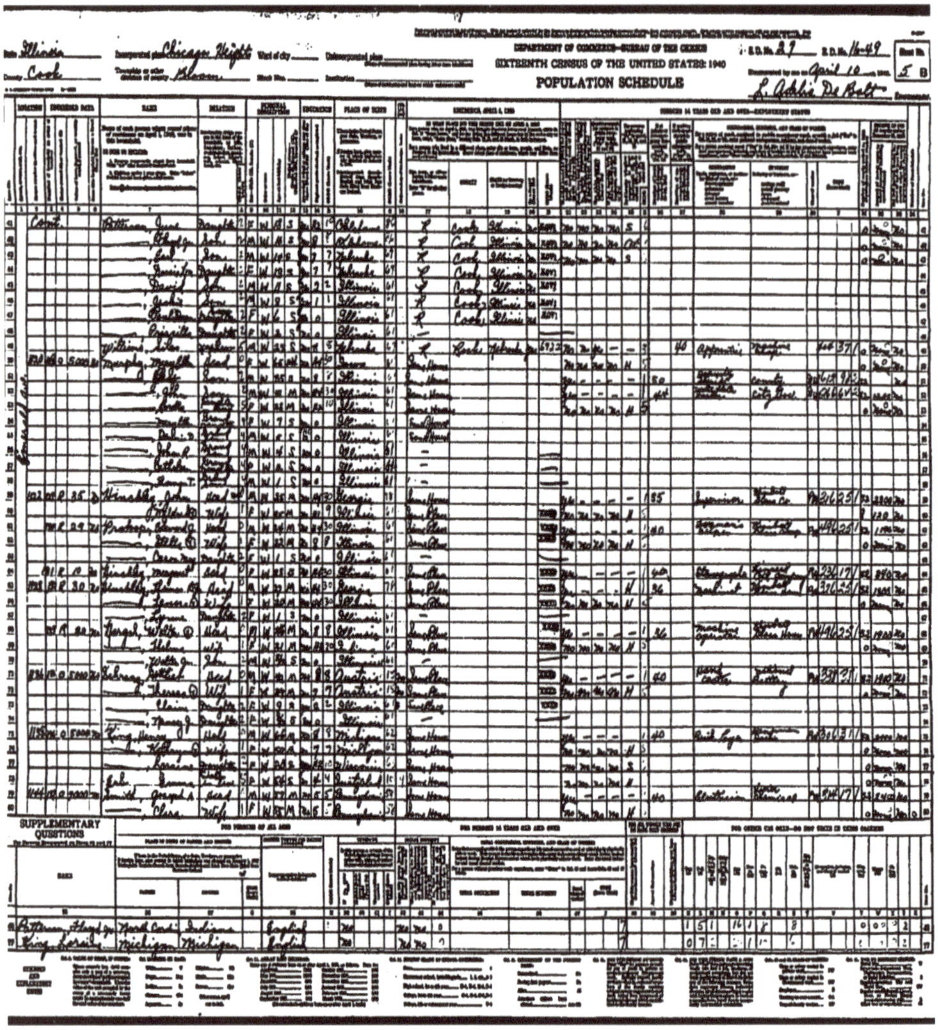

Figure 171. **1940 Federal Census Page 1 for Smith Family: Joseph and Clara Smith Are On the Last Two Lines of the Main Section on the Page.**

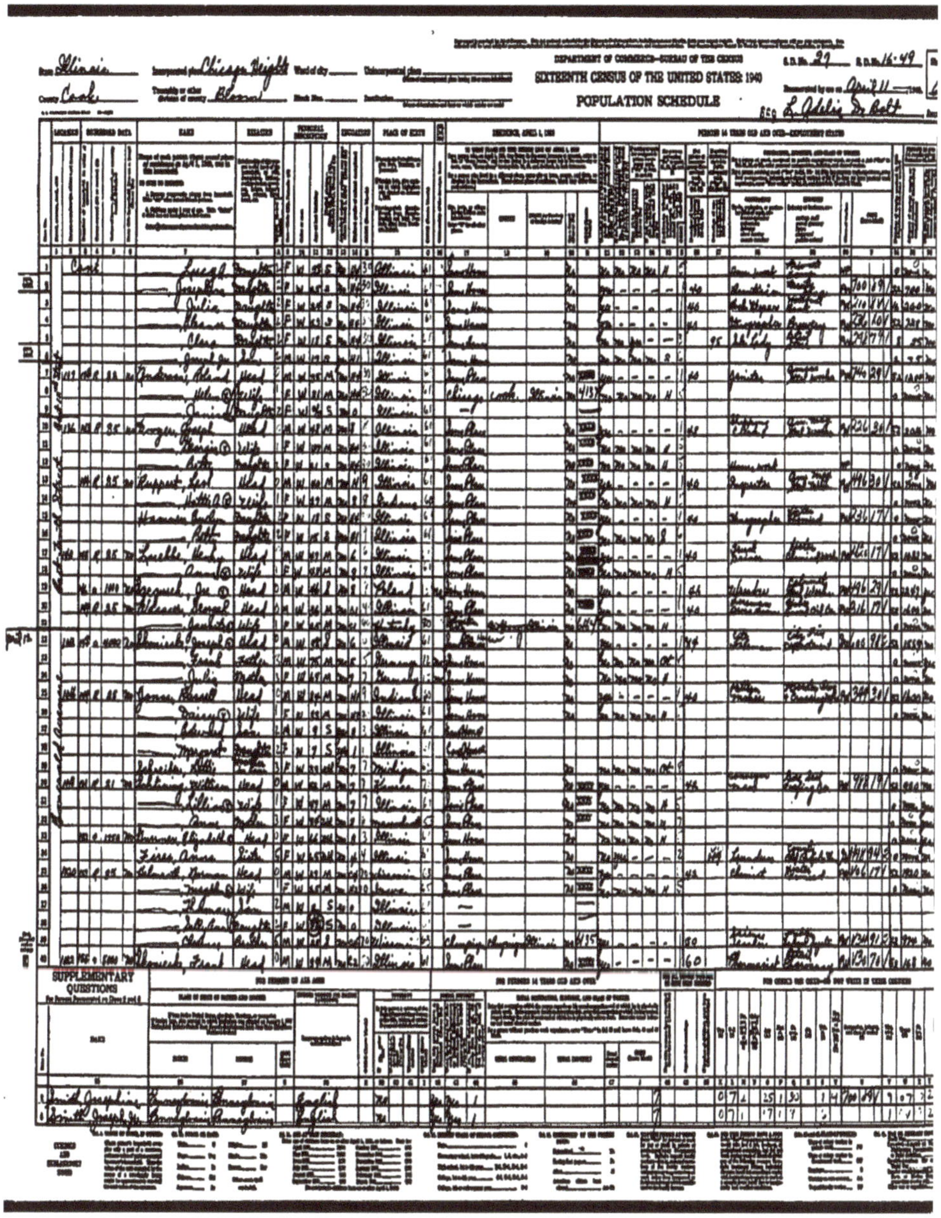

DEPARTMENT OF COMMERCE—BUREAU OF THE CENSUS

SIXTEENTH CENSUS OF THE UNITED STATES: 1940

POPULATION SCHEDULE

SUPPLEMENTARY QUESTIONS

Figure 172. **1940 Federal Census Page 2 for Smith Family: Smith Children are Listed at the Top of the Main Section on the Page.**

After the 1940 Federal Census was taken, a second addition to the Novak family arrived, namely **Robert (Bob) Clement Novak**, grandchild # 4, born 11 September 1940.

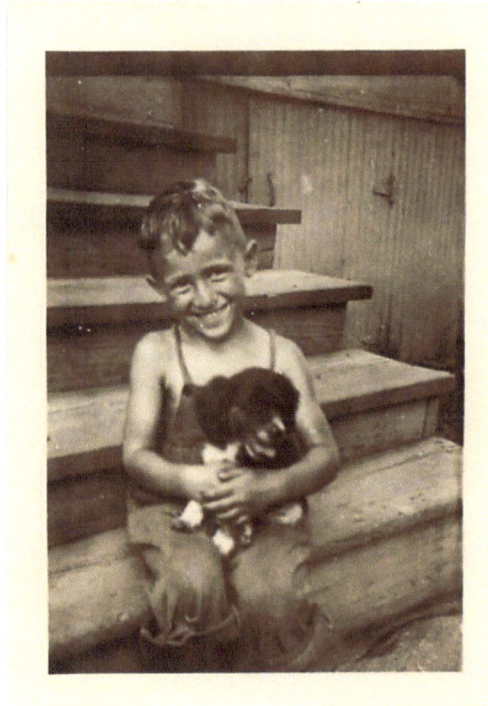

Figure 173. **Undated Photo of Robert (Bob) Novak with Puppy**

By 1942 when Bob Novak was just two years old, his uncle **Joseph Anthony Smith, Jr. (Smitty)** had completed high school. Smitty did not attend the same high school as his sisters. Instead, he went to **Leo High School** located on 79th and Sangamon Street in Chicago. This was an all-boys Catholic School built in 1926 to serve the working-class families. It was 22 miles from Emerald Avenue. Smitty is listed on the Senior Class 1942 roll as Joseph John Smith, and his diploma has the same incorrect middle name.

The following is a copy of the second page of the 1942 Senior Class List for Smitty.

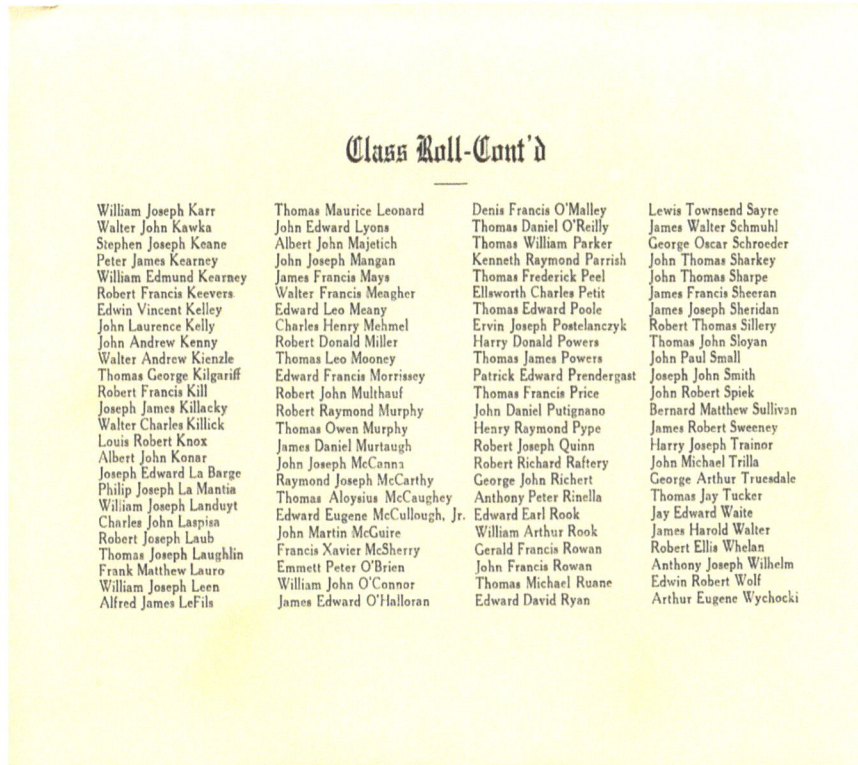

Class Roll-Cont'd

William Joseph Karr	Thomas Maurice Leonard	Denis Francis O'Malley	Lewis Townsend Sayre
Walter John Kawka	John Edward Lyons	Thomas Daniel O'Reilly	James Walter Schmuhl
Stephen Joseph Keane	Albert John Majetich	Thomas William Parker	George Oscar Schroeder
Peter James Kearney	John Joseph Mangan	Kenneth Raymond Parrish	John Thomas Sharkey
William Edmund Kearney	James Francis Mays	Thomas Frederick Peel	John Thomas Sharpe
Robert Francis Keevers	Walter Francis Meagher	Ellsworth Charles Petit	James Francis Sheeran
Edwin Vincent Kelley	Edward Leo Meany	Thomas Edward Poole	James Joseph Sheridan
John Laurence Kelly	Charles Henry Mehmel	Ervin Joseph Postelanczyk	Robert Thomas Sillery
John Andrew Kenny	Robert Donald Miller	Harry Donald Powers	Thomas John Sloyan
Walter Andrew Kienzle	Thomas Leo Mooney	Thomas James Powers	John Paul Small
Thomas George Kilgariff	Edward Francis Morrissey	Patrick Edward Prendergast	Joseph John Smith
Robert Francis Kill	Robert John Multhauf	Thomas Francis Price	John Robert Spiek
Joseph James Killacky	Robert Raymond Murphy	John Daniel Putignano	Bernard Matthew Sullivan
Walter Charles Killick	Thomas Owen Murphy	Henry Raymond Pype	James Robert Sweeney
Louis Robert Knox	James Daniel Murtaugh	Robert Joseph Quinn	Harry Joseph Trainor
Albert John Konar	John Joseph McCanna	Robert Richard Raftery	John Michael Trilla
Joseph Edward La Barge	Raymond Joseph McCarthy	George John Richert	George Arthur Truesdale
Philip Joseph La Mantia	Thomas Aloysius McCaughey	Anthony Peter Rinella	Thomas Jay Tucker
William Joseph Landuyt	Edward Eugene McCullough, Jr.	Edward Earl Rook	Jay Edward Waite
Charles John Laspisa	John Martin McGuire	William Arthur Rook	James Harold Walter
Robert Joseph Laub	Francis Xavier McSherry	Gerald Francis Rowan	Robert Ellis Whelan
Thomas Joseph Laughlin	Emmett Peter O'Brien	John Francis Rowan	Anthony Joseph Wilhelm
Frank Matthew Lauro	William John O'Connor	Thomas Michael Ruane	Edwin Robert Wolf
William Joseph Leen	James Edward O'Halloran	Edward David Ryan	Arthur Eugene Wychocki
Alfred James LeFils			

Figure 174. Smitty's Name is Shown as Joseph John Smith.

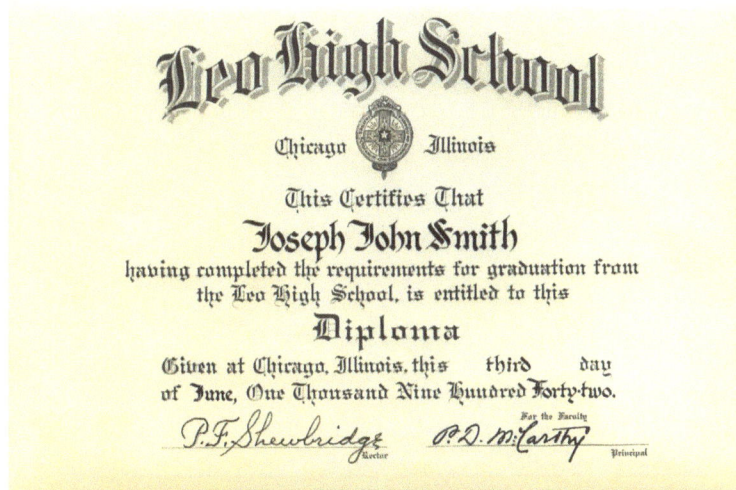

Figure 175. The Original Diploma from Leo High School Graduation on 3 June 1942

Smitty's sister Josephine recalled that Smitty worked at The KarmelKorn Shop sometime during his teenage years, taking orders from customers. The shop was located next door to the Lincoln-Dixie Theater in Chicago Heights (which opened in 1921) on Chicago Road. The theater was demolished in 1972 after a fire, but the candy shop is still in existence to this day.

In a 1995 journal entry of **Josephine**, she talked about the many times that the Smith siblings would call their friends and "...off we went to a movie. Only 10 cents a ticket and we could sit for 2 or 3 movies if we wanted. No popcorn was sold in the show. A

KarmelKorn shop was right next door, so we bought things there…We'd stay all afternoon, walk home and on time for supper."

From the Smiths' house on Emerald Avenue, it was a one-mile walk. Some of the old-time candy favorites are still available for purchase today. Josephine remembered one treat in particular--the Peanut Butter Bar (made by Atkinsons). The candy usually would cost 1 cent per piece, so the owners felt confident they could be successful even during the Depression years, because their theory was that everyone could afford to spend a penny. (In 2024, on Amazon.com, an online purchasing website, nowadays the price is 15 cents per piece if you buy say, a two-pound bag.)

The Smiths all seemed to have a sweet tooth, so this KarmelKorn shop was quite a popular place for the entire family. The movie theater matinées were a big attraction for the Smiths in those years of Emerald Avenue living.

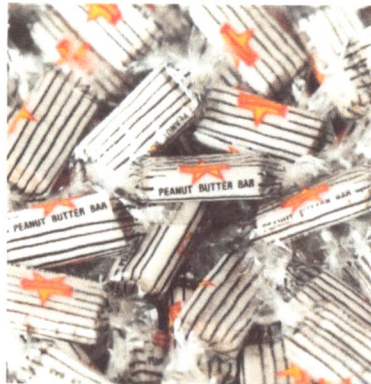

Figure 176. **Peanut Butter Bars: One of the Smiths' Favorite Candy Treats**

Figure 177. KARMELKORN SHOP Chicago Heights Where Smitty Worked. It is to the Left of the Lincoln-Dixie Theater. The Lower Part of the Awning on the Left Says "THE KARMELKORN SHOP." This is from Images of America Chicago Heights by Dominic Candeloro and Barbara Paul.

Figure 178. Joseph and Clara Taking a Moment to Relax at Emerald Avenue in 1942

Figure 179. **Joseph and Clara in their Emerald Avenue Dining Room Before Dinner**

Mealtimes were important gathering times for the Smith family. Usually after dinner, recalled **Josephine** (Daughter #5) in her 1995 journal, her dad would listen to the news on their radio set. On the night of 7 December 1941, "...he called us into the living room to hear President Roosevelt tell of the declaration of World War II. We were all scared thinking it was the end of the world."

Chicago Daily Tribune 8 Dec 1941 WWII

Figure 180. Newspaper Front Page, December 8, 1941

Josephine continued:

> I was almost 28 years old, working in a beauty shop in Chicago. The following year, my brother decided to go into the Navy, rather than be drafted into the Army. When I heard that they were to form a Women's Auxiliary Unit in the Army, I was extremely anxious to go to war also. In July of 1942, I had my first experience of what lay ahead. I had to go to Chicago for aptitude tests, medical tests, and physical tests. I did well on all, but was told that I was 8 pounds underweight, so had a couple of months to gain that much. I was sworn in the United States Women's Army Auxiliary Corps 11 October 1942 at Fort Sheridan, IL.

Josephine's enlistment date was 17 September 1942. She weighed the required 100 pounds and was 5 feet 1 inch tall.

Her dad's registration card for 1941 shows his name as Joseph Antony Smith at the 1144 Emerald Avenue address, his age as 59, place of birth Wilmerding, PA, employer Victor Chemical Works. He signs his name Joseph A. Smith.

Joseph Sr.'s son's registration card shows his name as Joseph Anthony Smith Jr, age 19 with the same address as his mom and dad, and his employer was Victor Chemical Works. He weighed 120 pounds, was 5 feet 4 inches tall, had blue eyes, and blond hair. He signed the card on 29 June 1942.

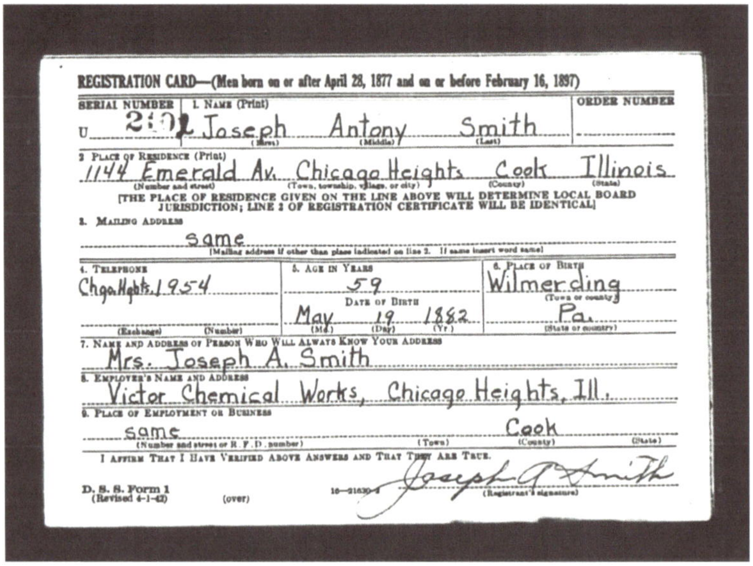

Figure 181. **Joseph A. Smith Sr. WWII Draft Registration Card**

Figure 182. **Smitty in his Navy Uniform with His Mom and Dad**

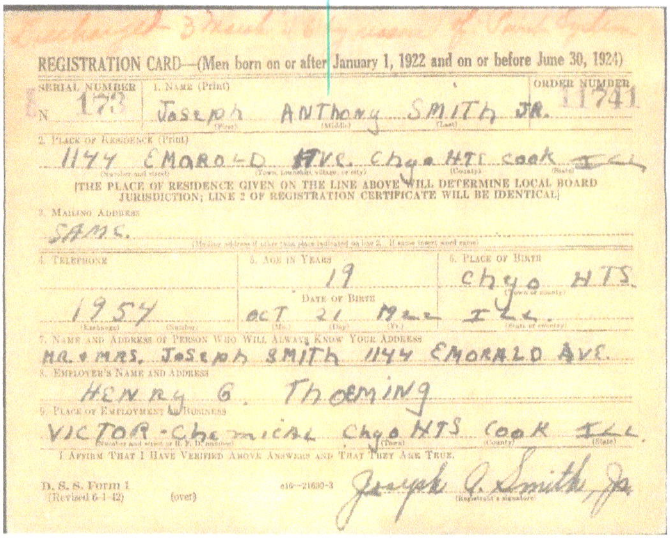

Figure 183. **Joseph A. Smith Jr. (Smitty) WWII Draft Registration Card**

Smitty received a certificate dated 12 February 1945 showing he completed the course of study at the Technical Storekeeper School, (Internal Combustion Engine Spares), Naval Supply Depot, Mechanicsburg, Pennsylvania, signed by the Supply Officer in Command. Additionally, he received a certificate signed by President Harry S. Truman shown below.

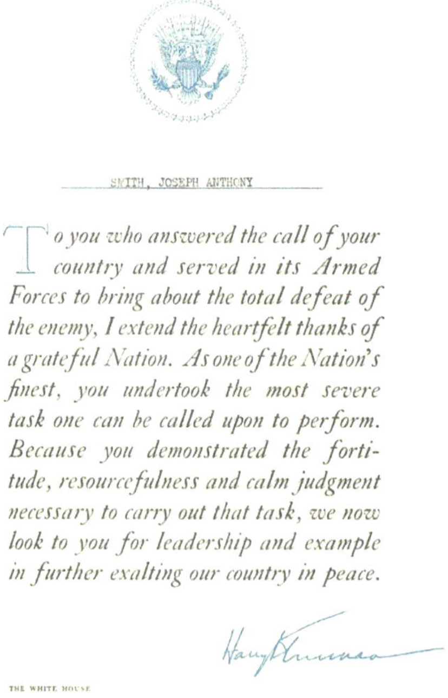

Figure 184. **Certificate of Military Service Signed by President Truman**

Figure 185. **Josephine in WAC (Women's Army Corps WWII**

Figure 186. **Josephine in Army Uniform with Her Mom and Nephew Don Novak 14 June 1944**

Josephine's length of duty (beginning in 1942) was for three years, three and a half months. She spent 3 months in Des Moines, Iowa and because there were no uniforms, she had to wear a utility dress until a correct-sized uniform could be made. The Army did not know where to put her. She was asked to start up a beauty shop, to run a laundry shop, to do radio work, or to go to France. She refused all those assignments and temporarily ended up working in a supply room and in an office. Then she was assigned to an Arkansas dental school where she learned how to make false teeth and worked in a lab. She loved Arkansas, especially seeing roses in December. She was then sent to Fort Knox to continue working in a dental lab with men. She worked with German prisoners and later with Italian prisoners. She made the rank of corporal and then sergeant.

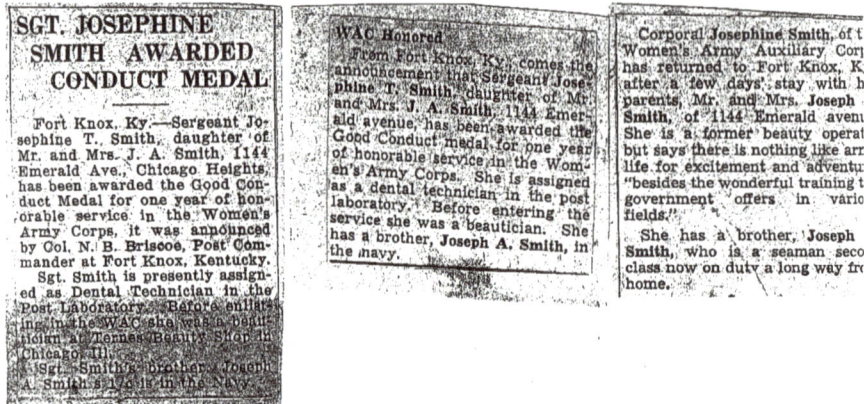

Figure 187. **Newspaper Articles About Josephine Smith's Time in the Women's Army Auxiliary Corp During World War II.**

Figure 188. **Photo Taken of Josephine in WWII for Newspaper**

Figure 189. **Josephine Leaning Against WAAC Garbage Can in WWII.**

Meanwhile, while **Smitty** and **Josephine** were serving in the war efforts, other family members were carrying on with their respective lives. **Eleanor**, who had completed her high school education in 1935 at Bloom Township High School, had been working in Chicago for Philips Petroleum, and during World War II, she was a USO dance instructor. She excelled at dancing and had danced with Lawrence Welk's band at the Trianon Ballroom in Chicago.

Daughter **Clara** on 6 November 1944 married Jeremiah Gerard Foley (born 6 June 1915 in Worcester). The marriage took place in Chicago Heights at St. Agnes Catholic Church.

Here is a photo featuring daughter Clara on her wedding day and another photo a few days later.

Figure 190. Daughter Clara on Her Wedding Day, 6 November 1944

The photo below shows **Clara** and her husband Jerry Foley (right side of photo) on 8 November 1944 with sister **Elizabeth** and her husband Gerry Baker (on the left side of the photo).

Figure 191. **Clara and Jerry Foley Shortly After Their Wedding**

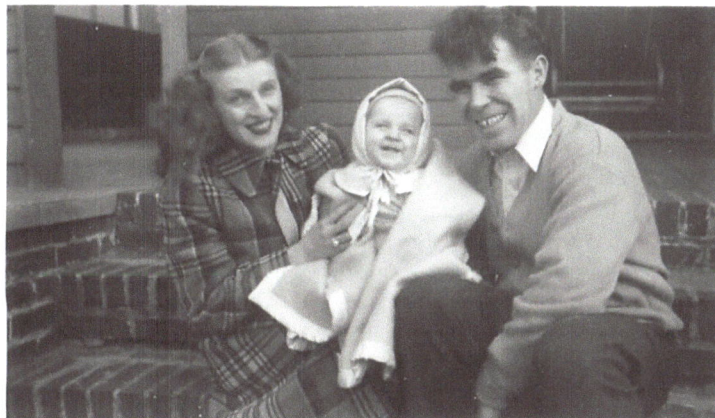

Figure 192. **Clara and Jerry Foley with First Born Son Michael. Photo dated 7 March 1946. Michael Gerard Foley, Grandchild #5, Was Born 22 September 1945.**

The next wedding in the family was that of **Julia Gertrude Smith** on 4 February 1945 to Florian F. ("Dick") Yanikoski of Berlin, Wisconsin in Chicago Heights, Illinois.

Figure 193. **Julia Smith's Wedding Day. Top left: Ellie, Teenie, Amanda. Bottom: Lucy, Julia. 4 February 1945**

Figure 194. **Julia's Wedding Day: Parents Clara and Joseph Smith February 1945**

In that same year of 1945, namely on 11 November 1945, Marie and Wally Novak gave birth to their third son **James Joseph Novak** (grandchild #5 for Clara and Joseph). Here's a picture of Jim as a toddler.

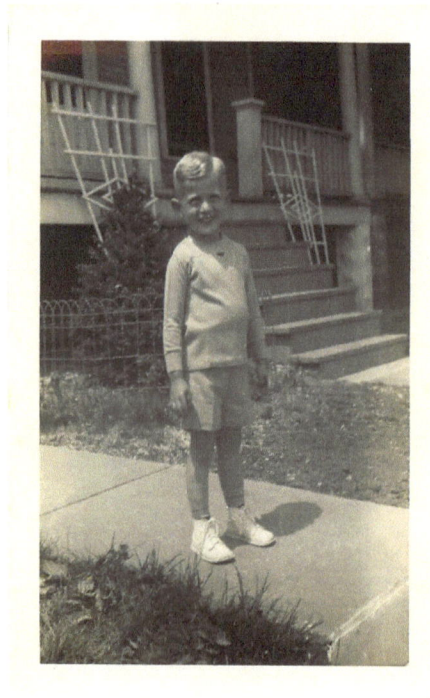

Figure 195. James Joseph Novak as a toddler (Grandchild #6 for Clara and Joseph Smith)

Here's a picture of **Julie and Dick Yanikoski** on 15 August 1946, about a year and a half after their wedding.

Figure 196. Julie and Dick Yanikoski Standing in Front of Scenic Area

About a year after Jim Novak's birth, **Julia and Dick Yanikoski** gave birth to **Richard Alan Yanikoski** on 30 November 1946. He is grandchild #7 for Clara and Joseph Smith.

Figure 197. Julia holding Rick (6 Months) 30 May 1947. Richard Alan Yanikoski (Grandchild #7) born 30 November 1946

Another year passed, and daughter **Clara and Jerry Foley** gave birth to **John Joseph Foley**, their second son (**grandchild #8** for Joseph and Clara Smith).

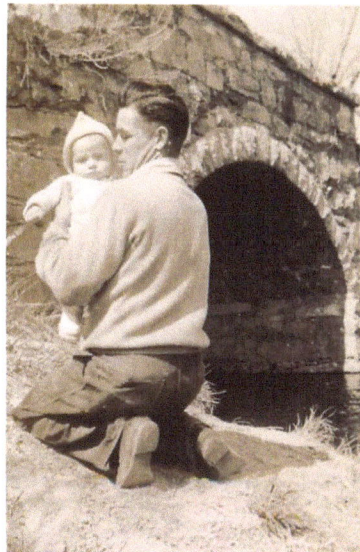

Figure 198. Jerry Foley Holding John Joseph Foley (4.5 months old). Photo May 1948, Grandchild #8. Born 27 December 1947

Around the time that Rick Yanikoski was six months old and before John Foley was born, his grandfather Joseph Smith retired from his job at Victor Chemical Works with the intention of moving down to Orlando, Florida to live out his years with Clara there. He was 65 years old, and Clara was 63 years old. The move was most likely influenced by the encouragement of their son Smitty who had been stationed at the US Naval Base in Orlando, Florida during World War II.

The date of Smitty's Honorable Discharge from the United States Navy was 3 March 1946. Here is a copy of the certificate and notice of separation from the U. S. Naval Service.

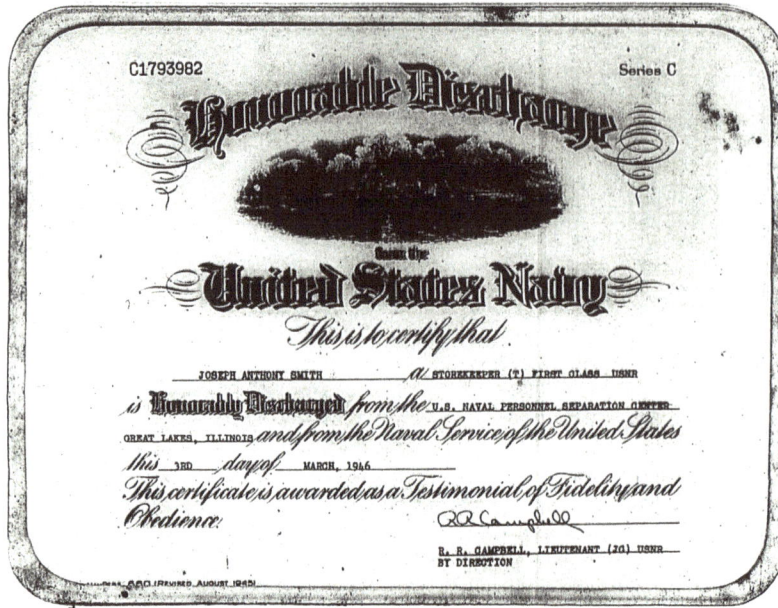

Figure 199. Smitty's Honorable Discharge 1946

Figure 200. Smitty's Notice of Separation from U. S. Naval Service (Note: #24 Service Includes US Naval Base Navy 824 Which is Based in Orlando, FL)

According to a conversation with Josephine in 2019, Smitty's enthusiastic opinion of Orlando, FL was instrumental in the decision for Joseph and Clara to make that their next destination for their later years. Ellie and Josephine made plans to move from Chicago Heights to Chicago and rent an apartment on 67th Boulevard since the Emerald Avenue house was to be vacated. Smitty and Lucy made plans to move to Orlando with their parents and get jobs there.

Here is the letter from the President of Victor Chemical Works, Walter B. Brown, dated 15 May 1947 upon Joseph A. Smith, Sr. retirement after 32 years of employment with the company, having started there on 4 January 1915.

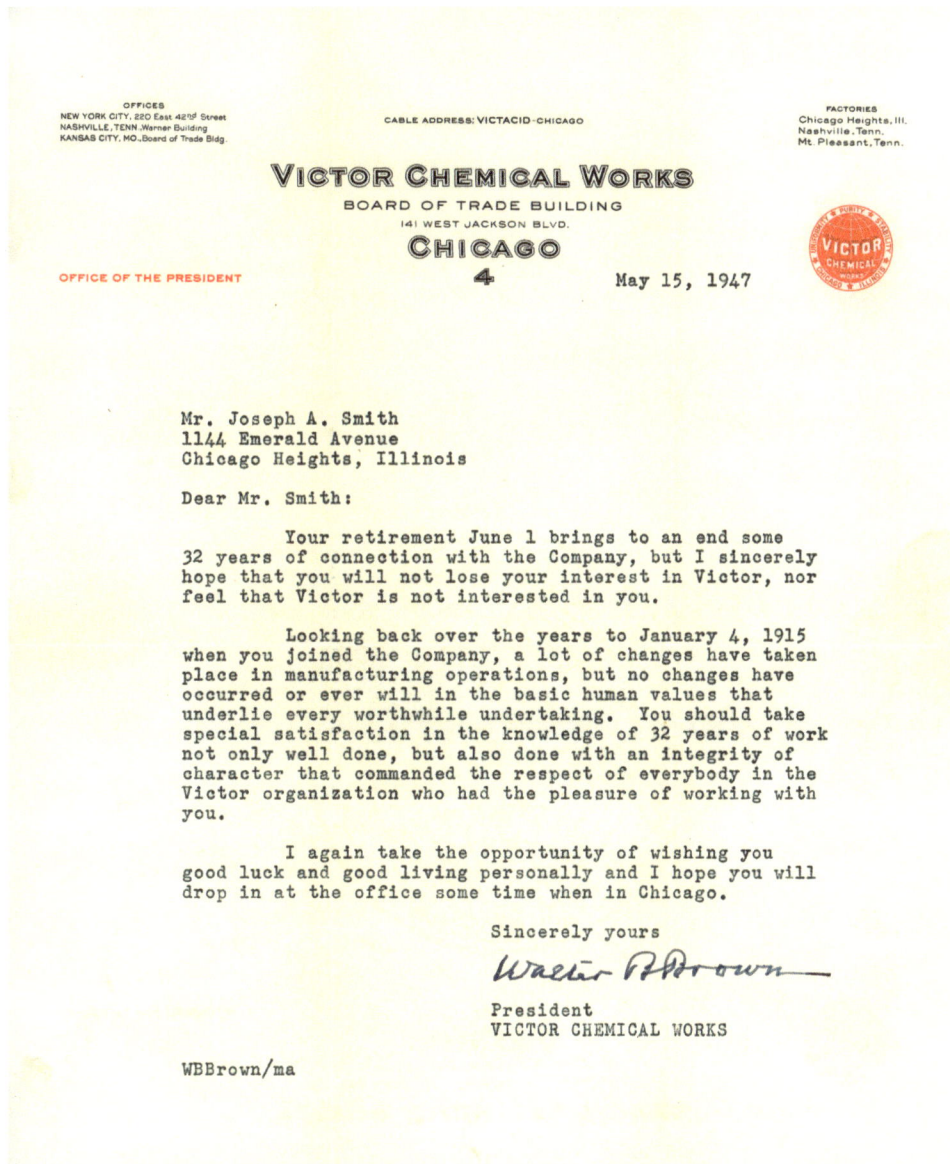

Figure 201. **Victor Chemical Works Letter (Above) and Envelope (Below) to Joseph A. Smith, Sr.**

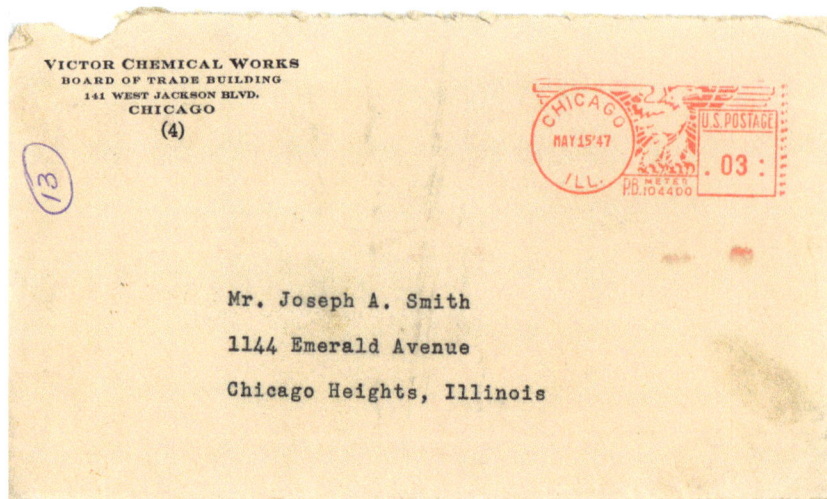

Figure 202. **Copy of 15 May 1947 Envelope (with Postage of Three Cents) from Victor Chemical Works**

The president of the company thanked Joseph Smith for "...32 years of work well done but also done with an integrity of character that commanded the respect of everybody in the Victor organization who had the pleasure of working with you."

Shortly after the receipt of the retirement letter on 15 May 1947, Clara and Joseph Smith packed up their bags and headed to Orlando, Florida for their future life away from the Chicago Heights cold winter climates. Smitty and Lucy also were eager to travel to their new state of Florida where previously Smitty had been stationed at the Naval Base during WWII. Lucy was looking for a change of climate with warmer weather to improve her health.

An undated clipping from a Chicago Heights newspaper (possibly sometime in June 1947) has a story about a farewell party given for Lucy Smith. She was the guest of honor at a farewell party in the Golden Glow room at St. Agnes, and honors at games went to her and one other person. The clipping says that "Miss Smith will leave this week to make her home in Orlando, Fla."

Orlando, Florida

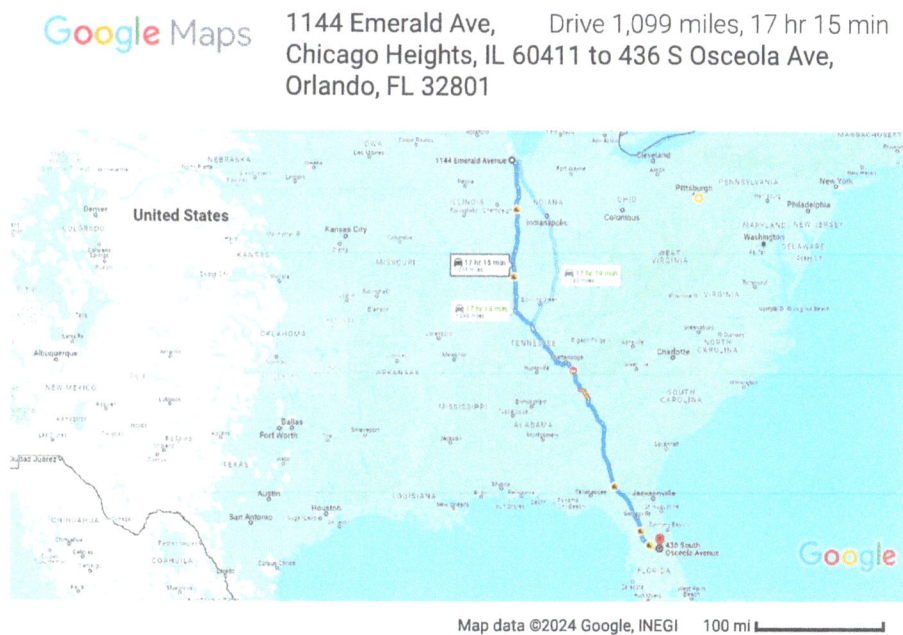

Figure 203. **The trip from Chicago Heights, Illinois to Orlando, Florida was about 1,100 miles.**

The city of **Orlando** was established in 1875. Back in 1843, Fort Gatlin was built to protect the settlers from the attacks by the Seminole Indians, and by 1875 there were about 85 residents in the area. As time progressed, the area expanded to be more than just cattle and cotton land. Around 1950 the population was about 52,000, and it was called the City Beautiful, attracting more and more people as time progressed. The city was characterized by many lakes, warm year-round temperatures, and plentiful citrus fruit—just what the Smith family was looking for. They purchased their Orlando house on 7 July 1947.

436 S. Osceola Avenue, Orlando, Florida

The new home was located at 436 S. Osceola Avenue near Lake Eola. The deed for the property is dated 8 July 1947, Document #19470180736 in the Orange County, Florida public records. It was a two-story house with an enclosed front porch, a side garage, and a large palm tree to the left of the house. It was large enough to have guests and visitors and large enough to have room for Lucy and Smitty. Here is a picture of the house at that time in 1947.

Figure 204. **436 S. Osceola Avenue, Orlando, Florida**

(Note: This house is no longer in existence and has not been there for quite a few years as rapid development of the area took place. The area is downtown Orlando with high-rises and commercial buildings. Coincidentally, the Smith house would have been only 1/tenth of a mile from the 2024 location of one of the later-born grandson's condominium in a high-rise complex in downtown Orlando.)

Enlargement of a negative of a photo shows a close-up of the sign appearing on the open garage at the house: It says: "J. A. SMITH Electric Motors and Appliances Repaired." Joseph Smith was always the industrious one!

Figure 205. **Osceola Avenue, Orlando, FL Sign Above Garage with Two of the Smith Sisters About 1947**

Figure 206. **Joseph Smith Wearing his Suspenders Standing in Front of his House on Osceola Avenue, Orlando**

Figure 207. **Clara Smith Standing in Front of Osceola Avenue House, Orlando, FL**

Figure 208. **Clara and Joseph Smith Standing to Front Left of Osceola Avenue House**

Figure 209. **Smitty at Osceola Avenue House in Orlando**

Figure 210. **Lucy in Front of a Palm Tree in Orlando, FL**

The Smith family settled quickly into their new home and kept in touch with their friends and family in Chicago Heights. Lucy received many letters from various priests and nuns with postmarks starting on 30 July 1947, addressed to her at the Smith's Osceola address, and thanking her and her mom for sending a basket of Florida citrus fruit to the convent in Chicago Heights. There was mention in one letter of the beautiful doily that Clara made for the St. James Hospital. One writer wished Smitty success in his new employment. Smitty had started up a Karmel Corn shop near where he lived in Orlando, with Lucy helping him out for a while.

Figure 211. **Lucy, Joseph, Clara, and Smitty Smith at Osceola House**

Family Visits

Joseph and Clara soon began receiving visits from family members including a visit from Eleanor Smith who brought toddler **Rick Yanikoski** along with her to visit his grandparents. When Joseph and Clara moved to Orlando, Ellie was living and working in Chicago, the Emerald Avenue house was vacant, and Josephine had no place to live and so moved into the apartment with Ellie in Chicago. The address was 7322 S. Blackstone Ave, Chicago 19, IL. Josephine worked at a beauty shop nearby.

Figure 212. **Eleanor (Ellie) Smith Visiting her Mom at Osceola House in Orlando. Sitting on Back Fender of Parents' Buick**

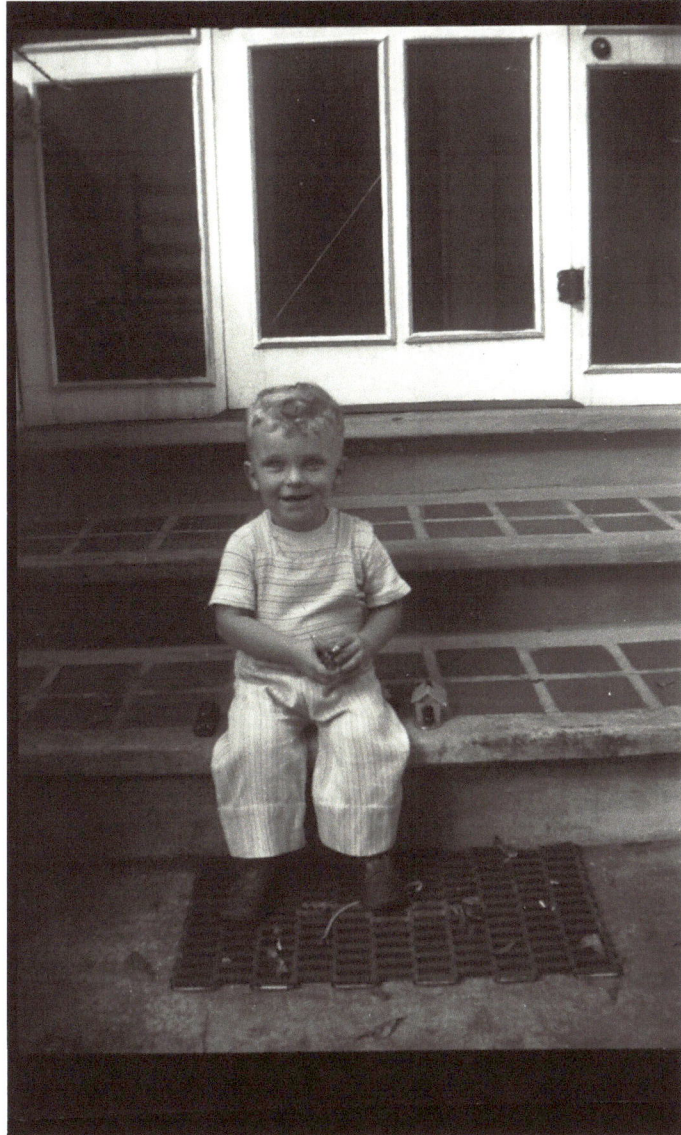

Figure 213. Rick Yanikoski (grandchild #7) Sitting on Front Porch Visiting his Grandparents with His Aunt Ellie in Orlando About 1949

Figure 214. Lucy and Her Mom Clara Sitting on Back Fender of Buick Car at Osceola House

The large sticker on the back of the car advertises Orlando Springs, Central Florida's Favorite Resort, Tropical Park. This was a tourist attraction often visited by the Smiths, as evidenced by the large number of photos taken at the site. The Springs became known as Sanlando Springs because the springs were located in between the cities of Sanford and Orlando. The Sanlando Springs are now privately owned, but in the times of the Smiths' visits to the resort, the springs were open to the public and had beautiful scenery, a place to swim, scenic trees, paths to walk on, and great places for picnics. The first picture below shows Sanlando Springs in 2022 and the remaining ones show the Smiths at the park in the late 1940s.

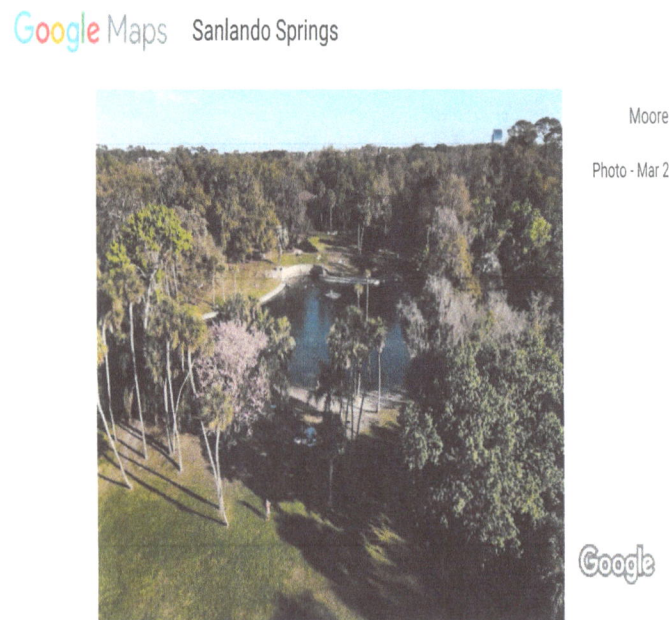

Figure 215. **2022 Google Maps Photo of Sanlando Springs**

Note that in the far back of the water, there is a concrete semi-circle structure like a guard rail. In the picture below, about 72 years earlier, Joseph and Clara are standing in front of that guard rail. The beach where swimmers would enter is in the closer-up section of the picture.

Figure 216. **Joseph and Clara Smith in Front of Guard Rail at Sanlando Springs**

Figure 217. **Josephine (Teenie) Smith Visiting Her Mom and Dad at Sanlando Springs in Early 1949**

Another destination for relaxation and enjoyment for the Smiths, especially when their adult children came to town, was the beach. Here are some beach pictures from that same time around 1949. (The identification of this particular beach is unknown to the author because there are no actual photos to check markings on the backs, only negatives to examine; however, the scenery is not familiar to the author. It does not look like Daytona Beach or New Smyrna Beach, which were other later destinations.)

Figure 218. **Joseph Smith at Beach**

Figure 219. **Clara and Joseph Smith**

Figure 220. **Clara and Joseph Smith**

Figure 221. **Ellie and Lucy**

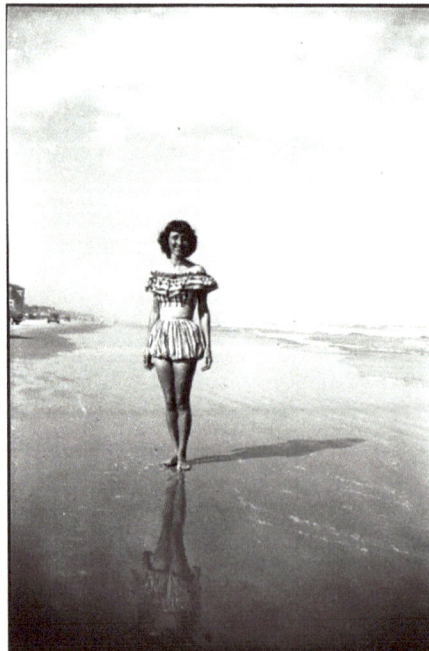

Figure 222. **Josephine at Beach on Her Visit to Her Mom and Dad's House in Orlando in 1949**

In addition to the beaches, the many lakes and natural springs of the area were enjoyed by the Smiths and their visitors. Very close to the Smith house was Lake Eola, which was less than a mile walking distance away. Here's a map showing the closeness of Lake Eola to the Smith house.

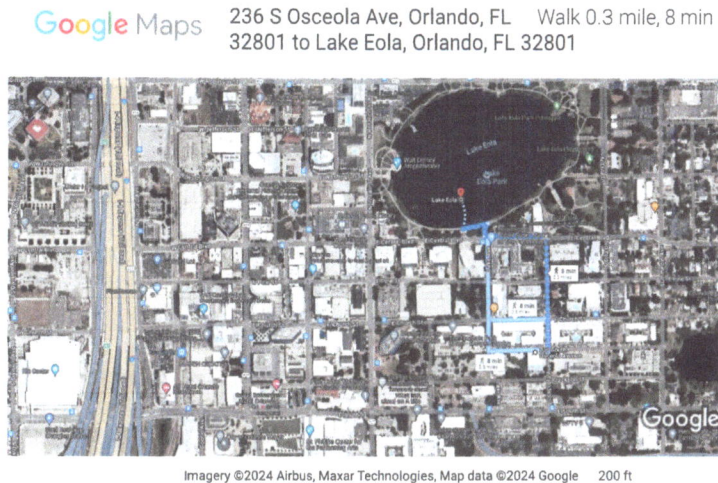

Figure 223. **Google Map Showing Distance from Lake Eola to the Smith House**

Lake Eola had benches and shady trees surrounding it and was the perfect place for strolls, walks, picnics, and family gatherings. The land became a public park in 1888 and is still a popular destination for cultural events, concerts, jogging, relaxing, and other activities. The distance around Lake Eola is about a mile and could be walked leisurely in less than thirty minutes.

Figure 224. **Josephine (Teenie) Sitting on a Bench at Lake Eola in Early 1949. Orlando, FL**

Smitty's KarmelKorn shop turned out to be a strategic meeting place for Teenie, who happened to be in the shop when Smitty was working, and his friend Harold Stonitsch stopped in. Harold was from Chicago but had recently moved to Orlando. Teenie was living in Chicago in an apartment with Ellie at the time. On 29 January 1949 Teenie and Harold had their first date at a General Electric Electrical Show in Orlando which had followed a dance at the Angebilt Hotel with a group from St. James Youth Club. He was 28 and worked as a radio engineer at WORZ in Orlando, and she was 34 and working as a beautician in Chicago. Harold was already known by Clara and Joseph through Smitty. Teenie returned to Chicago but had left her heart in Orlando, where she returned for a visit again in April and became engaged to Harold on 18 April 1949 while at the movies. She went back to Chicago to finish out her Easter time beautician work, packed her bags and bid farewell to her friends. She and Harold wed on 4 June 1949 at St. James Catholic Church. Father David B. Cronin officiated at the ceremony. The couple began their new life together in a cottage on Old Cheney Highway, about five miles from the Smith house on Osceola Avenue.

St. James Catholic Church was the church that Joseph and Clara attended, and it was located only one mile from their home. (See Google Map below.) It was completed in 1891 and was a wooden structure. The church was rebuilt in 1951, and is still in existence, although now it is the Cathedral of St. James.

Figure 225. **Google Map Showing Distance from Smith House to St. James Church**

Figure 226. **St. James Church**

Figure 227. **Joseph Smith at Central Florida Deanery Rally Holy Name Society of St. James Church on 8 July 1951.**

Here's a picture of **Teenie** and **Harold** on their wedding day at the Osceola House on 4 June 1949 before heading to St. James Catholic Church for their wedding.

Figure 228. Ringbearer Michael Foley (Grandchild #5 of Clara and Joseph Smith), Bride Josephine, Groom Harold, and Bridesmaid Lucy Smith on 4 June 1949

Without Teenie as her roommate now, Ellie moved from her apartment in Chicago to live in Natick, Massachusetts with the Yanikoski family around 1950, where she worked as a bookkeeper for Fenwal Inc. Rick Yanikoski in 2024 remembers that as a four-year old, he shared his room with his Aunt Ellie for several years up until 1953. When Charlie took Ellie away in April of 1953, Rick recalled that he was "...feeling a bit miffed..."

More Grandchildren

Eight more grandchildren were added to the family between 1950 and 1953, including **Harold William Stonitsch** (grandchild #9 born on 19 February 1950), the firstborn of Josephine and Harold; **Mary Christine Yanikoski** (grandchild #10 born on 3 April 1950), second child of Julie and Dick Yanikoski; **Brian Francis Foley** (grandchild #11 born 8 February 1951) third child of Clara and Gerry Foley; **Mary Josephine Stonitsch** (grandchild #12 born on 5 May 1951), second born of Harold and Josephine Stonitsch; **Margaret Marie Novak** (grandchild #13 born on 8 February 1952), fourth child of Marie and Wally Novak; **Joseph James Stonitsch** (grandchild #14 born on 26 July 1952), third child of Josephine and Harold Stonitsch; **Charles Stephen Yanikoski** (grandchild #15 born 8 August 1952), third child of Julie and Dick Yanikoski; and **Gerald James Foley** (grandchild #16 born 21 September 1953), fourth child of Clara and Jerry Foley.

Figure 229. **Clara Smith with Grandson Harold (Skip) William Stonitsch 1950 Osceola House   Grandchild #9**

Figure 230. **Harold William (Skip) Stonitsch (Grandchild #9) 1950**

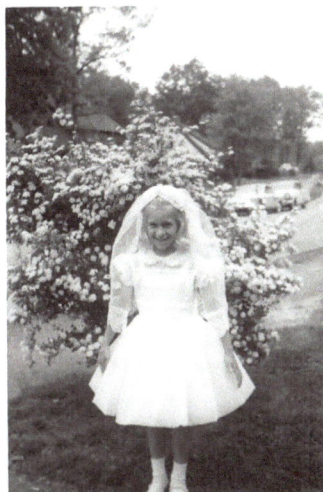

Figure 231. **Mary Christine Yanikoski, 2nd Child of Julie and Dick Yanikoski (Grandchild #10) on First Communion Day June 1957**

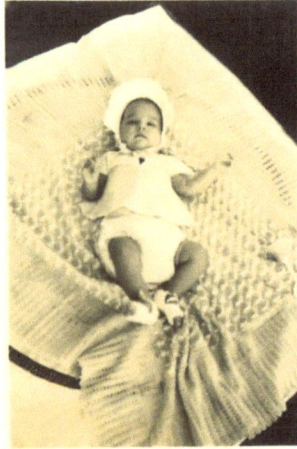

Figure 232. **Mary Josephine Stonitsch (Grandchild #12) 3 Months Old 5 August 1951**

The last addition to the Marie and Wally Novak family was **Margaret (Meg) Marie Novak**, born on 8 February 1952. She was **Grandchild #13** for Clara and Joseph Smith.

Figure 233. **Margaret (Meg) Marie Novak (Grandchild #13) in Stroller, Brother Jimmy, and Grandfather Joseph Smith on 24 August 1952. Meg 6 ½ Months Old**

APR • 55

Figure 234. Margaret (Meg) Marie Novak (Grandchild #13) Visiting Grandparents and Uncle Smitty at Osceola House in Orlando on 2 November 1954. Meg About 2 ½ Years Old

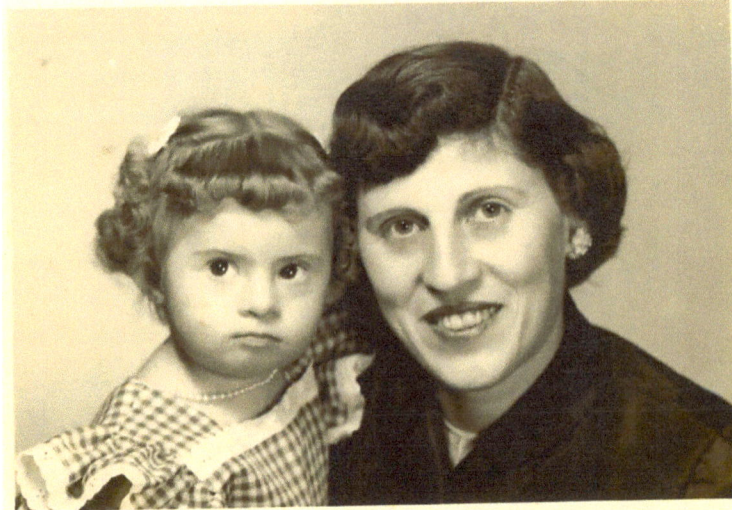

Figure 235. Meg and her Mom Marie Novak

Figure 236. Meg and Brother Don Novak on 2 February 1956

Figure 237. **Meg and Brother Jimmy Novak on 8 February 1956**

The next **grandchild #14** in the Smith family was **Joseph James Stonitsch**, born to Josephine and Harold Stonitsch on 26 July 1952.

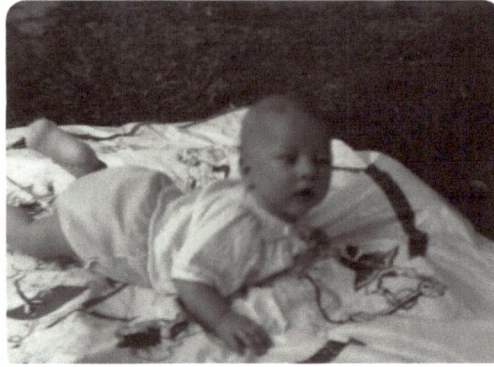

Figure 238. **Joseph James (Jay) Stonitsch (Grandchild #14) 1952**

Next in line was the third child of Julie and Dick Yanikoski, **Charles (Chuck) Stephen Yanikoski**, who was born on 8 August 1952 (**grandchild #15**) in Natick, Massachusetts. This is a photo of him taken on Easter Sunday, 18 April 1954.

Figure 239. **Charles Stephen Yanikoski (Grandchild #15) on 18 April 1954**

Adding to the Foley family, in addition to Michael and John were **Brian Francis Foley (grandchild #11)**, born 8 February 1951 and **Gerard James Foley (grandchild #16)**, born 21 September 1953.

Figure 240. **Brian Francis Foley (Grandchild #11) on Left, John Joseph (Grandchild #8), Dad Gerard (Middle), Toddler Gerard James Foley (Grandchild #16) in Front, and Michael Gerard (Grandchild #5) (Photo Taken in Massachusetts)**

Here are the **Foley** boys a year later in 1955.

Figure 241. **The Top left is John, then Michael. The Bottom Left Sitting in Chair is Gerard and Next to Him is Brian (Grandchild #11). (Photo Taken in Massachusetts)**

To complete the Foley family are the last two of the twenty-one grandchildren of Clara and Joseph Smith: **Mary Claire Foley** (grandchild #20), born 6 June 1957 and **Julie Therese Foley** (grandchild #21), born 19 March 1960. The first photo was taken in early 1961 of Julie Therese (right) and her sister Mary Claire (left). The next is a photo of **Julie Therese** at about seven months old taken 21 October 1960. Both pictures were taken in Massachusetts.

Figure 242. **The Foley Girls, Mary Claire (Grandchild #20) and Julie Therese (Grandchild #21), January 1961**

Figure 243. **Julie Therese Foley (Grandchild #21) on 31 October 1960**

In August 1952, although older brother Rick Yanikoski now had his younger brother Chuck around, he still was miffed to lose his roommate Eleanor in 1953; however, Charles (Charlie) Henry Audet was more than happy to have **Eleanor Barbara Smith** as his wife on 18 April 1953.

Figure 244. **Eleanor Barbara Smith and Charles Henry Audet Wedding 18 May 1953**

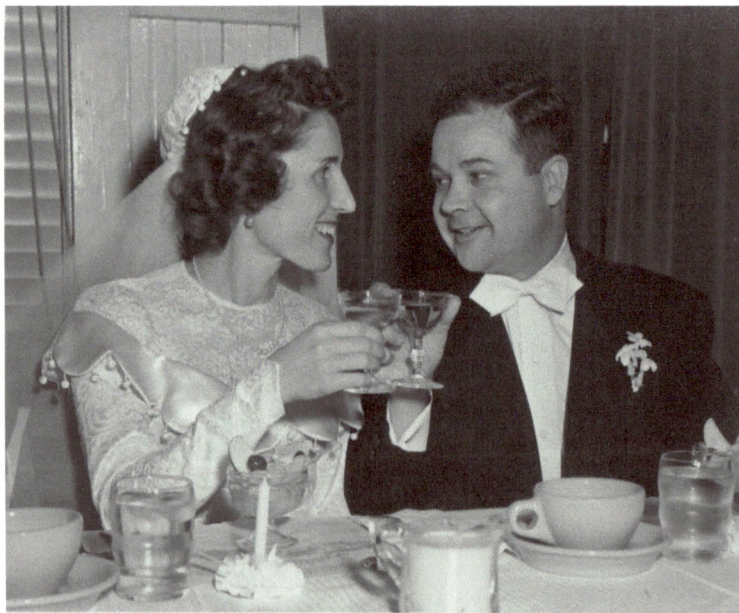

Figure 245. **Newlyweds Ellie and Charlie Audet at Their Wedding Dinner 18 April 1953**

After the wedding, the Audets got an apartment in Leominster, Massachusetts and lived there until their move to Framingham in 1957. In Leominster, Ellie worked as a bookkeeper at a plastics factory, and Charlie worked at Leominster General Electric plant. Ellie remained close to her sisters, Julie and Clara, and their families who were also living in Massachusetts. The couple made numerous yearly trips to visit Ellie's parents, Joseph and Clara, and those siblings who were living in Orlando.

Even More Grandchildren and More Gatherings/Visits

The next group of 5 grandchildren born between 1954 and 1960 included the following: **Clenise (Lindy) Ann Stonitsch (grandchild #17)**, born 21 April 1954 to Harold and Josephine Stonitsch; **Rita Ellen Stonitsch (grandchild #18)** born 22 October 1955; **Joseph Anthony Yanikoski (grandchild #19)** born 31 January 1956 to Julie and Dick Yanikoski; **Mary Claire Foley (grandchild #20)** to Clara and Gerry Foley born 6 June 1957; and **Julie Therese Foley (grandchild #21)** also to Clara and Gerry Foley born 19 March 1960. (Mary Claire and Julie Therese were pictured under the Foley discussion earlier as the last two of the Smith grandchildren.)

Figure 246. Grandma Smith, Lucy Smith, and Clenise (Lindy) Ann Stonitsch (Grandchild # 17) Born 21 April 1954, Pictured at Nine Months Old at Osceola House on 31 January 1955

Whenever there was a holiday or birthday or any other reason to celebrate, the Smith family would have a gathering centered around food and fun times. When Ellie and Charlie came for a visit sometime around the summer of 1955, the famous dull green thermos, a woven picnic basket, and blankets would be piled into the trunk of the cars, and off the group would go to a picnic or park destination. (Mary Jo Zkiab remembers this one below as being at Cocoa Beach.) Those present on the left back side were Ellie and Charlie in their bathing suits, Mary Jo, and Joseph (Jay) sitting next to Grandma, Grandpa standing with a plate of food in his left hand, Aunt Lucy sitting on the blanket eating a piece of chicken, infant Clenise sitting in front of her, Smitty looking in the trunk of the car, and Harold Stonitsch with sunglasses on the right side of the photo.

Figure 247. Smith Gathering with Ellie and Charlie Audet, Grandpa and Grandma Smith, Lucy and Smitty, Harold Stonitsch, and Children Mary Jo, Jay, and Clenise 1955

Figure 248. Grandpa and Grandma Smith (Back Left Corner) Celebrating Birthday of Jay Stonitsch Along with Smitty, a Person Blocked by Smitty, Mary Jo, Skip, Big Grandma Knebelsberger (Who Was Like a Mother to Harold Stonitsch), Lucy Smith, and Harold Stonitsch in Kitchen of Stonitsch House on Old Cheney Highway

Figure 249. **Grandma and Grandpa Smith with Baby Rita Ellen Stonitsch (Grandchild #18) Born 22 October 1955. Picture Taken at Stonitsch Home on Old Cheney Highway**

Figure 250. Baby Rita Ellen Stonitsch (Grandchild #18) Fifth Child of Josephine and Harold Stonitsch, Sitting on Lap of Aunt Lucy Smith. Brother Skip on Left, Grandma Smith on Right, Mary Jo, Joseph, and Clenise Stonitsch February 1956. At Stonitsch Old Cheney Highway home.

Figure 251. **Grandma and Grandpa, Lindy, Aunt Lucy, Skip, Uncle Smitty, Mary Jo and Jay on Lap of Harold Stonitsch Celebrating Skip's Birthday with Cake and Presents in Living Room at Stonitsch Old Cheney Highway Home. February 1956**

Figure 252. **Ellie and Charlie Audet Visiting Smith and Stonitsch Family in Orlando, FL Lake Barton About 1954**

The last of the Yanikoski family, **Joseph Anthony Yanikoski (grandchild #19)** was born on 31 January 1956 to Julie and Dick.

Figure 253. **Joe Yanikoski (Grandchild #19) About Age 3 Dressed in Sister's Ballet Outfit.**

Grandchildren #20 and #21 are discussed under the Foley family above.

2305 Ann Arbor Avenue, Orlando, FL

In June of 1956 Clara and Joseph sold their house on Osceola Avenue and moved to 2305 Ann Arbor Avenue, about 5 miles away. (See Google Map below.)

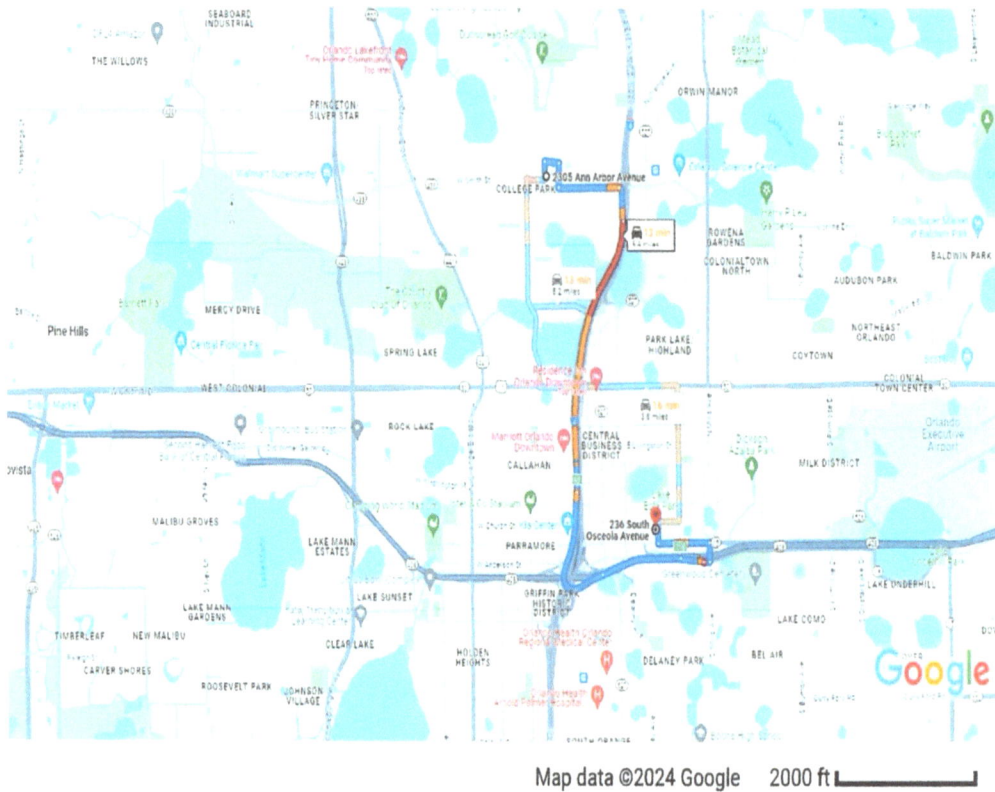

2305 Ann Arbor Ave, Orlando, Drive 5.4 miles, 13 min
FL 32804 to 236 S Osceola Ave, Orlando, FL 32801

Figure 254. **Google Map Showing Distance Between Ann Arbor and Osceola Houses**

The Orange County Comptroller's records of mortgages and deeds shows that the purchaser of the Osceola house took out a mortgage for $11,500 to buy the house on 6 June 1956 for $11,500 which included the following house furnishings:

together with the following items situated on said premises:
FRONT PORCH: 1 Wicker couch and cushion, 1 Wicker chair and cushion, 1 Wicker planter, 1 Wicker magazine rack, 1 Wicker stack table, 1 wrought iron seat, 1 smoking stand, 1 end table, 2 throw rugs, 1 flower pot, 2 wall plaques, LIVING ROOM: 1 couch, 2 cushions, 1 chair and ottoman and cushion, 1 chair and cushion, 1 end table, 1 chair, 1 TV table, 2 floor lamps, 1 table lamp, 1 smoking stand, 1 fire screen, 1 clock, 1 cigar box, 6 trinkets, 1 large rug, 2 throw rugs, 5 pair white curtains, SUN PORCH: 6 sets cafe curtains, SOUTHWEST BEDROOM: UPSTAIRS: 1 chest of drawers, 1 dressing table, 1 chair, 2 table lamps, 2 throw rugs, 1 set curtains, SOUTHEAST BEDROOM: 1 bed-spring & mattress & spread, 2 end tables, 1 chair, 1 rug 6 x 9, 1 throw rug, 1 set drapes (Panels - 2), HALLWAY AND HALL CLOSET: 1 6 x 9 rug, 2 throw rugs, 1 telephone table and chair, 1 hat rack, 1 mirror, CLOSET: 1 G.E. vacuum cleaner, 1 carpet sweeper, 1 dust mop, DINING ROOM: 1 dining room table, 1 dining room table pad and cloth, 6 dining room chairs, 1 buffet, 1 mirror, 1 rug 9 x 12, 1 throw rug, 3 pairs curtains, KITCHEN: 1 Servel gas refrigerator, 1 Magic Chef gas range, 1 Vesco electric roaster, 1 electric toaster, 1 exhaust fan, 1 steel chair, 1 Autohot gas hot water heater, 1 throw rug, LAUNDRY ROOM: 1 set double laundry tubs, NORTH BEDROOM: 1 bed, spring mattress, spread, 1 vanity, 1 chest of drawers, 1 chair, 1 9 x 12 rug, 2 throw rugs, 2 pair drapes (panels) BATHROOM: 3 throw rugs, 1 rubber mat, 1 shower curtain, 1 pair bathroom scales, 1 stool,
    Venetian blinds throughout the house, exhaust fan, carpeting on stairway

Figure 255. **Computer Display of Furnishings at Osceola House to Convey with Sale of House**

The 2305 Ann Arbor house was built in 1946 (the same year as the Osceola house that the Smiths sold) and was on .14 acres. The backyard was shady and had a fence around the back. It also had a small shed in the back left corner, a backyard picnic table, a brick cook fireplace, and a small patio near the back door. The concrete/cinder block house was considerably smaller than their previous house on South Osceola Avenue, but it was the right size for them. Lucy and Smitty moved with them. The residence still exists today in the year 2024 and looks quite similar in structure to what it looked like under the ownership of the Smiths. Of course, it has a new roof, different awnings and different vegetation, and a new garage door, but the stairs, sidewalk, driveway, and basic shape of the house appear to be the same.

Figure 256. **2305 Ann Arbor Avenue, Orlando, Florida. About 1955.**

Figure 257. **Google Maps Photo of 2305 Ann Arbor Avenue, Orlando, Florida. May 2022**

This house was the center of many happy events which included Thanksgiving and Christmas dinners, Easter egg hunts, birthday parties, cook-outs and dinners in the backyard at the large concrete picnic table, fun games, and card parties for the adults with games of pinochle or bunco. There were always large gatherings of relatives and friends of the family. The front yard had a great sidewalk that extended all the way down the street.

One memorable event that included most of the relatives (except Clara Foley and her family who were expecting another baby soon) took place when Clara and Joseph Smith celebrated their Golden Wedding Anniversary. The anniversary was on 18 April 1957 and was celebrated on Saturday, 27 April 1957, beginning with a Mass at St. Charles Catholic Church on Edgewater Drive. This was Clara and Joseph's parish when they moved to Ann Arbor Avenue.

Figure 258. **St. Charles Catholic Church About 1957, Edgewood Dr., Orlando, FL**

St. Charles Church was less than a mile away from the Ann Arbor Avenue house, and the Smiths were quite active in the various goings-on of the parish.

You are cordially invited

to attend an

Open House Celebration

in honor of

The Fiftieth Wedding Anniversary

of Mr. and Mrs. Joseph A. Smith

Saturday, April twenty-seventh

3 until 5 o'clock

College Park Woman's Club

714 Dartmouth Avenue

Orlando, Florida

Figure 259. **Invitation to the Smiths' Golden Wedding Anniversary Celebration**

After morning Mass at St. Charles Catholic Church, the family met at the Louis' Restaurant and later in the day went to dinner at the College Park Woman's Club. There were about eighty people who signed the guest book. Those in attendance were relatives and friends from Chicago, Chicago Heights, and South Chicago, Illinois; Logansport, Indiana; Framingham and Natick, Massachusetts; and Orlando, FL.

Figure 260. **Clara and Joseph Smith at Golden Anniversary 18 April 1957**

The **<u>Our Golden Wedding Anniversary</u>** scrapbook, which was a gift from Elizabeth Smith Baker to her mom and dad, contains cards, letters, lists of guests and gifts received, photos of members of the family, and poems from each of the Smith grown-up daughters. Below are copies of some of these items.

What follows is a poem written by daughter Elizabeth.

Mom & Dad: April, 1957

Though fifty years have come and gone,
And times and styles have changed,
The Smiths' eleven still are quite
A family! -- slightly rearranged!

You know, Smith history was first made
When you, our folks, were wed;
'Twas 1907, one April day,
Your marriage vows were said.

Now ends a whole half century
Of success as man and wife;
And comes a new year that we pray
Brings joy and grace into your life.

Elizabeth

Written by Pat Baker.

P.S. I love you both very much.

Figure 261. **Poem Written by Elizabeth Baker**

Figure 262. **Smith Family at 50th Anniversary: Marie, Mandy, Smitty, Teenie, Beth, Julie,Lucy, Joseph, Clara, and Ellie. April 1957**

Figure 263. Charlie Audet, Smitty Smith, Dick Yanikoski, Wally Novak, Harold Stonitsch, Joseph and Clara Smith. 50th Wedding Anniversary. April 1957

Figure 264. Joseph and Clara Smith with Grandchildren at 50th Anniversary in 1957. Starting on Left Back Side and Going Clockwise: Jay Stonitsch, Ricky Yanikoski, Bob Novak, Jim Novak, Skip Stonitsch, Mary Chris Yanikoski, Mary Jo Stonitsch, Chuck Yanikoski, Rita Stonitsch, Lindy Stonitsch, Meg Novak.

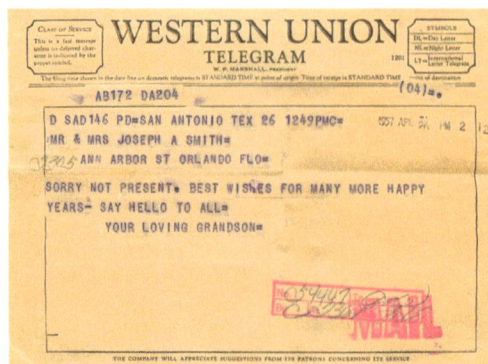

Figure 265. Don Novak's Telegram to His Grandparents on Their 50th Anniversary

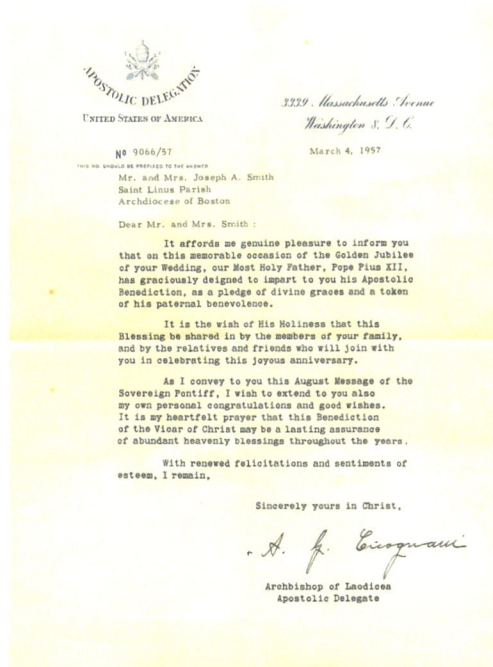

Figure 266. Apostolic Benediction from Pope Pius XII upon 50th Anniversary 1957

RT. REV. MSGR. WALTER E. CROARKIN
ST. AGNES CHURCH
1515 CHICAGO ROAD
CHICAGO HEIGHTS, ILLINOIS

April 11, 1957

Mr. & Mrs. Joseph A. Smith
2305 Ann Arbor Street
Orlando, Florida

Dear Friends,

Congratulations on your 50th wedding anniversary which I understand is this Wednesday,
April 18th. When you were in Chicago Heights,
you and your children were the outstanding family
in St. Agnes Parish. The fact that you reared
such a large and especially fine group of children
is proof of your own sterling qualities. Truly,
you are deserving of heartiest congratulations for
those fifty fruitful and admirable years. May God
fill your heart with the joy you so richly deserve
and continue to bless you and yours in every way.

Sincerely yours in Christ,

Rt. Rev. Msgr. W. E. Croarkin

Figure 267. **Congratulatory Letter From Msgr. Croarkin on 50th Anniversary**

Figure 268. **Clara and Joseph Smith Sitting on Couch at 2305 Ann Arbor Avenue About 1958**

Figure 269. **Joseph Smith in Backyard at 2305 Ann Arbor Avenue Around 1958**

The Smith family members living at Ann Arbor were very active at St. Charles Church. Joseph was a member of the Knights of Columbus for many years, and he also was a long-time member of the Holy Name Society in the parish. Clara was a member of the St. Charles Parish Council, and Lucy and Smitty were quite involved in volunteer work at the church.

The next major gathering of the extended family occurred on the occasion of the funeral of Joseph Sr. who was 77 years old. His date of death was 5 September 1959, and he died from acute myocardial infarction and coronary heart disease at Orange Memorial Hospital at 8:58 a.m., Saturday. He had not been bed-ridden or sick prior to the occurrence of the heart attack. Relatives came from near and far to participate in the funeral, with the Rosary service taking place in the evening at Fairchild Chapel on Monday 7 September at 8:30 p.m. The funeral Mass was held at St. Charles Catholic Church with Father Bartok officiating. Joseph was survived by his wife Clara, his son Smitty, 8 of his daughters

(Marie, Beth, Lucy, Mandy, Josephine, Julie, Ellie, and Clara); and 20 (not 18 as written in the obituary) grandchildren—Don, Bob, Jim, and Meg Novak; Loral Beth and Pat Baker; Skip, Mary Jo, Jay, Lindy, and Rita Stonitsch; and Rick, Mary Chris, Chuck, and Joe Yanikoski; Michael, John, Gerard, Brian, Mary Claire Foley. The last of the grandchildren to be born was Julie Theresa Foley who was born in 1960 after Joseph's death in 1959. The burial was in Greenwood Cemetery.

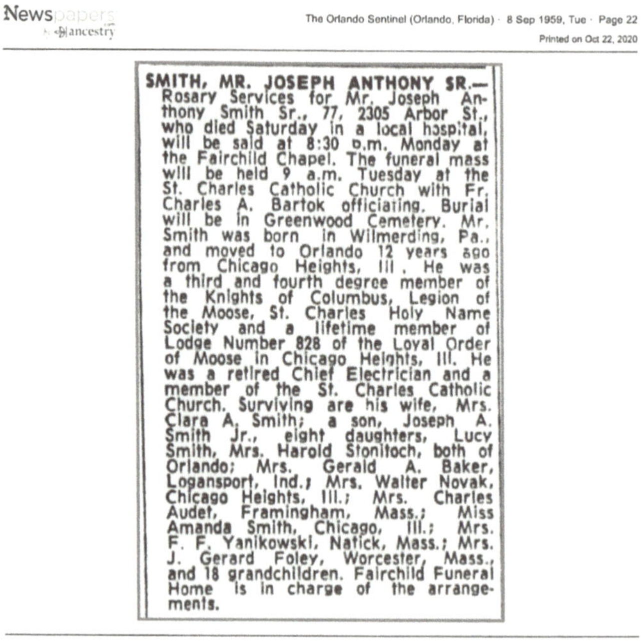

Newspapers by Ancestry — The Orlando Sentinel (Orlando, Florida) · 8 Sep 1959, Tue · Page 22 — Printed on Oct 22, 2020

SMITH, MR. JOSEPH ANTHONY SR.— Rosary Services for Mr. Joseph Anthony Smith Sr., 77, 2305 Arbor St., who died Saturday in a local hospital, will be said at 8:30 p.m. Monday at the Fairchild Chapel. The funeral mass will be held 9 a.m. Tuesday at the St. Charles Catholic Church with Fr. Charles A. Bartok officiating. Burial will be in Greenwood Cemetery. Mr. Smith was born in Wilmerding, Pa., and moved to Orlando 12 years ago from Chicago Heights, Ill. He was a third and fourth degree member of the Knights of Columbus, Legion of the Moose, St. Charles Holy Name Society and a lifetime member of Lodge Number 828 of the Loyal Order of Moose in Chicago Heights, Ill. He was a retired Chief Electrician and a member of the St. Charles Catholic Church. Surviving are his wife, Mrs. Clara A. Smith; a son, Joseph A. Smith Jr., eight daughters, Lucy Smith, Mrs. Harold Stonitoch, both of Orlando; Mrs. Gerald A. Baker, Logansport, Ind.; Mrs. Walter Novak, Chicago Heights, Ill.; Mrs. Charles Audet, Framingham, Mass.; Miss Amanda Smith, Chicago, Ill.; Mrs. F. F. Yanikowski, Natick, Mass.; Mrs. J. Gerard Foley, Worcester, Mass., and 18 grandchildren. Fairchild Funeral Home is in charge of the arrangements.

Obituary for MR. JOSEPH ANTHONY SMITH (Aged 77)

Figure 270. **Joseph Anthony Smith Sr. Obituary**

More Additions to the Family and More Get-Togethers

Life, love, and get-togethers continued for the Smith family after Joseph's death in September 1959 with one last grandchild **Julie Therese Foley** being born in 1960, and six great grandchildren born from December 1959 to December 1963.

The **great grandchildren** included the following:

3 December 1959 **Donald Lewis Novak** (Parents: Donald Louis Novak and Kathryn Irene Horning)

6 June 1961 **Susanne Miller Novak** (Parents: Robert Clement Novak and Susanne Miller Novak)

11 September 1961 **Dana Allene Novak** (Parents: Donald Louis Novak and Kathryn Irene Horning)

24 March 1962 **Kelly Gerard Kirke** (Parents: Loral Beth Baker and Robert James Kirke)

10 November 1962 **Robert Michael Novak** (Parents: Robert Clement Novak and Susanne Miller Novak)

31 December 1963 **Elizabeth Allen Kirke** (Parents: Loral Beth Baker and Robert James Kirke)

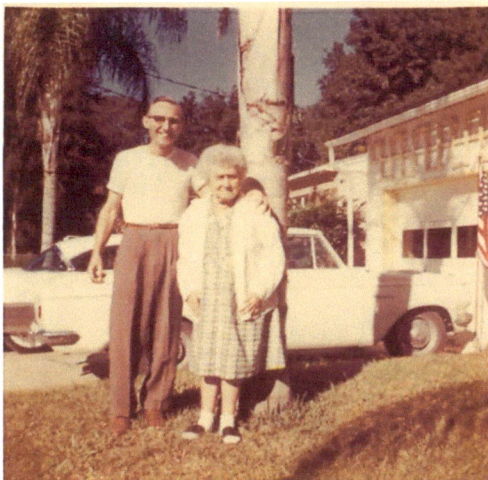

Figure 271. **Smitty and Clara at Ann Arbor in Front Yard About 1960**

Figure 272. **Grandma with Rita, Lindy, Mary Jo and Jay Stonitsch at Stonitsch Manor Drive House Around 1960.**

A large gathering took place at Daytona with members of the Yanikoski family (Dick, Julie, Rick, Mary Chris, Chuck, and Joe), Mandy, the Stonitsch family (Harold, Josephine, Skip, Mary Jo, Jay, Lindy, and Rita), and Lucy and Smitty. This was at Daytona Beach around 1962.

Figure 273. **Harold Stonitsch, Clara Smith, Julie Yanikoski, Amanda Smith at Daytona Beach About 1962**

Figure 274. **Mary Jo Stonitsch, Mary Chris Yanikoski, Jay Stonitsch, Lindy Stonitsch, Rita Stonitsch at Daytona Beach About 1962**

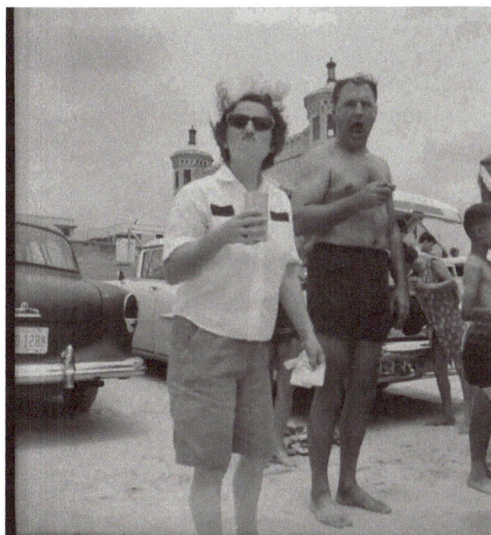

Figure 275. **Julie Yanikoski and Harold Stonitsch, and Jay Stonitsch (to Right)**

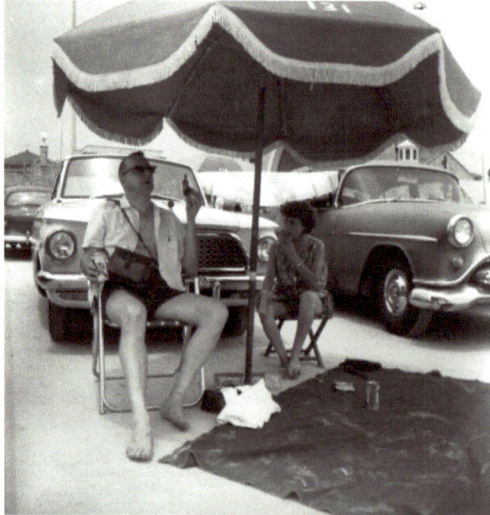

Figure 276. **Dick Yanikoski and Lucy Smith**

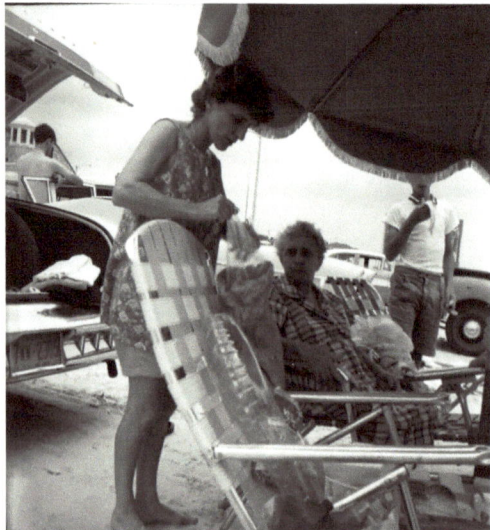

Figure 277. **Lucy and Clara at Daytona Beach**

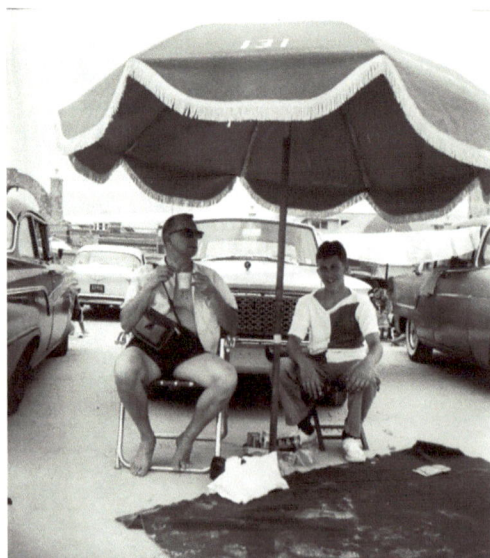

Figure 278. **Dick and Rick at Daytona Beach**

Figure 279. **Smitty is at Daytona Beach Grabbing a Drink from the Trunk of His car.**

Figure 280. **Lucy Smith, Clara Smith, Mary Jo Stonitsch, Skip Stonitsch, Lindy Stonitsch, Joe and Chuck Yanikoski, Mandy Smith, Jay Stonitsch, Mary Chris Yanikoski, and Rita Stonitsch at Daytona Beach**

Lucy used to drive Grandma to the Manor Drive house to spend the day with the Stonitsch family while Lucy worked as a medical secretary for Dr. Howarth, and Uncle Smitty was occupied with his work as a painter. Each day Grandma would come to the house with a loaf of store-bought bread, and she mostly sat and played bunco with Lindy or Rita who were not in school yet. Sometimes she would fall asleep during the day and would have meals with the family. At the kitchen dinner table, Harold would get Grandma laughing so hard that Teenie was afraid her mom would have a heart attack.

Grandma's health began to suffer around this time, and Mandy Smith came to the Ann Arbor house to help with the care of Grandma. Grandma was eventually in a wheelchair and then bed-bound at Ann Arbor.

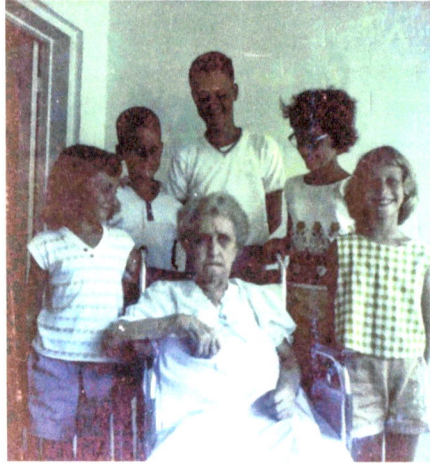

Figure 281. **Ann Arbor House: Grandma with Lindy, Jay, Skip, Mary, and Rita Stonitsch (About 1963)**

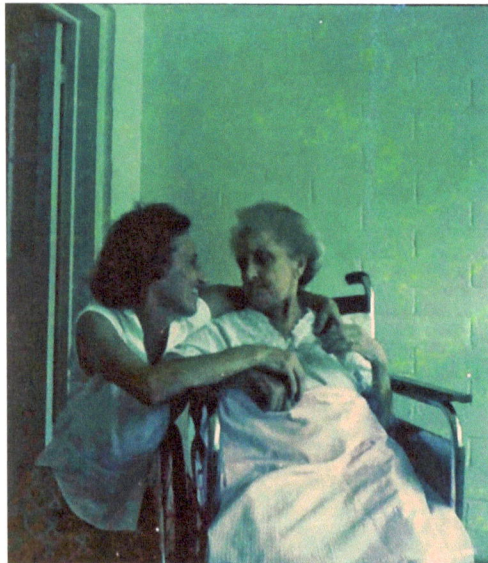

Figure 282. **Teenie with Grandma at Ann Arbor House About 1963**

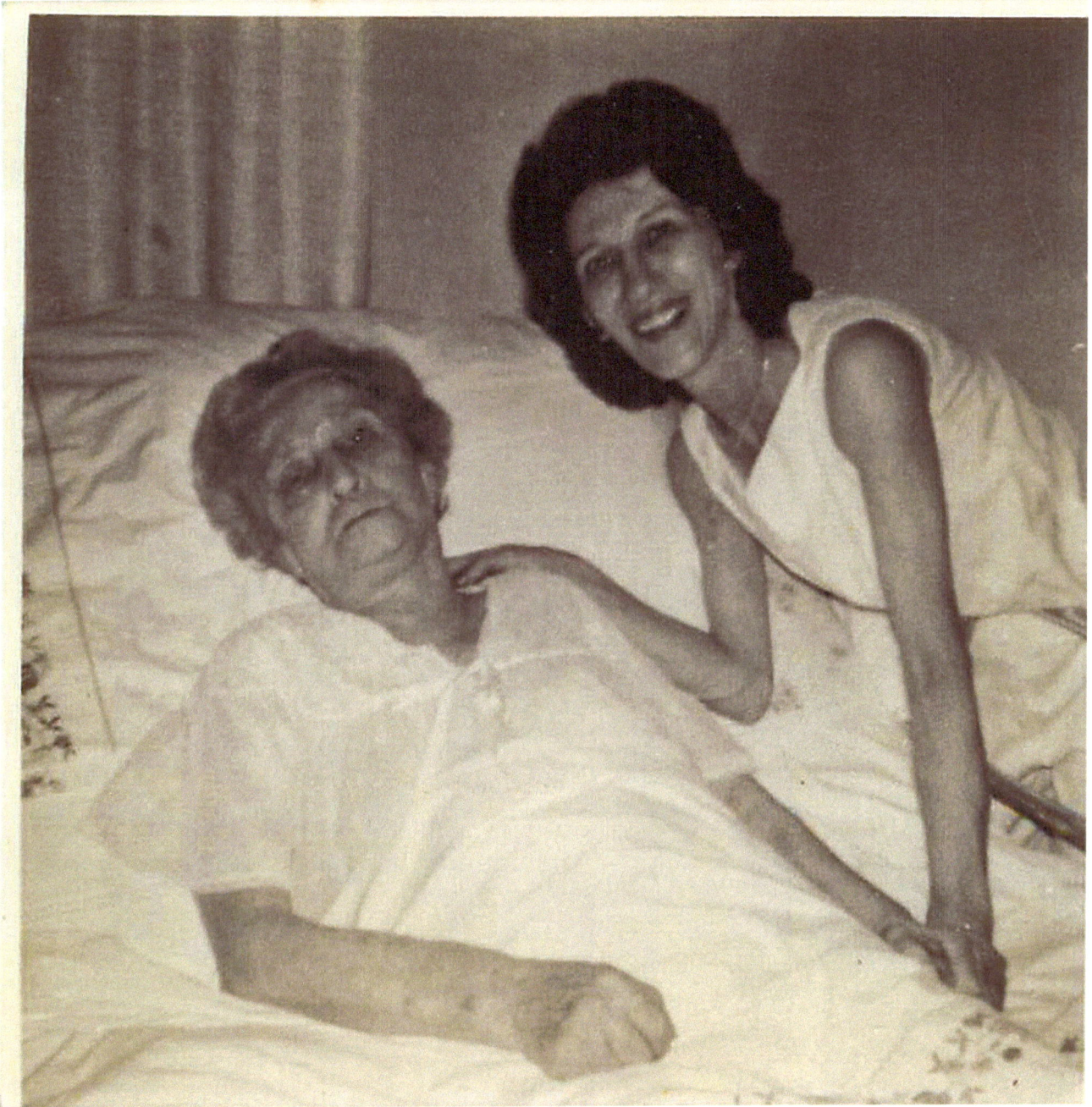

Figure 283. **Grandma and Mandy at Ann Arbor Avenue House Late 1963**

The family came together for the services related to Grandma Clara A. Smith's death which happened on Thursday, 2 January 1964 at age 79. She had been living at 2305 Ann Arbor Avenue in Orlando, Florida with Smitty, Lucy, and Mandy Smith. Her Orlando residency was for seventeen years. The death certificate says that the cause of death was encephalomalacia due to cerebral arteriosclerosis with arteriosclerotic heart disease contributing to her death. She suffered with this condition for about a year. Her Rosary Service was held at Fairchild Funeral Home; the funeral Mass was held at St. Charles Catholic Church; and the burial at Greenwood Cemetery.

Deaths And Funeral Notices

MRS. CLARA A. SMITH, 79, 2305 Ann Arbor Ave., died Thursday.

She had lived in Orlando since 1947 and attended St. Charles Catholic Church. She was a member of the St. Charles Parish Council.

Son, Joseph A. Jr., Orlando; daughters, Mrs. Marie Novak, Chicago Heights, Ill., Mrs. Elizabeth Baker, Williamsport, Ind., the Misses Lucy, Amanda Smith, Mrs. Josephine Stonitsch, Orlando, Mrs. Julie Yanikoski, South Braintree, Mass., Mrs. Eleanore Audet, Framingham, Mass., Mrs. Clara Foley, Worcester, Mass.; 21 grandchildren; five great-grandchildren survive.

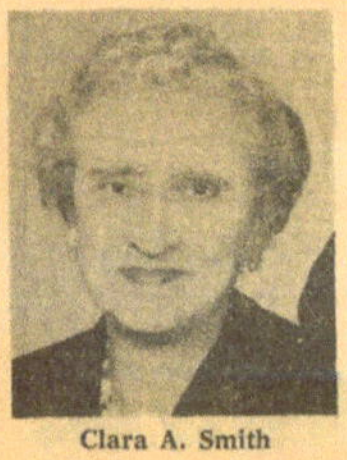

Clara A. Smith

Fairchild Funeral Home is in charge.

SMITH, MRS. CLARA A. — A Rosary service for Mrs. Clara A. Smith, 79, 2305 Ann Arbor, who died Thursday, will recited Sunday night at 7:30 p.m. at the Fairchild Funeral Home Chapel and the funeral Mass will be celebrated Monday at 9 a.m. at St. Charles Catholic Church with Monsignor Charles A. Bartok officiating. Interment will be at Greenwood Cemetery. Mrs. Smith came to Orlando in 1947 from Chicago Heights Ill., and was a member of St. Charles Catholic Church and the St. Charles Parish Council. She is survived by a son, Joseph A. Smith, Jr., Orlando; daughters, Miss Lucy Smith, Miss Amanda Smith, Mrs. Josephine Stonitsch, of Orlando, Mrs. Marie Novak, Chicago Heights, Ill. Mrs. Elizabeth Baker, Logansport, Ind. Mrs. Julie Yanikoski, South Braintree, Mass., Mrs. Eleanore Audet, Framingham, Mass., Mrs. Clara Foley, Worcester, Mass.; 21 grandchildren and five great-grandchildren. Pallbearers will be Edward Henz, William O'Brien, Harry Grimm, Al Alibeti, Art Pleva, Bill Heil. Fairchild Funeral Home, Lake Ivanhoe, in charge of arrangements.

Figure 284. **Obituaries for Clara A. Smith**

At the time of death, there were nine of her children who survived her, twenty-one grandchildren (including Julie Therese Foley born in 1960), and six great grandchildren, not five as written in both obituaries above.

Greenwood Cemetery, Orlando, Florida

The final resting place for Grandma and Grandpa Smith is **Greenwood Cemetery**, 1603 Greenwood Street, Orlando, Florida, Block 10. The cemetery was founded in 1888 and has scenic views and is of historical importance. It is 86 acres. The Smiths purchased the plot when they lived at 236 S. Osceola Avenue on 14 January 1953. When they moved to 2305 Ann Arbor Avenue, their house was 5.4 miles from the cemetery.

Figure 285. **Marked by lives of Faith and Family**

Causes of death listed on available Smith family members' death certificates:

Acute myocardial infarction; coronary heart disease.

Encephalomalacia; cerebral arteriosclerosis; arteriosclerotic heart disease.

Acute myocardial infarction; hypertensive arteriosclerotic cardiovascular disease.

Acute cardiac arrhythmia; arteriosclerotic cardiovascular disease.

Multi organ failure; acute hypoxic respiratory failure; aortic occlusion.

Heart disease.

2024 Memories of Some of Florida Descendants of Grandparents Joseph and Clara

Mary Jo Stonitsch Zkiab 2024 Memories of Little Grandma

Little Grandma:

--was short and sweet.

--always wore a dress. I never saw her in slacks or shorts.

--walked very slowly, careful not to fall. I remember the "scraping sound" of her heels on the kitchen floor.

--didn't talk very much. I do remember her saying Lutsee. (Lucy).

--loved to play bunco with me when I came home from school. (3rd grade).

--scratched her head a lot. ("They" said it was shingles, but not sure if it was.)

--took naps in my bed during the day when Mom was grammy-sitting her.

--fearful of the bathroom mirror.

--fearful of riding in the car towards Lake Ivanhoe.

--loved Daddo, who could always make her laugh.

When Little Grandma was visiting our house, we girls (Lindy, Reet or myself) would walk her to the bathroom, as she didn't like to be by herself. (or, for safety reasons, as she could easily fall?)

One memory of Grandma's funeral was that dad had a difficult time finding the funeral parlor for the vigil. He drove around in circles... not sure how he eventually located it. I also remember during/after the Rosary at the vigil our aunts started laughing uncontrollably. We didn't know what to think as kids...

****

Clenise Stonitsch White 2024 Memories of Little Grandma and Little Grandpa

My earliest memories of Little Grandma and Grandpa were of those activities that took place in the second house that we moved into at 1020 Manor Drive. We moved there on 21 April 1957, on my birthday and around the time that they were celebrating their 50th Anniversary at 2305 Ann Arbor Avenue. Our new house which my dad had built was about 4 or 5 miles from theirs, and they and Lucy and Smitty came often for celebrations and family events, and we, in turn went to many parties and events at their Ann Arbor house. In particular, I remember that Grandpa used to come regularly to get his haircut by my mom. He would sit in a chair in the kitchen with a protective towel over his shoulders facing the window towards the backyard. He usually had a pipe with him and would tap down the tobacco in it. I often got treated to a walk outside around the house with him holding my hand and showing me the bean plants that grew at the side of the house. It made me feel very special that he took the time to just be with me sometimes. I also remember him playing the game of horseshows in our backyard with my dad.

Because I didn't travel well in the car (due to car sickness), a few times, instead of going on a vacation with my family, I was dropped off to spend a few days or so with Grandma and Grandpa, and Aunt Lucy and Uncle Smitty. Grandma was a bit of a stickler and wanted me to get up early in the morning, but Grandpa would say, "Oh, let the little dear sleep." I liked that plan much better. Also, I remember that Grandpa had a special glass jar in the kitchen cabinet under the sink area to the right that was hidden away, and he used to sneak out cookies to give to me—white oreo-type cookies. He was soft-spoken and very gentle. It was fun being spoiled.

I don't remember much about when Little Grandpa died. He always seemed healthy to me. It was 5 September 1959. I was 5 years old. It seems that shortly after he died, Grandma had more health issues and maybe that's when Aunt Mandy moved to the Ann Arbor house to help Lucy and Smitty take care of her. Often, Lucy would drop Grandma off at our Manor Drive house, and I would help to entertain her throughout the day, helping her walk, playing bunco with her, sitting with her on the sofa, listening to her, walking her to the bathroom. It wasn't easy to understand her, but once she told me about where she grew up and that the ladies would wear black and walk to the town square, and something about baking bread. I didn't go to kindergarten, so I was free to just be around her for those few years.

She loved talking to our parakeet Whiskers and would call the bird Pappagallo (the Italian word for parrot). She would move her finger up and down on the cage, trying to get Whiskers to follow her movements.

Grandma didn't hear well. I was named after her, and she thought my name was the same as hers, Cleonice. When I was about two years old, she gave me a framed picture of Jesus that she wrote on the back: "With all my love To my granddaughter Cleonice from Grandnona Smith 1956."

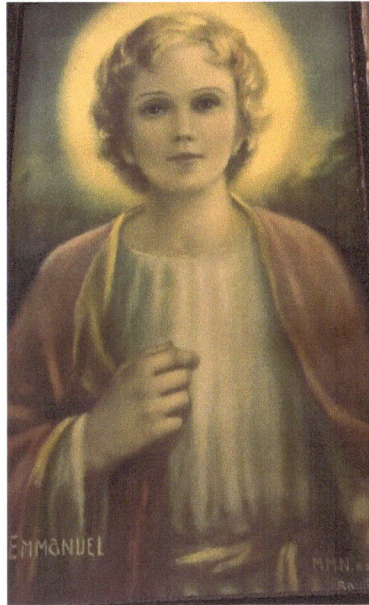

Figure 286. **Picture of Jesus with Halo**

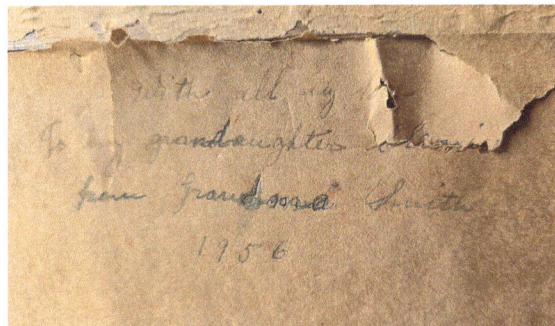

Figure 287. **My Mom's Over-writing of "Cleonice"**

My mom wrote over the Cleonice and made it Clenise, and she also overwrote the Grandnona and made it Grandma.

Figure 288. **Front of Valentine's Day Card to Clenise from Grandma, About 1957**

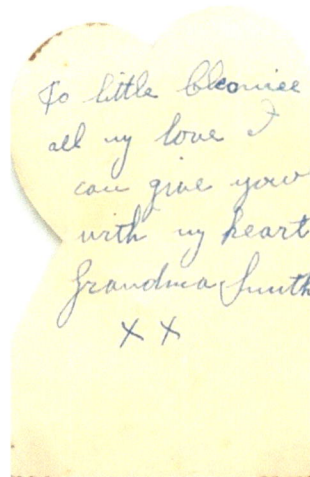

Figure 289. **Back of Valentine's Day Card, Showing Grandma's Handwriting**

I distinctly recall the funeral wake for Little Grandma. I was nine years old, and Grandma's casket was open. Aunt Lucy brought me close to the casket and made me touch Grandma's nose. It was very cold and made me feel uncomfortable. I also remember that the atmosphere was not very solemn. There was a lot of talking and some laughter. I just thought that perhaps people were sad and were disguising it with laughter or maybe that that's how most get-togethers were in the family, mostly light-hearted with a bit of humor. I couldn't tell one way or another.

****

Rita Ellen Stonitsch Lepinskie's 2024 Recollections of Gramma and Grampa Smith

As a little girl, I remember Aunt Lucy bringing Little Gramma to spend the day with us. She was a plump little lady who was always dressed nicely and was well cared for. We were always happy when she came over because she played games with us while Mom did work around the house. Bunco and dice were what stood out in my mind.

Lindy and I (maybe my sibs were in school at that time) thought she was cheating when she kept rolling the dice after each time until someone would grab the dice for the next one's turn. Of course, Little Gramma would never have cheated, but as kids we didn't know. I think Lindy brought it up to Mom later and she explained that Little Grandma's eyesight was very poor, and she couldn't see out of one eye. We just had to be faster at grabbing the dice when it was supposed to be our turn.

Another time I asked Mom why Little Gramma talked funny, and she answered that it was due to her false teeth. As a kid with no experience in foreign language, I had no clue that the real reason Little Gramma didn't "talk right" was because she wasn't a native English speaker!

Little Gramma was very patient and loving. I remember being hugged by her many times…the benefits of being the Baby of the family. She was very loving and smiled a lot. She was quite cheerful, smelled good, and sat a lot but loved to watch us kids play. I remember seeing her with a rosary in her hands.

When Little Gramma was bedridden and under the care of Aunt Lucy and Aunt Mandy, I remember she was lying in bed. I didn't know she was dying. She passed away and later Aunt Lucy or Mom told me that she had a miracle happen to her close to her end. She woke up and pointed her finger at the crucifix and uttered the words St. Therese, for whom she had shown great love. Then she closed her eyes and went to eternal sleep. (This is the reason I eventually chose St. Therese of the Little Flower as my confirmation name.)

Little Grampa was a slim man who seemed tall to me, but as a little girl, everyone was taller than me! He was active and loved to participate in throwing the ball to us kids. His English was easily understood, and he spoke gently. He loved to laugh and reminded me of Uncle Smitty with his looks and humor. Between Little Grampa, Uncle Smitty, and Daddo, they could masterfully turn a conversation into great laughter.

It was obvious from the gifts of chocolate that both grandparents loved my dad and chocolate! Little Gramma was very selective in choosing her chocolates and took her time as though she was a connoisseur.

****

AFTERTHOUGHTS

As a result of compiling this book, I have had the opportunity to interact with many more of my cousins and have grown in appreciation for the many sacrifices made over the years by our ancestors. There is a tendency to lament the trials and hardships of the present days such as the scams, wars, pandemic, crime, illness, and other maladies confronting us. The conditions in Italy in these rural areas such as Castelpetroso and Roccamandolfi were certainly arguably even more difficult. Poverty was rampant and opportunities for advancement and survival were often not possible given the economic and political oppression. Farmers, many of whom were our ancestors, were not able to enjoy the fruits of their labor, but they were instead taken advantage of by the rulers and landowners. The rate of infant mortality was quite high. The circumstances were desperate enough that there were large numbers of Italians during the late 1890's to the early 1930's who were willing to take the unpredictable risk of the long voyage to America with the hope of a better life. Despite the hardships encountered, Grandpa and Grandma Smith (Giuseppe and Cleonice) dedicated themselves to the best of their abilities to making their family life one of togetherness, love, religious devotion, and loyalty, and never gave up hope for a better tomorrow. Although the "family secret" may have caused some descendants to think there was something scandalous or bad that was being covered up, there was no stone left uncovered in searching for any evidence of such a negative aspect of their lives. I found nothing of the sort. The secret is no longer: they and we have Italian ancestors!

<h2 style="text-align:center">WHAT'S NEXT?</h2>

The next possible step of this research could be for the current and future interested persons/scientists in the family to look at the genetic aspects of the family tree. As of June 2024, at least three of the Smith descendants have used the Ancestry.com DNA testing kit.   The results for the author's DNA test show that of the 50% of the DNA inherited from her mom's Giancola/Mastrantuoni side of the family, 37% of her DNA is derived from ancestors who were from Southern Italy, 11% from Northern Italy, and 2% from Wales. There are books available that discuss detailed analyses relating to genetics and genealogy that could be pursued. One example is <u>Research Like a Pro with DNA: A Genealogist's Guide to Finding and Confirming Ancestors with DNA Evidence</u>, by Diana Elder, Nicole Dyer, and Robin Wirthlin (Family Locket Books 2021).

The culmination of the many hours of researching Italian civil records for Giuseppe Giancola's and Cleonice Mastrantuoni's sides of the family going back to the 1700's is presented below in charts on the next four pages: one chart of two pages for the Giancola side and one chart of two pages for the Mastrantuoni side. The Italian civil records include volumes and volumes of information (in Italian, of course), of birth, marriage, and death information, only some of which are indexed, but not always correctly. The records were written with quill pens and smeared when exposed to liquids. To say that the writing is illegible would be an understatement! The writers of the documents sometimes had disastrous penmanship, and there was no white-out to fix errors.

The charts are one popular way of displaying genealogical information, and they are called Ahnentafels, from the German words, "ancestry tables." The chart display is limited to seven generations, so Giuseppe and Cleonice are being considered as Generation 1 to make room for the other six preceding generations. Generation 2 in each Ahnentafel are the parents of the preceding generation, so Generation 2 has 2 ancestors for each Ahnentafel. Generation 3 ascends to the parents of those in Generation 2, for a total of 4 ancestors in each of the two tables. Generations 4 through 7 continue in the same manner. Those in higher generations are the most distant relatives for which records were found. So, for example, Cleonice's Ahnentafel shows Number 63, Mariangela Cicchino, the 5th great-grandmother to the author. Subtract 1 from 63, and you get her spouse Marino d'Andrea (5th great-grandfather), Number 62 in the chart. Note that the numbering system has even numbers as males and odd numbers as females. Now if you want to find the 4th great-grandfather, you go from Number 62, the 5th great-grandfather, you go from Number 62, the 5th great-grandfather, and divide by 2 and get 30. Number 30 is Liberato di Filippis, the 4th great-grandfather. (The female's spouse number is one more than her husband's number.) Liberato's spouse is Number 30 plus 1, so Number 31 is Elsabetta d'Andrea, the 4th great-grandmother. The same methodology works for Giuseppe's Ahnentafel.

The final page shows the ThruLine example generated by Ancestry.com for Mariangela Cicchino, the 5th great-grandmother to the author.

With sharing the Smith/Giancola/Mastrantuoni family life and history, the hope is that whose in the present and future generations will have an appreciation for those who went before us, and as Giuseppe Giancola Sr. used to often say: "God will provide. There's always room for one more.[1]

---

1   I will admit that I am taking this comment out of context! He was referring to providing a meal for anyone who would appear to be homeless who would come to the Smith house looking for food during the Great Depression. Josephine thought for sure that their house was marked on the street as being one that would provide a free meal for the needy.

AHNENTAFEL 1

Generated on June 17th, 2024

Giancola/Mastrantuoni Family Tree

Giuseppe Antonio (Joseph Anthony) Giancola (Smith)

Ahnentafel

Generation 1

1: Giuseppe Antonio (Joseph Anthony) Giancola (Smith) was born on 19 May 1882 in Castelpetroso, Isernia, Molise, Italy and died on 5 Sep 1959 in Orlando, Orange, Florida, USA.

Generation 2

2: Diamante Giancola was born on 1 March 1839 in Castelpetroso, Isernia, Molise, Italy and died in Castelpetroso, Isernia, Molise, Italy.

3: Concetta Illuminata Giancola di Genesio was born on 18 Jun 1841 in Castelpetroso, Isernia, Molise, Italy and died in Castelpetroso, Isernia, Molise, Italy.

Generation 3

4: Giuseppe Giancola was born on 12 July 1811 in Castelpetroso, Isernia, Molise, Italy and died on 13 June 1881 in Castelpetroso, Isernia, Molise, Italy.

5: Mariangela Cifelli was born on 23 Feb 1810 in Castelpetroso, Isernia, Molise, Italy and died on 09 Feb 1887 in Castelpetroso, Isernia, Molise, Italy.

6: Genesio Giancola was born on 14 Jun 1814 in Castelpetroso, Isernia, Molise, Italy and died on 16 Nov 1887 in Castelpetroso, Isernia, Molise, Italy.

7: Francesca Irene de Angelis was born on 27 April 1816 in Castelpetroso, Isernia, Molise, Italy and died on 14 Oct 1867 in Castelpetroso, Isernia, Molise, Italy.

Generation 4

8: Antonio Giancola was born in about 1777 in Castelpetroso, Isernia, Molise, Italy and died on 12 June 1856 in Castelpetroso, Isernia, Molise, Italy.

9: Maria Giancola was born in about 1786 in Castelpetroso, Isernia, Molise, Italy and died on 10 Jun 1815 in Castelpetroso, Isernia, Molise, Italy.

10: Cosmo Cifelli was born in Abt. 1766 in Castelpetroso, Isernia, Molise, Italy and died on 18 Sep 1824 in Castelpetroso, Isernia, Molise, Italy.

11: Anna Maria Cicchino was born in about 1775 in Castelpetroso, Isernia, Molise, Italy and died on 20 Jan 1820 in Castelpetroso, Isernia, Molise, Italy.

12: Pasquale Giancola was born in about 1766 in Castelpetroso, Isernia, Molise, Italy and died on 12 Feb 1833 in Castelpetroso, Isernia, Molise, Italy.

13: Domenica Armenti was born in about 1774 in Castelpetroso, Isernia, Molise, Italy and died on 4 Feb 1824 in Castelpetroso, Isernia, Molise, Italy.

14: Berardino de Angelis was born in 1784 in Castelpetroso, Isernia, Molise, Italy and died on 9 Jun 1844 in Castelpetroso, Isernia, Molise, Italy.

15: Rachele Armenti was born in Abt. 1783 in Castelpetroso, Isernia, Molise, Italy and died on 23 Jan 1850 in Castelpetroso, Isernia, Molise, Italy.

Generation 5

16: Francesco Antonio Giancola was born in Castelpetroso, Isernia, Molise, Italy.

17: Gertrude d' Angelis was born in Castelpetroso, Isernia, Molise, Italy.

18: Carlo Giancola was born in Castelpetroso, Isernia, Molise, Italy and died in Castelpetroso, Isernia, Molise, Italy.

19: Catarina Paoletti was born in Castelpetroso, Isernia, Molise, Italy.

20: Innocensio Cifelli was born in Castelpetroso, Isernia, Molise, Italy and died on 28 Nov 1810 in Castelpetroso, Isernia, Molise, Italy.

21: Martina Vacca was born in Castelpetroso, Isernia, Molise, Italy.

22: Giovanni Cicchino was born in Castelpetroso, Isernia, Molise, Italy.

23: Maddalena Paoletti

24: Domenico Giancola was born in Castelpetroso, Isernia, Molise, Italy and died in Castelpetroso, Isernia, Molise, Italy.

25: Susanna Arcaro was born in Castelpetroso, Isernia, Molise, Italy and died in Castelpetroso, Isernia, Molise, Italy.

26: Nicola Armenti was born in Castelpetroso, Isernia, Molise, Italy.

27: Margarita Vacca was born in Castelpetroso, Isernia, Molise, Italy.

28: Elia de Angelis

29: Francesca d'Uva

30: Vincenzo Armenti was born in Castelpetroso, Isernia, Molise, Italy.

31: Costanza Cicchino was born in Castelpetroso, Isernia, Molise, Italy.

Generation 6

40: Pasquale Cifelli was born in Castelpetroso, Isernia, Molise, Italy.

41: Catarina Vacca was born in Castelpetroso, Isernia, Molise, Italy.

AHNENTAFEL 2

Generated on June 17th, 2024

Giancola/Mastrantuoni Family Tree

Cleonice Mastrantuoni

ancestry

Ahnentafel

Generation 1

1: Cleonice Mastrantuoni was born on 11 Nov 1884 in Roccamandolfi, Isernia, Molise, Italy and died on 02 Jan 1964 in Orlando, Orange, Florida, USA.

Generation 2

2: Pasquale Mastrantuoni was born on 11 Feb 1847 in Roccamandolfi, Isernia, Molise, Italy and died in about 1926 in Roccamandolfi, Isernia, Molise, Italy.

3: Elisabetta Martelli was born on 14 Apr 1855 in Roccamandolfi, Isernia, Molise, Italy and died in about 1930 in Roccamandolfi, Isernia, Molise, Italy.

Generation 3

4: Domenico Angelo Mastrantuoni was born on 7 Jun 1823 in Roccamandolfi, Isernia, Molise, Italy.

5: Elisabetta Carmina Di Filippo was born on 22 Jan 1823 in Roccamandolfi, Isernia, Molise, Italy.

6: Berardino Pasquale Martelli was born on 26 Mar 1826 in Roccamandolfi, Isernia, Molise, Italy and died on 1 Jan 1872 in Roccamandolfi, Isernia, Molise, Italy.

7: Angela Maria Bruno was born on 30 Jan 1832 in Roccamandolfi, Isernia, Molise, Italy and died in after 1873 in Roccamandolfi, Isernia, Molise, Italy.

Generation 4

8: Pasquale Mastrantuoni was born on 17 May 1797 in Roccamandolfi, Isernia, Molise, Italy and died on 11 Dec 1839 in Roccamandolfi, Isernia, Molise, Italy.

9: Concetta Ricciordone was born on 8 Dec 1800 in Roccamandolfi, Isernia, Molise, Italy.

10: Donato Di Filippo was born in about 1766 in Roccamandolfi, Isernia, Molise, Italy and died on 27 Jan 1836 in Roccamandolfi, Isernia, Molise, Italy.

11: Angela Rosa Innamorato was born in about 1785 in Roccamandolfi, Isernia, Molise, Italy and died in Roccamandolphi, Isernia, Molise, Italy.

12: Antonio Martelli was born in about 1792 in Roccamandolfi, Isernia, Molise, Italy and died on 5 Sep 1850 in Roccamandolfi, Isernia, Molise, Italy.

13: Elisabetta Innamorato was born in Abt. 1795 in Roccamandolfi, Isernia, Molise, Italy and died on 21 Apr 1843 in Roccamandolfi, Isernia, Molise, Italy.

14: Giacomo Bruno was born on 20 Apr 1814 in Roccamandolfi, Isernia, Molise, Italy and died on 01 Aug 1835 in Roccamandolfi, Isernia, Molise, Italy.

15: Rachele di Filippis was born on 18 Feb 1812 in Roccamandolfi, Isernia, Molise, Italy.

Generation 5

16: Dominico Mastrantuoni was born in About 1741 in Roccamandolfi, Isernia, Molise, Italy and died on 9 Oct 1817 in Roccamandolfi, Isernia, Molise, Italy.

17: Cristina Gianfrancesco was born in Roccamandolfi, Isernia, Molise, Italy.

18: Pasquale Ricciordone

19: Giovanna Costrilli

20: Eggidio (sp?) Di Filippo was born in Roccamandolfi, Isernia, Molise, Italy and died on 28 March 1819 in Roccamandolfi, Isernia, Molise, Italy.

21: Pasqua Baccaro was born in Roccamandolfi, Isernia, Molise, Italy and died in Roccamandolfi, Isernia, Molise, Italy.

24: Berardino Martelli was born in about 1744 in Roccamandolfi, Isernia, Molise, Italy and died on 28 Aug 1817 in Roccamandolfi, Isernia, Molise, Italy.

25: Catarina d' Andrea was born in Abt. 1761 in Roccamandolfi, Isernia, Molise, Italy and died in about 1805 in Roccamandolfi, Isernia, Molise, Italy.

26: Pasquale Innamorato was born in Roccamandolfi, Isernia, Molise, Italy and died in before 1843 in Roccamandolfi, Isernia, Molise, Italy.

27: Teresa was born in Roccamandolfi, Isernia, Molise, Italy and died in before 1843 in Roccamandolfi, Isernia, Molise, Italy.

28: Liberato Bruno was born in Roccamandolfi, Isernia, Molise, Italy.

29: Margarita Mazzuto was born in Abt. 1778.

30: Liberato di Filippis was born in Abt. 1784 in Roccamandolfi, Isernia, Molise, Italy and died in Abt. 1831.

31: Elisabetta d' Andrea was born in Abt. 1784 in Roccamandolfi, Isernia, Molise, Italy and died in Abt. 1817 in Roccamandolfi, Isernia, Molise, Italy.

Generation 6

32: Giuseppe Mastrantuoni was born in Roccamandolfi, Isernia, Molise, Italy.

33: Antonia was born in Roccamandolfi, Isernia, Molise, Italy.

40: Donato Di Filippo was born in Roccamandolfi, Isernia, Molise, Italy and died in Roccamandolfi, Isernia, Molise, Italy.

41: Domenica Rizza was born in Roccamandolfi, Isernia, Molise, Italy and died in Roccamandolfi, Isernia, Molise, Italy.

48: Antonio Martelli was born in Roccamandolfi, Isernia, Molise, Italy.

56: Giantonio Bruno was born in About 1782.

57: Alesandra Lombardi

60: Michele di Filippis was born in Abt. 1747 in Roccamandolfi, Isernia, Molise, Italy and died on 19 Jul 1784 in Roccamandolfi, Isernia, Molise, Italy.

61: Domenica Martelli was born in Roccamandolfi, Isernia, Molise, Italy.

62: Marino d' Andrea was born in Roccamandolfi, Isernia, Molise, Italy.

63: Mariangela Cicchino was born in Roccamandolfi, Isernia, Molise, Italy.

Generation 7

120: Sebastiano di Filippis

121: Francesca Ianatelli

ThruLines® for Mariangela Cicchino

ThruLines® uses Ancestry® trees to suggest that you may be related to Mariangela Cicchino.

⌖ **Relationships**   ☰ **List**

Mariangela Cicchino
5th great-grandmother

Elisabetta d' Andrea
4th great-grandmother
1784-1817

⌃

Rachele di Filippis
3rd great-grandmother
1812-

Angela Maria Bruno
2nd great-grandmother
1832-1873

Elisabetta Martelli
Great-grandmother
1855-1930

C Mastrantuoni
Maternal grandmother
1884-1964

www.ingramcontent.com/pod-product-compliance
Lightning Source LLC
Chambersburg PA
CBHW041549260326
41914CB00016B/1592